D0643753

How to Design and Teach a Successful School String and Orchestra Program

How to Design and Teach a Successful School String and Orchestra Program

by

Jacquelyn A. Dillon
Casimer B. Kriechbaum, Jr.

Photographs courtesy of Scherl and Roth, Inc.
Drawings by Michael S. Meek

Kjos West/Neil A. Kjos, Jr., Publishers
4382 Jutland Drive
San Diego, California
1978

Published by Kjos West
4382 Jutland Drive, San Diego, California 92117

International Standard Book Number 0-8497-5400-3
Library of Congress Card Number 78-54217
Printed and Bound in the United States of America
Edition Number WS5

Foreword

This book was written to fill several needs that became apparent as the authors presented string-class and orchestra teaching clinics and workshops to university level music education students and public school music teachers across the United States and Canada. The needs were for: (1) A method of teaching string technique in large, heterogeneous classes rather than depending on private teaching or small, like instrument classes; (2) A concrete analysis of the many factors necessary to consider in the organization of an orchestra program including, setting up a new program with the school administration, recruiting students for an orchestra program, and maintaining the orchestra program once it is started; (3) A comprehensive overview of the many facets of teaching necessary for an efficient instruction on *all* levels – elementary through high school; and (4) A statement concerning the most important administrative problems that face the director and/or supervisor of an instrumental group and/or music department.

The need for a successful class method to teach to *all* strings at the same time is very apparent, because at the present time, most so-called class teaching is *not* class teaching but rather private teaching with many students in front of the teacher. There is a singular lack of books treating the development of string technique within a class situation upon all instruments from beginner up through the secondary level and culminating in the development of a complete symphonic orchestra.

As the clinics and workshops of the authors were adapted to meet the expressed needs of the individual students and teachers, it became apparent that the instructors needed to know not only *how* to teach the string classes in large, heterogeneous groups but also how to handle the great concerns that existed among them about a myriad of other string and orchestra teaching problems. As there was also a lack of books treating everyday problems such as: the psychology of rehearsals; the recruiting of string students; retention of students in the program; how to teach musicianship to young students; how to choose music for groups; ad inifitum, it was necessary to add sessions in the clinics and workshops to meet these needs.

It is hoped that by writing this book, the information, procedure, and philosophy developed and examined by the authors will be disseminated more rapidly, conveniently and universally than they could be through presenting individual clinics and workshops.

The authors have strived to make the book so pragmatic and detailed that any music teacher with the desire to learn can take it, follow the "recipe" and obtain excellent results even if they have not had the benefit of an extensive background in string performance.

Jacquelyn A. Dillon and Casimer B. Kriechbaum, Jr.

Contents

Part One

ORGANIZATION OF AN ORCHESTRA PROGRAM

Part One

Organization of the Orchestra Program

2

Organization of the Orchestra Program

Setting Up the Orchestra Program 1

INTRODUCTION

Why Every School Should Have An Orchestra Program

Orchestra is a necessary part of the school program and should be included in the music curriculum for the following reasons:

(1) Music cannot be taught properly and completely without an orchestra, as almost every great composer has spent a great deal of his time writing for the orchestra.

(2) Most state boards of education and accrediting agencies recognize that a music curriculum is not complete without an orchestral program.

(3) Orchestras are more than ever the coming thing We presently are experiencing a tremendous resurgence of interest in professional and school orchestras across the United States. Especially in smaller communities one finds many new string programs. In the past ten years, sales of string instruments to school systems has more than doubled. In 1975 alone, the number of stringed instruments sold in the United States hit an all-time high as sales increased 43% over the sales of 1974.[1]

The above arguments for having orchestras in the curriculum are fairly well-known and probably accepted by most educators. But yet, according to a survey made by the American Music Conference in 1975, 78% of the schools responding to a questionnaire indicated that they do not have orchestral programs.[2]

Reasons that people give for not having orchestral programs are:

(1) The school is not big enough for both a band and orchestra.

(2) They fear that adding a string program will hurt the existing band program.

(3) There is no interest.

[1] *The Instrumentalist,* Volume XXXI, No. 5, December 1976, p. 98.

[2] Telephone Conversation, American Music Conference, Chicago, Illinois, June 29, 1976.

The above reasons for not having an orchestral program are well meant and undoubtedly sincere; however, when the facts are examined it soon becomes obvious that these obstacles are more imaginary than real.

Any secondary school large enough to have a band program of fifty members will also be able to have a forty-piece orchestra without hurting the existing instrumental program. A band of fifty members would be ordinarily drawing from a school population of, at the very least, two-hundred and fifty students. A forty-piece orchestra needs about twenty-four strings and sixteen winds and percussion. This means that only twenty-four additional members need to be recruited from the remaining two-hundred students to fill the string section. Experience has shown that orchestra attracts students who are not in either band or choir, just as a choir attracts members outside of band as well as those in band. There are plenty of students for everyone!!

The orchestra does not *hurt* the band program, it *helps* it. This is because the wind players in an orchestra will be provided an extra chance to play, plus the opportunity to learn a soloistic style of playing.

The idea that *only* a string major can teach strings and direct an orchestra program is one of the most widely held misconceptions in educational circles today! Anyone who is a musician, organizer, promoter, and teacher enough to handle a good music program of any kind can have a good string program. Stringed instruments, properly taught, are really easier to teach (not necessarily to play) than woodwind or brass instruments. There are a comparatively few basic fundamentals that need to be known to teach strings. (See Chapter II, Part II.) In teaching strings, all problems of tone production, intonation, and articulation will be obvious (both as to cause and cure) because everything that a string player does, right or wrong, is visible to the observer. There are no hidden tongue movements, closed throats, improper use of inner muscle apparatus – everything is exposed for all to see.

Just as it is felt that wind majors can and should teach strings, it is felt that string majors are well-advised to realize that they need to be able to teach winds as adequately as the strings. Obviously, if a string major is to teach a full orchestra (hopefully he will), a large part of the orchestra and its problems are going to be in the wind section. Also, from a practical viewpoint, most jobs available to beginning instrumental music teachers are going to require that the teacher be able to teach something besides the strings. Many opportunities available to graduating string majors will be in smaller communities or in systems where there may not be enough work exclusively in strings to justify hiring a full-time person. Therefore, the choices available to a graduate very well may be to take a part-time teaching position, to teach something else along with strings (band, vocal, general music, etc.) or simply *not* to teach at all.

As to the concern about the cost of equipping a string program – it is surprisingly *much* less than the cost of equipping a band program. The only things that are necessary to buy are the string basses, because the wind instruments will already be available while the rest of the stringed instruments *should be student-owned*. (See Privately Versus School-owned Instruments, p. 14.)

To counter the statement that there is no interest in stringed instruments and orchestra – repeatedly, experience has shown that the only real interest needed for successful music instruction is the interest of a teacher who *wants* to teach the string program. There are many students that really would like to do something in music and they may not want to play in the band or sing in a choir. When one considers the number of students playing guitars, drums and piano but not enrolled in music courses at school, it is obvious that there is a great interest in music that is not being fulfilled with the bands and choirs presently in the school music curriculum.

STEPS TO BUILDING AN ORCHESTRA PROGRAM

Seeing The Superintendent

Many decisions must be made that involve people other than the string teacher before the first class in school can be taught. Many of these must be made on a system-wide basis by someone in authority at a higher level than the string teacher or even a building principal. Some of these decisions involve such areas as: structure of the program, length and number of classes per week, grade level(s) at which beginners may start, will privately or school-owned instruments be used, who will be in charge of recruiting, and who will handle and supply the instruments?

In most school systems, the person making these decisions will be the superintendent of schools although very large systems may have an assistant superintendent in charge of curriculum to take care of such matters. These decisions *should not* be a matter of negotiation between the individual string teacher and the different principals. If all students are going to be expected to end up at a predictable level in junior and senior high, then all students must start in the *same* grade, have *equal* time with their teachers and cover *stated* materials each year. At best, there will be a spread of ability levels; but if time spent with the teacher and materials to be covered are not controlled as much as possible, an even wider spread of ability levels will occur. If this is allowed to happen, there will be almost insurmountable problems in the second and third year classes.

The Structure of the Orchestra Program (Grades 5-12)

The authors propose the following outlines of string programs that can be used as guides to what can reasonably be asked for when setting up a new program or reorganizing an existing one. Obviously, no single structure can fit all situations, therefore several possibilities are described. It is hoped that one of them will be close enough to any existing situation to be applicable.

When approaching the superintendent, it will be necessary for the prospective teacher to have an overall plan in mind of where the program is going to go in the future. While the entire structure of the future program should be in mind when talking with the superintendent, it probably would be wise not to go into as much detail at first as is set forth in this book. The information must be available if the superintendent asks, but it is not necessary to frighten him with many unnecessary details unless he *asks* for them. It is well to bear in mind that it gives the superintendent a feeling of confidence to understand that he is not going to be personally involved in *all* the details of running the program.

If ones' ideals cannot be achieved in setting up the program some alternatives are better than others. The authors will indicate their best choices in case a compromise plan must be used.

TRADITIONAL SCHOOL PLAN (6-3-3)

Elementary School (1-6) – Fifth grade (beginning string class) should meet three to five days a week in a heterogeneous string class (mixed instruments) for a minimum of thirty minutes per lesson. The purpose of this class is to build technique rather than to perform.

Sixth grade (second year string class) should also meet three to five days a week as a heterogeneous string class for thirty minutes. Its main purpose should be to build technique but performance should begin to assume some importance. Some supplementary *string orchestra* music should be used in this class.

Junior High School (7-9) – Seventh grade (third year string class) should meet five days a week for a *minimum* of forty minutes daily. This group should be involved about two-thirds of the time in expanding technique and one-third of the time as a performance string orchestra. It is an absolute necessity during the third year to use string orchestra materials along with technique method books, otherwise the students will find the material dull which can cause students to drop out of the program.

Eighth and ninth grade (fourth and fifth year class) should meet five days a week (two or three days with selected winds in a full orchestra and two or three days with strings only). This group should meet in regularly scheduled periods a *minimum* of forty minutes daily, and will be primarily a performing group with about two-thirds of the time spent on performance materials and the other one-third on technique expansion.

High School (10-12) – This orchestra will include students from three grades (10, 11, 12) and will be primarily a performing group meeting five days a week (three with selected winds and two days with strings only). On this level, because of the type of literature and the performance demands, forty minutes is really not sufficient. A minimum of fifty minutes is more realistic for high school.

MIDDLE SCHOOL PLANS

Sixth, Seventh and Eighth Grade Plan (5-3-4)

Elementary (1-5) – Beginning string class should still start in the fifth grade and meet three to five days a week in one-half hour periods. The purpose of this class is again primarily to build technique rather than to perform.

Middle School (6-8) – As a middle school schedule is set up more like a junior high school schedule than an elementary school schedule, the sixth grade class (second year string class) should meet five days a week for one period a day as a string orchestra class. It will be mainly a technique class with 60% of the work spent in technique expansion and 40% in performance activities.

The seventh grade and the eighth grade orchestra can be scheduled separately or as a combined class. This will depend on size of the classes and/or the availability of personnel. If the personnel is available and the classes are big enough, probably separate classes are the best choice. If the seventh and eighth grades meet separately, then the seventh grade should spend about 60% of the available time on technique building materials and about 40% on performance materials. The eighth grade should be about 40% on technique building materials and 60% on performance materials. If the seventh and eighth grades are combined as a string class or an orchestra, the amount of technique building materials and performance materials should be about even.

High School (9-12) – This group is principally a performing orchestra and should meet five days a week (three with selected winds and two with strings alone).

Fifth, Sixth, and Seventh Grade Plan (4-3-2-3)

Middle School (5-7) – The fifth grade (beginning string class) should meet three to five days a week. The sixth grade (second year string class) should meet five days a week so that these students will be ready to be in a performing organization in the seventh grade. These classes should be primarily technique building classes, otherwise the students will not be ready to perform as an orchestra when they reach the seventh grade. In the seventh grade, class should be held five days a week and continue to expand technique with considerable emphassis on performance. About two-thirds of the time should be spent on performance materials and one-third on technical materials.

Junior High School (8-9) – This group (fourth and fifth year string class) should meet five days a week (two or three days in full orchestra with selected winds and two or three days a week strings only). About three-fourths of the time should be spent on performance and one-fourth on technical materials.

High School (10-12) – This class should meet five days a week (three days with selected winds and two days with strings only). This group will be primarily a performance group.

OVERVIEW OF SCHEDULING PRINCIPLES)

All of the sample schedules are essentially the same – *beginning classes start in the fifth grade.* For the first two years, the string classes are treated mainly as technique classes rather than performing groups. Expansion of string technique is continued in the third year but there is increased emphasis on performing as a string orchestra.

Winds should be added from the fourth year on and a complete orchestra experience with concert and contest activities should be provided. To maintain interest and allow the opportunity to play different styles of music, full orchestra is an absolute necessity for the strings. Obviously, it is a must if the winds are to have any orchestral experience at all. Also, to prevent the frequently few boy string players from feeling that all musicians are girls, it is good to bring the wind players in by the fourth year as brass players particularly tend to be boys. On the secondary level, it is imperative to schedule the orchestra five days a week (with selected winds, and at least two days a week with strings only) if the result to be accomplished is to be of top quality.

Why Not Start Beginners Earlier? – It will be noticed that in every case the fifth grade has been designated as the grade to start the beginning string classes rather than the fourth grade (or lower) that many teachers favor. The reasons that the authors feel strongly that the fifth grade is the grade to begin string students are:

(1) By the fifth grade, the child is larger physically and fewer changes of instrument size are necessary, cutting overall cost to the parents. (Usually only one change will be necessary if the students are started in the fifth grade.)

(2) The percentage of children succeeding, and, as a result, staying in the program, will be considerably greater when they are started later.

(3) The added physical, mental, and social maturity of the older children generally far outweighs the advantage of the additional time gained from starting them earlier.

(4) Every year that the children are in the program (before reaching a performance group) increases the problem of keeping the students interested in the string program. If interest lags, drop outs increase. To prevent this, the activities of a *performance-oriented* group are needed by the beginning of the third year.

(5) Each additional year that the children are in the program increases the expense to the school system. Unless money is no object, the authors feel that starting lower than the fifth grade *cannot* be justified financially.

All of the above reasons given for starting in the fifth grade are equally valid reasons to postpone the starting of beginners until the sixth (or even the seventh) grade except for one vital consideration! *It takes about three years of properly taught string-class lessons to prepare students to play in an orchestra.* If beginning classes are postponed beyond the fifth grade, the students will not be ready to play in an orchestra until the ninth grade and this is too late for them to begin to participate in a performing orchestra. In the case of the seventh grade orchestra in a 4-3-2-3 middle school plan, an adjustment *must be* made if there is to be a performing group at this school. If the seventh grade students are to be ready to play in an orchestra during the third year, then the sixth grade students *must* meet five days a week as additional technical materials need to be covered to enable them to be able to handle performance type music.

Why Not Start Strings Before the Winds? – Starting the strings a year or more ahead of the winds is probably a mistake. Although starting them a year earlier does get students in the string program before the band personnel recruit, many will want to change to a band instrument the next year regardless of how good the teacher is. This is true, because by the end of the first year, the novelty has worn off. The string students know that work is involved in learning to play. Then, when the band director recruits, the band seems to them to be more exciting, new and easier and some will want to try it.

If the winds and strings are not to be recruited in the same year, it is probably better to recruit strings a year after the winds (contrary to what most people believe). Experience has shown that starting earlier may recruit a few more in the program originally, but this does not usually result in larger numbers participating in the orchestra program later on.

Reduced Scheduling – If the ideal cannot be attained and a reduced schedule is needed, it should be remembered that *the first year is the most important one.* So, if there should be a shortage of personnel or reluctance by the administration to allow the music program adequate time, propose that the first cuts be made in the second and/or third year string classes rather than during the first year. Satisfactory progress can be maintained with less time during second and third years, provided the first year has established solid fundamental habits.

If for some reason the secondary school orchestra must meet less than five days a week, rehearse the strings during the regular school day and schedule full orchestra after school (or an evening) once a week for a two-hour rehearsal. Other alternatives that have been found to work well in some school systems are to use the lunch period(s), activity periods, or before-school period for full orchestra.

A reduced, but workable schedule, might resemble this:

(1) Fifth grade (beginning) class – three days a week with one half-hour classes.

(2) Sixth grade (second year) class – two days a week with one-half hour classes.

(3) Seventh grade (third year) class – three days a week with forty-five minute periods.

Starting Late Students – It is a common practice with orchestra programs that start in the fifth grade to allow additional beginning string students from the sixth grade to start at the same time. This has not been particularly successful for several reasons. First, the additional maturity of the sixth graders causes problems if they are put in with the fifth graders. (*note:* The authors strongly believe it is unwise to mix-up different grade levels (ages) in the same beginning class at school). Second, when the sixth grade beginners reach the seventh grade they are a year behind the seventh graders who started in the fifth grade. This situation forces the teacher to go back and cover second year material with all, go on to the third year materials with the late starters, or set up a special class for those who started in the sixth grade. The last alternative is the best solution, but it requires more personnel.

A better solution is to set up a beginning class five days a week on the seventh grade level. Students at this age, with classes five days a week and a judicious editing of materials, can learn enough technique to be ready to participate in a fourth year full orchestra program by the end of the seventh grade. However, string technique classes *must* be continued for reinforcement and review two days a week with all the students on the eighth and ninth grade level.

In the event that the beginning classes are on some level other than the fifth grade, the authors feel even more strongly that late beginners should wait to start until they are in some sort of a secondary situation (junior high or middle school) where they can be given lessons five days a week and can progress very quickly to enable them to join the other students in a performing group as soon as possible. It is definitely not a good idea to put them in the performing group *before* they have learned the missed technique as they will be no asset to the group and will, of course, get very discouraged. *Warning:* Do not mix up students of different grade levels in the first three years of playing.

Scheduling of Classes Within The School Day

ELEMENTARY LEVEL

On the *elementary level*, when the school is using the conventional self-contained classroom type scheduling, make sure that *everyone*, including the classroom teachers, principals, students, and parents understand that instrumental lessons are not meant to take the place of any other subject or to be used as an excuse to miss an academic subject. Students enrolled in the instrumental class should understand that they must do everything that everyone else does in *addition* to their instrumental music class.

In an ordinary elementary school there are many times during the day when the classroom teachers are not presenting new materials or reviewing for a test. To avoid as much conflict as possible, schedule instrumental music at those times when students are left on their own to read, study with others, or go to the library or resource center. Request that the principal ask the classroom teachers to schedule this kind of activity when instrumental music will be held in that building.

If for some reason the teacher cannot schedule instrumental music during the time slots mentioned above, another possibility is to schedule during part of a recess period. Be careful, however, not to make the students miss all of a recess period all of the time, because it is important that the students get at least part of their recess most of the time. Other times that can be used that will not cause instrumental students to miss academics are parts of lunch periods and, as a last resort, general music. Another idea that has been very successful in some school systems is to place all students taking instrumental music in one classroom so that the entire class goes to band or orchestra leaving the classroom teacher with planning time while they are gone.

Most administrators and teachers will be able to tolerate students leaving their classes if the instrumental music lessons don't spread over such a big time period that students are apparently "coming and going" all day.

A successful way to minimize the number of interruptions to the regular school schedule and thus facilitate scheduling of time for the lessons is to have two or three teachers scheduled in one building at the same time and hold two or three classes at once. Obviously, only a system with two or more instrumental music teachers can take advantage of these options. (See sample schedule in Figure No. 1.)

8:30 – 9	**Monday**	**Tuesday**	**Wednesday**	**Thursday**	**Friday**
Teacher A	Beginning Woodwind 5	Advanced Winds 6	Beginning Woodwind 5	Advanced Winds 6	Beginning Woodwind 5
Teacher B	Beginning Brass 5		Beginning Brass 5		Beginning Brass 5
Teacher C	Beginning Strings 5	Advanced Strings 6	Beginning Strings 5	Advanced Strings 6	Beginning Strings 5
9 – 9:30	**Monday**	**Tuesday**	**Wednesday**	**Thursday**	**Friday**
Teacher A	Advanced Winds 6				
Teacher C	Advanced Strings 6				

Three Teacher Schedule
Figure No. 1

With the schedule shown in Figure No. 1 there are only six interruptions a week of the regular school schedule (three in the fifth grade and three in the sixth grade). All instrumental classes are out of the way in one-half hour's time four days of the week and one hour's time on one day of the week. At first glance, it would seem that Teacher B could teach Tuesday and Thursday at 8:30 and eliminate Teacher A and C teaching the second half hour period on Monday, but there are several reasons why it is better not to do this. If Teacher B would teach these students on Tuesday and Thursday this would mean that the students would have one teacher two days a week and a different teacher on the third day. To change teachers in this manner would confuse the students because, especially at this age, different personalities, procedures, and pace could really upset them. Supposing Teachers A and C were assigned to their respective classes because they were in their areas of greatest competency, it would be foolish to change to a teacher of lesser ability.

8:30 – 9	Monday	Tuesday	Wednesday	Thursday	Friday
Teacher A	Beginning Brass 5	Beginning Strings 5	Beginning Brass 5	Beginning Strings 5	Beginning Strings 5
Teacher B	Beginning Woodwind 5	Advanced Winds 6	Beginning Woodwind 5	Advanced Winds 6	Advanced Winds 6
9 – 9:30	**Monday**	**Tuesday**	**Wednesday**	**Thursday**	**Friday**
Teacher A	Advanced Strings 6		Advanced Strings 6	Advanced Strings 6	Beginning Brass 5
Teacher B					Beginning Woodwind 5

Two Teacher Schedule
Figure No. 2

It will be noticed in Figure No. 2 that there are now nine interruptions in the school week instead of only six as in Figure No. 1. This schedule presupposes that both teachers teach winds and strings. All classes are out of the way in a half hour's time, one day a week, and within one hour, four days a week. However, for the fifth graders four days a week there is only a half hour's interruption and during only one day a week are classes interrupted for an hour. The same is true of the sixth grade.

9 – 9:30	Monday	Tuesday	Wednesday	Thursday	Friday
Teacher A	Beginning Winds 5	Advanced Winds 6	Beginning Winds 5	Advanced Winds 6	Beginning Winds 5
Teacher B	Beginning Strings 5	Advanced Strings 6	Beginning Strings 5	Advanced Strings 6	Beginning Strings 6

Alternate Two Teacher Schedule
Figure No. 3

In Figure No. 3 Teacher A is a wind specialist and Teacher B is a string specialist. This schedule is usually found in use in smaller school systems. It does not require that the wind personnel teach strings or the wind personnel teach winds. The disadvantage of this schedule is that it forces the band person to teach all the winds together.

8:30 – 9	Monday	Tuesday	Wednesday	Thursday	Friday
Teacher A	Beginning Woodwind 5	Beginning Strings 5	Beginning Woodwind 5	Beginning Strings 5	Beginning Woodwind 5
9 – 9:30	**Monday**	**Tuesday**	**Wednesday**	**Thursday**	**Friday**
Teacher A	Beginning Brass 5	Advanced Strings 6	Beginning Brass 5	Beginning Brass 5	Beginning Strings 5
9:30 – 10	**Monday**	**Tuesday**	**Wednesday**	**Thursday**	**Friday**
Teacher A	Advanced Strings	Advanced Winds 6	Advanced Winds 6	Advanced Strings 6	Advanced Winds 6

One Teacher Schedule
Figure No. 4

With the schedule shown in Figure No. 4 there are now fifteen interruptions in the school week instead of the six interruptions a week for the three teacher schedule or the nine interruptions for the two teacher schedule. This schedule is planned so that the same person can handle all the wind and string teaching in this school. It will also be noticed that as fewer teachers are used the number and length of the interruptions to any one class are increased. In order to minimize this effect, even with one teacher making fifteen interruptions a week, the fifth grade classes are scheduled consecutively so that the interruptions are kept within one hour time slot as are the sixth grade classes.

It should be understood that the foregoing schedules apply only to the scheduling within any one school. It is possible within a larger system to have a one-teacher schedule in one school and have a multiple teacher schedule in other schools.

SECONDARY LEVEL (MIDDLE SCHOOL, JUNIOR HIGH OR HIGH SCHOOL)

The seventh grade string class (third year) should be scheduled a *minimum* of three days a week (preferably five) for a full period during the regular school day just as band or any other class would be scheduled. To facilitate scheduling on the seventh grade level, it is sometimes possible for instrumental music to be substituted for fine arts, general music or an exploratory enrichment type course.

The eighth and ninth grade strings should be placed in a full orchestra situation, with the strings meeting daily and the best wind players joining them two or three times weekly. Depending on the number of string players available, they can be either organized into one orchestra of eighth and ninth grade players or a separate orchestra for each grade. Probably a minimum of twenty-five strings in each group would be advisable before splitting into two orchestras.

On the high school level, the orchestra experience should include the best winds available, one on a part, meeting two or three days a week with the strings rehearsing every day.

Orchestra should be scheduled as a subject with its own time slot just as band is. It is *not* a *good solution* to schedule *orchestra* at the *same time as band* because this causes competition between the teachers for the top players that are needed by both groups. Besides, these outstanding students certainly need both types of experience! Also, while it may seem like two mature directors can share students, it usually does not work this way. No matter how it is handled, the students will feel frustrated and as if they are being pulled between the two directors. If the directors are conscientious, they (the directors) are bound to feel that their opportunity to do their job properly is being jeopardized.

If the school day has at least seven scheduling periods (plus lunch period), an administrator who really wants to can set up a schedule that will allow for band and/or orchestra plus four or five other major subjects. If there are less than seven periods, then the student may have to choose between orchestra and some other subject unless full orchestra is scheduled outside the regular school day (not recommended). It has been found that many students will take such classes as Driver Education, Typing, etc., during summer school to make room in their regular term schedules for orchestra if it is suggested to them by the orchestra director.

Another solution that eliminates the competition between directors is to have the *same person direct both groups*. If a competent, qualified person is available, this has been found to be an excellent solution by many school systems. This is so, because the most important qualifications necessary for success are common to both good band and orchestra directors.

SCHEDULING OF INSTRUMENTAL MUSIC PERSONNEL (HORIZONTAL VERSUS VERTICAL)

At first, when the orchestra program is small, there is no choice of how to schedule the personnel. However, as the program grows, a crucial decision that will effect many things will have to be made and the teacher should give thought to this matter well in advance. There are, in general, two ways to schedule in larger systems – *horizontally and vertically. Horizontal* organization is when a teacher is assigned to teach only on one level, i.e., elementary, middle (or junior high), or senior high. *Vertical* organization is when a teacher teaches on *two* or more levels, i.e., elementary and one or more of the secondary levels.

The authors feel very strongly that *vertical utilization* of staff allows by far the *best quality of teaching.* The horizontal scheduling (unfortunately the most common) has one advantage (to administrators) and that is that a teacher can be assigned either to *one* building (or one level) making the scheduling less complicated and possibly more efficient timewise. The disadvantages of horizontal scheduling are so numerous that it is appropriate that they be discussed one by one.

First of all, because in horizontal scheduling no teacher has the students for more than a year or two, it becomes extremely easy for *every* teacher along the line (except the first year teacher) to blame all the problems that the students have on the teachers who had them before they reached his class. The previous teacher(s), of course, feel that there is no point in trying too hard because they feel that the teachers at the secondary level won't do anything with them when they get them. Voila! Human Nature. *Everyone* is in free! *No one* can be blamed for the teaching failures. Obviously, with the vertical scheduling, this cannot happen because the teacher that had the students last year will have them again the next year and will probably have them several more years as well. Therefore, blaming the previous teacher is simply self-defeating.

Second, with horizontal scheduling there is very little continuity from one grade level to the next as the elementary teacher(s) probably doesn't know and may not even care what is happening on the junior high or middle school level. Likewise, the junior high or middle school teacher may be unaware of what is happening at the high school and elementary school level, etc. On the other hand, with vertical scheduling of personnel, the elementary teacher knows what is happening on the secondary level because he is also the secondary teacher.

Third, with horizontal scheduling, the students are usually graduating to teachers that they do not know and this makes many of them feel very insecure and can cause some unnecessary drop-outs. With the vertical organization, the students are *all* going on to a teacher that they have known somewhere along the line and thus they feel less fearful of what is ahead.

Fourth, with horizontal scheduling, teachers often show less concern about students dropping out of the orchestra program because they feel that fewer students are easier to teach. With vertical scheduling, however, the teacher realizes right from the beginning that any student lost is a student that he will not have in the orchestra program at the secondary level later on. This gives an added incentive to the teacher to go that "extra mile" with borderline students – to do whatever needs to be done to help them to succeed and stay in the program.

Vertical scheduling is more complicated to arrange than horizontal scheduling and may require somewhat better and more dedicated teachers. But, the authors feel strongly that if the program is to develop into an outstanding one, *mediocre teachers cannot be tolerated at any level.*

Planning For Necessary Equipment and Other Expenses

Another thing that must be arranged for at the outset with the Superintendent is the equipment that it will be necessary for the school system to provide for the string program.

PRIVATELY-OWNED VERSUS SCHOOL-OWNED INSTRUMENTS

The authors feel very strongly that the *best results* are obtained when the students *furnish their own instruments.* Parents *will* furnish instruments for the students unless they are somehow conditioned to expect that the school will do it. Surprisingly, it has been found in almost all successful instrumental music programs today that the students furnish all but the very largest and most expensive instruments. One can only guess why this is true, but it would seem that the parents and students who own their own instruments feel more committed to the program. Apparently buying the instrument initially, and assuming the responsibility for its maintenance, makes them have a completely different attitude about the music program than those who depend on the school to furnish the instruments.

The common assumption is that poorer families cannot or will not buy instruments for thier children. Experience has shown, however, that this is not true. The authors feel that people tend to value a program according to what it costs in terms of financial effort and responsibility. People are also prone to feel that anything given free doesn't have much value.

When the students furnish their own instruments the drop-out rate has been found to be less, the level of achievement higher, and the program to be more meaningful to everyone. The students furnishing their own instruments, of course, save the school board money, but equally important, is that it makes the Superintendent (and the school board) think twice before deciding to cut the program when individual parents have a fairly large financial investment. This initial commitment is made easier for the parents by the rental-lease (with option to buy) plan that most music stores make available.

Who Should Handle The Recruiting? – The authors feel that to avoid misunderstandings with the administration, the parents, and the music dealers, the recruiting of students should be handled and completely controlled by the teacher(s) who are going to teach the class. The teacher's first and only responsibility is to the students and their parents, and must be to see that they (the students) are obtaining and using first-quality instruments.

ELEMENTARY LEVEL

String Basses – The biggest and most important item(s) that will be required are *half-size* string basses. Basses are absolutely necessary for a complete orchestra program. Most generally parents will not purchase them for the students in the beginning so they need to be secured by the school board.

One half-size bass, French bow, and case will be needed for each elementary school the first year. It must be kept in mind that the second year another bass will be needed per school. Recognize at the outset what this implies in future years so that plans can be made. If the system has four grade schools, there would be the possibility of four basses in the seventh grade orchestra, eight basses in the eighth and ninth grade orchestra and twelve basses in the senior high orchestra, barring moveouts or dropouts. These do not need to be bought all at one time, of course, but must be *planned* for from the beginning. If there are more than four schools feeding a junior high, it might be wise to only start bass beginners every other year in some of the schools to save money and avoid a surfeit of basses later.

If money to buy instruments is seen as a problem by the Superintendent, it is suggested that the school buy the basses and rent them to the students for the same rental charged by the music store for cellos, saxophones, and oboes. In this way the expense of the basses can be amortized over about a seven year period.

Music Stands – Music stands will be needed and the authors prefer one stand per student at the elementary level. It is recommended, therefore, that the students supply their own folding music stands to use both at school and at home for practicing – thus eliminating the school having to store and maintain them. The money saved can be used to better advantage in many other areas.

Method Books – Method books should be the responsibility of the individual students enrolled in the program. Some supplementary music will be needed but the expense to the school is minimal – perhaps the price of two arrangements and thirty-five books per school for the first year and less in subsequent years as the library is built for this age level.

SECONDARY LEVEL

String Basses – At the secondary level enough 3/4 size basses (the size commonly used by adults), French bows, and cases will be needed to allow all bass players started in the fifth grade to continue playing.

Cellos – Many schools forbid the transportation of cellos on school buses. If this is so, it will be necessary that the school provide enough cellos for the students to use in school. This will allow the cellists to keep their own instruments at home for practice purposes thus eliminating the problem of damaging their instruments (or the schools) while transporting them.

Music Stands – Durable, school type music stands will be needed at this level. String bass and wind players will each need their own stand while the string players (except for the string basses) traditionally look two to a stand.

Tuning Device – A standard A-440 tuning bar is necessary and is superior to tuning to unstable oboes.

Cello and Bass Storage Racks – Storage racks for the cellos and basses are available commercially or can be made in the school shop department. These racks allow the instruments to be stored up-right thus eliminating the danger of damage while not in use.

String Bass Stools – At this level, it is strongly recommended that stools be provided for the string bass players. They can be purchased relatively inexpensively from furniture supply houses. While many music accessory catalogues show special stools for string basses, it has been found that it is really not necessary to purchase a special bass stool.

Sheet Music Budget – The sheet music budget will need to be large enough to provide music for all performing organizations at the secondary level.

Repair Budget – A repair budget can be kept to a minimum by having the students be responsible for their own repairs and the purchase of new strings and bow rehairing.

Seeing the Elementary Principal(s)

All of the scheduling proposals, options, attitudes, etc., that were expressed and explained to the Superintendent in regard to scheduling string classes during the day must now be repeated to the various principals. There is one very important difference, however, and that is that the Superintendent has already decided that the schools *will* offer the string classes and how much time is to be allotted for them. There should be no need of further discussion on this point.

Individual Building Schedules

It should be the elementary principal's role to decide *when* the teacher is to come to his building within the limits of the times that are available. If more than one school is involved, a joint meeting with *all* of the principals is a good idea. At this meeting a schedule of the times available can be presented, and each can then choose the one that will be best for him. By doing it this way, the principals don't have the option of telling the teacher that they can't use him when he has the time. The Superintendent has already decided that the teacher is going to come to their schools so they are in the position of fighting the other principals for the teacher's time. It might also be well to include the Superintendent in this meeting. The string teacher's attitude can then be something like: "Here are the times I have available, you (the principals) divide it up to suit yourselves; I am at your service." Obviously, the times during the school day that would not be available are when the secondary classes meet (if the string teacher teaches at that level). Be careful to not let *anyone* decide that elementary instrumental classes should be held before or after school. *Remember: All* instrumental music classes should be held during the *regular* school day.

Teaching Facilities and Room Equipment

It is very important that it be made clear to each principal at the very beginning what will be needed to teach properly at his school. The teacher should not be afraid to ask for whatever is really needed or he may find himself teaching in some very undesirable places and with no equipment.

Rehearsal Room – Ideally, a rehearsal room should be a place that will be accessible before class starts so that the teacher can tune the instruments and have the chairs ready for class. Some possible rehearsal places are all purpose rooms, the vocal music room (when not in use), the cafeteria (at times of the day when it is quiet), and kindergarten rooms (at certain times of the day and/or days of the week).

Some other places that might be available to hold class, if the above-mentioned rooms are not available, are hallways, boiler rooms (if large enough), the teacher's lounge, and regular classrooms during times that they are not used. *Warning:* Don't ask for these places because they certainly are not ideal – only suggest them as a last resort! If awkward places like these *must* be used, it does not need to be all bad as the teacher's plight is so obviously terrible that a lot of attention will be received from the principal, fellow teachers, and students. This attention can be a positive thing as the students, seeing a class held in odd places, often think that it looks interesting and may want to enroll in the class. The principal may be embarrassed or impressed enough by the work that is done under such conditions, that he might strive to find a better place for the class to be taught. Another idea that has often helped a teacher to gain a place to teach is to set the *beginning* class up in the hall near the principal's office. Usually it isn't long until he finds some place else for the class to meet.

Chairs – Chairs of the proper size and design (See Part II, Chapter II) will be needed for the students. Simply using the regular classroom chairs or folding chairs, although often done, is *not* the best solution to the chair problem as they don't really fit young string students.

Chalkboard – A chalkboard and an eraser are quite necessary for efficient teaching. If the class is to be taught in a place that doesn't have a permanent board, then the teacher should obtain a portable one.

Instrument Storage – A place to store instruments before and after class is needed. Ideally, this should be the classroom that will be used for the string class. Obviously, if this room is to be used throughout the day, then another place will be needed – preferably a place that can be locked or where an adult can keep a watchful eye on the instruments to make sure they are safe.

Student Recruiting Program and Parents Meeting

A meeting time(s) will have to be scheduled to present a recruiting demonstration for prospective first year students during the school day and another time, probably in the evening, for a meeting with the parents and their interested children.

A stringed instrument demonstration program for the fifth grade students (or whatever grade level beginners are started) is absolutely necessary to secure sufficient new students each year. This should take place in a setting where the students can be as close to the instruments and the teacher presenting the program as possible. If time allows, schedule a meeting for every home room so that the groups are small and personal. If the teacher cannot go to the individual classrooms, then he should arrange to hold the recruiting demonstration in a large room without chairs.

The teacher should have the students sit on the floor around and close to the instruments and the teacher. If it is necessary to combine several classrooms together for the demonstration, then it is wise to limit the number of students to no more than sixty at a time. The actual mechanics and description of the recruiting program for the students will be covered thoroughly in Part II, Chapter II.

Seeing the Secondary Principal(s)

There are relatively few problems that need to be discussed with the secondary principal(s). As most schools already have band programs, there should be no problem with the school needing rooms, stands, chairs and room equipment. It will be necessary, however, to discuss the scheduling of classes, the music budget, and the need for a place for storage of the stringed instruments (particularly racks for the cellos and basses).

Scheduling

All orchestras should be scheduled five days a week for one full period (forty to fifty-five minutes) preferably at a time *other* than when the band meets. (If the wind players are to get the greatest amount of benefit from both band and orchestra, they should not have to miss one to participate in the other.) The teacher should be sure to schedule *only* the best wind players available as orchestral playing is basically soloistic and demands the best players. Also, because it is recommended that winds be in the orchestra only two or three days a week, it takes the best possible players to learn the music with the limited number of rehearsals. Only as a last resort should there be *only* string orchestras in the curriculum at the secondary level. If full orchestra cannot be scheduled during the day, the teacher *must* use an evening or before-school or after-school as the rehearsal time with the full orchestra.

Music Budget

Funds will have to be budgeted for sheet music for the orchestra. About the same amount of money will need to be budgeted for an orchestra as is needed for a concert band. The first year, however, it is wise to allow some extra funds because there will be no library of previously used music to fall back on.

Seeing the Music Dealer(s)

The teacher and the local music dealers are mutually interdependent, and therefore, they *must* work together. Without a cooperative music dealer to service the school, it is very difficult to institute or continue a strong music program. On the other hand, without the teacher(s) doing a good job, the dealer obviously cannot stay in the music education business. The dealer can only do his job if he understands exactly what is expected of him in the way of instruments, music supplies, stands, strings, rosin, etc.

Most music dealers are very willing to cooperate with a teacher who is knowledgeable and gets results. To a dealer this means that students rent instruments and rarely return them. A dealer stays in business by selling things. He cannot afford to rent out instruments equipped exactly as specified and stock the necessary accessories if most of the students do not continue in the instrumental music program once they begin (85-100%). The dealer *must be* supported through the string teacher sending students into the store for the equipment the teacher requested him to stock. For instance, a dealer should not be asked to stock 1/2 and 3/4 size strings, if the students are to be allowed to use full-size strings on small-size instruments. Or, he should not be asked to stock instruments with patented adjustable pegs and then have the teacher allow attic instruments and instruments from other music dealers in the classes without them.

It is very important for the success of the orchestra program that the music dealer *know exactly* what accessories the teacher expects the students to have so that the parents can get everything they need in one trip. Also, he will need to know *when* they will be needed. It really causes problems in the class when the dealer doesn't have the equipment that is needed and the parents have to visit the store several times to get it. (Students will be in the class for weeks without the proper equipment.)

The string teacher *must* see the music dealer(s) as soon as possible (hopefully as early as three or four months ahead) before the opening of school to give him the date that he can expect students and parents to start coming into the store for rental of instruments. The teacher should get a verbal commitment that the dealer agrees to have *all* of the instruments that will be needed on hand and equipped as the teacher as specified.

Quantity and Proportion of Instruments Needed

As a starting point for estimating how many stringed instruments the dealer will need to order, the teacher can figure that at least twenty-five percent of the school system's band beginners for the year before (if it is a new program) will start stringed instruments. Be sure that the music dealer has enough cellos and violas as well as violins. A minimum of one cello and one viola will be needed for every three violins to have a balanced beginning string class that will result in the right proportions later in the secondary orchestra. If the string program is started on the fifth grade level, a class of twenty-five beginners will need a ratio of instruments about as shown below in Figure No. 5.

	Full	Three-fourths	Half-size	Total
Violin	1	9	3	13
Viola	4(Int.)*	2(Jr.)*	--	6
Cello	1	3	2	6
Total	6	14	5	25

*The intermediate size viola is the same size as a full-size violin.
*The junior size viola is the same size as a three-fourth size violin.

Distribution of Instrument Sizes On Fifth Grade Level
Figure No. 5

If the teacher is forced to start beginners in the fourth grade it should be realized that more smaller instruments and fewer larger ones will be needed. If beginning in the sixth grade, more larger and fewer smaller instruments will be needed. There *will be* students interested in playing the larger instruments (viola and cello) *if* the teacher uses the size of the hand and size of the child as a criteria when counseling students on which instruments to play. (See Part I, Chapter II for more detail on the recruiting of students.)

Rental-Lease Program

It will be necessary to discuss with the dealer the rental, trial purchase or lease agreement that he will want the parents to sign so that it can be approved and then explained to the parents. The terms should be at least as good as the ones given for band instruments of equal value. If the classes are taught as advocated in this book, the return ratio will be much less than that of the band instruments (if the band instruments are taught traditionally).

While seeing the dealer, the teacher should also discuss the arrangements for "stepping up" to better quality instruments as it is almost impossible to have a really first-class orchestra tone with "student line" (lesser quality) instruments. This is much more critical with stringed instruments than band instruments. Many dealers will allow credit for all or most of the money spent on student line instruments, less a maintenance charge, if they are turned in on a larger or "better" instrument.

The teacher should suggest to the music dealer that when a student is ready for a full-size instrument (hopefully the second or third year) that he try to get the student to move up to a better instrument rather than go to a full-size student line instrument. This can usually be done if the parent is made to realize first that it is cheaper to buy *one good instrument* than it is to buy a student line instrument and then later have to get a better one.

Secondly, tell the parent that there is much difference in sound between a student line instrument and a better instrument and that the difference in sound is much greater than the difference in price between the two. A good way to convince the parents of the difference in sound is to have the music dealer keep some better instruments on hand for the students to try out. A five minute tryout of a better instrument will convince both the parent and the student of the reality of the difference in quality between a more expensive instrument and a student line instrument.

Instrument Specifications and Accessories

The importance of instruments properly adjusted and equipped cannot be over-emphasized. This factor alone can make a great difference in the dropout rate of the string classes. It is imperative for the teaching efficiency of the teacher, as well as for the ease of learning of the student, that all beginning instruments be equipped with four chrome wound steel strings, adjusters, patented adjustable pegs, well-fitted bridges and tail pieces. (For more detailed information see the MENC Specifications in Chapter I, Part III). The bows should be new (or newly rehaired) and every student outfit should include a music stand, rosin, pencil, polish and a properly fitted shoulder pad (violin and viola) or an end pin rest (cello and bass). It is also highly desirable for psychological reasons that the instruments and cases be attractive visually.

Educational and Recruiting Aids

Many educational and recruiting aids are available through the music dealer to help the teacher with the recruiting and teaching of the classes – posters, case stickers, pamphlets, music folders, movies, records, etc. The teacher should check with his local music dealer about what recruiting aids he can supply and make use of them!

Method Books for Class Instruction

The teacher will need to tell the music dealer what method books will be used in the classes and the approximate number that will be needed early enough so that he has time to order them from the publisher. This is essential if the dealer is expected to have them all in stock before school begins.

Instrument Accessories

In order for the string teacher to be able to run the classes efficiently, the students *must* have immediate access to various accessories as they are needed. These must be kept in constant stock and in sufficient quantity. The teacher will need to let the music dealer know the accessories he wishes to use throughout the year. The teacher should be careful to not ask the music dealer to stock things that he will very seldom use.

Strings

Besides full-size strings, the music dealer will need a supply of half and three-fourth size strings (if small-size instruments are used in beginning classes). Small-size instruments cannot properly use full-sized strings, so stress this fact to both the students and the music dealer. Only chrome wound steel strings are available in various sizes (gut wound strings are not); make sure that the dealer also has a stock of the adjusters that *must* be used with the chrome steel string. Using steel strings without adjusters makes it very difficult to tune the instruments and puts more pressure on the top of the instruments than they are designed to take. As the string program matures, the dealer will also need to stock gut-wound strings that should be used on better quality ("step-up") instruments. It is important to remember that gut wound strings *should not* be used on beginning instruments because they can't be replaced often enough to remain true and also that they are much more difficult to keep in tune. (For more information on strings and adjusters see Chapter II (Strings and Pegs).)

Mutes

The music dealer will also need to stock mutes – preferably the kind that attach to the strings behind the bridge and slide up on the bridge when they are used. These can't be dropped and lost as easily as the traditional kind that are removed from the instruments.

Rosin

The music dealer will need a generous supply of rosin as the students will break and lose it at a rate at first that makes one wonder if it is a secret part of their diets. For the first year or so they will need a harder rosin that is amber colored. After they have developed more bow control (when the rosin starts to fall on top of the instrument), they will need to start using the dark colored rosin which is softer and stickier and adheres to the string more than the light colored rosin. Bass players will need a special bass rosin (No. 2 or No. 3 depending on the climate it is used in). It is probably best to use No. 3 in the beginning as it is harder and No. 2 (softer) after they advance. For all instruments (with the exception of the bass), *rosin is the same* so that music dealer only needs to stock three kinds of rosin – light and dark (for violins, violas, and cellos) and bass rosin (No. 2 and No. 3).

Recruiting for Beginners 2

INTRODUCTION

The recruiting of new students for the string program is perhaps the single most important thing that the teacher does during the school year. Teaching methods, materials, techniques of building skills and enthusiasm for the program mean nothing if students cannot be secured for the classes to be taught.

When the teacher is recruiting, the goal *must be* to get the largest possible number of students involved in the program. *Quality can and will come from quantity.* Large numbers of students, properly taught, must and *will* result in top quality students emerging from the orchestra program. It should be clearly understood that the attempt to secure quality students by using tests to exclude those likely to fail is doomed. First of all, tests (when they do what they are designed to do) only measure where the child is *now.* Teachers are supposed to be specialists in "moving" a child from where he is now to where it is desired for him to be in a year, two years, etc. Teachers must accept the responsibility of teaching, instead of looking for failure-proof students.

Second, music (in this case playing a stringed instrument) is something that will enrich the life of *every* child given a chance to participate. For this reason, no one has a right to say to any student, "You will not be able to play well enough to be in my orchestra; therefore, you cannot start to play." They *all* have a right: to start, to be taught to the best of the teacher's ability, and to experience the amount of success they can achieve (which is much more than many people think). Even the most valid and reliable tests do not claim to be 100% accurate and so no teacher can dare, in good conscience, to deny even one student the opportunity to experience the joys of music on the basis of a test that can be wrong.

Third, the effect that the teacher has on the students is so great that the test predictions are irrelevant. The only honest way, then, is to take *all* students who are able to do acceptable work in academic subjects and have the necessary physical equipment to play (arms, fingers, etc.).

WHEN SHOULD RECRUITING BE DONE?

Recruiting is a full-time continuous activity! *Everyting* that the teacher does, directly or indirectly, affects the recruiting of future students.

Everytime the teacher enters an elementary school, he is having either a positive or negative effect on all the people he comes into contact with. His attitudes towards them, his physical appearance, his general disposition are constantly being evaluated by all. Therefore, it behooves him to realize that he is either helping or hurting his program with every person he meets – students, parents, teachers and principals.

Students have friends, brothers and sisters who will know about the teacher before he is even aware of them. Parents will tell other parents about him. Classroom teachers and principals obviously can have a great effect on whether or not the students enroll in the string classes.

One of the best ways to recruit, and at the same time encourage the students already in the program, is to have the older students perform for younger, potential students at *every* level. The fifth and sixth grade students can perform for the Kindergarten and primary grades; the junior high student can play for the upper elementary grades; and the high school students can play for the elementary students and the junior high students.

To help the elementary principals and teachers to feel as if they are a part of the instrumental music program, it is an excellent idea to list the students participating in the string classes in the printed program by homeroom teachers. In a concert involving more than one elementary school, they can be listed by school and principal. If printed programs are not used, another idea would be to introduce the string students and classroom teachers involved at the concert.

ELEMENTARY LEVEL RECRUITING

Before actually entering the classroom to talk to the prospective students, many preliminary steps will need to be taken. These steps all involve the cooperation of other people – principals, classroom teachers, classroom music teacher, instrumental music staff, and the news media.

Principal

As always, the elementary principal must be consulted as he will need to be involved in setting a time for the demonstration sessions with the students during the school day. He will also need to help with the students' and parents' meeting that will be held during the evening hours.

If possible, the principal should introduce the teacher to the prospective students and their teachers at the school demonstration, and to the parents at the evening demonstration. After all, the teacher is building the string program for his (or her) school and the principal's appearance at these meetings will indicate to the people his interest in the program.

Classroom Teachers

The time for the classroom meetings will be set up with the principal, but if possible, a trip to the room(s) of all the teachers of children to be involved is a very good idea. The string teacher must make sure that the classroom teachers understand *when* and *where* the demonstrations are to be held. It should be explained briefly to them what is going to be done and that each student will need to bring a pencil. It is also a good idea to get a list from them of the students' names, telephone numbers and some sort of indication of who they think the top students academically and socially are. There idea on these students can be very helpful later on.

Sending a brief written note (with the pertinent details) to the classroom teachers the day before the demonstration meeting is a good idea and, it serves as a reminder as the teachers and principals sometimes forget what has been said to them. A real interest builder is to get the classroom teacher and/or the principal to agree to participate in the demonstration by attempting to play one of the instruments. Explain to them that they are to do a terrible job of playing so the students laugh and feel good when they (the students) play and do it better.

Classroom Music Teacher

The classroom music teacher, if there is one, should also be informed about the forthcoming recruiting of students. He (or she) can help encourage the students to consider playing the stringed instruments by playing orchestra records, presenting a unit on the strings and just generally making the students aware of how they are used constantly on radio, television, and for movie background music. Most classroom music teachers are usually quite willing to do this, especially if the string teacher helps them by providing ideas and materials for this presentation. A list of the classroom music teacher's better students would also be helpful in making sure no potentially good students are overlooked later.

Other Instrumental Staff

The string recruiting should be coordinated with the wind recruiting for the band programs. If the strings are to be recruited separately from the winds (advisable if the same teachers are not teaching both), then the recruiting for the strings should be done *after* the winds and *not before*. It should not be done at the same time unless the same person(s) teach(es) both.

There are several good reasons why the string recruiting *must* follow the wind recruiting. They are:

(1) The last person to talk to the students has a natural advantage because he will be the one that they will remember the best (everything else being equal).

(2) The last person doing the recruiting doesn't have the problem of students already recruited changing their minds when another person comes to recruit.

(3) If there is already a band program in the schools, and the band people are concerned about the string program hurting them, they will be consoled by the thought that they have already done their recruiting. Even though this is true, there will be *plenty* of good students left. If a band director can recruit half of the class he is truly outstanding! Even if he is this good, this still leaves half of the class available for the string class.

(4) There will be students who really wanted to play an instrument but for some reason didn't quite make up their minds the first time around.

(5) There are students (and parents) who just don't want to be a part of a band program but who will want to play in the orchestra. For these students, it doesn't matter when they are recruited, they will be bound to sign up.

Recruiting Letter

A letter will have to be written and duplicated to send home with the students following their initial demonstration meeting at school. This letter must include a brief rationale for starting lessons on a stringed instrument as well as information about time, frequency, and cost of classes as well as the equipment that will be needed. (See Figure No. 1 (A) and (B) for sample recruiting letters that are used in two successful orchestra programs.)

NORMAN PUBLIC SCHOOLS
NORMAN, OKLAHOMA

OFFICE OF THE SUPERINTENDENT

Fall, 1976

Dear Fifth Grade Students and Parents:

The Department of Music is offering beginning classes in violin, viola, cello, and bass to all interested fifth grade students. The classes will begin on Monday, September 8, and will be held Monday through Thursday of each week thereafter. Classes are thirty minutes in length, they are held during school hours, and all fifth graders are encouraged to participate.

Learning to play a string instrument and belonging to the school orchestra opens up a whole new world of friendship and fun. As a string player, a child is able to take advantage of music performance with orchestras at the middle school, mid-high, and high school levels. The opportunities for playing a string instrument after high school are also abundant – university orchestras which offer generous scholarships to string players, community orchestras, chamber music groups, professional playing in metropolitan symphonies and television and movie studio orchestras. Orchestra students may participate fully in the academic offerings in school, athletics, and other extracurricular activities.

Students who are interested in learning to play a string instrument should bring their parents to one of the following consultation sessions any time between 7:00 p.m. and 9:00 p.m. at Norman High School: Wednesday, September 3rd, and Thursday, September 4th. Parents are asked to park in the lot east of the school and follow signs which will be posted to direct them to the consultation room. During these sessions, members of the music faculty will answer questions concerning the music program and counsel parents and students on instrument size and selection. You may fill out the enrollment blank below and bring it to the session with you. Students who started in summer beginning classes do not need to come to any of these sessions, but they should bring the enrollment blank to the first class with the necessary equipment.

Fees or tuition are not required to enroll in these classes. However, students must provide their own instrument, folding music stand, rosin, soft cloth, pencil, and music book. The title of the music book is *Muller-Rusch String Method, Book I.* Violinists and violists will need a shoulder pad, and cello and bass players will need an end-pin stop. Most parents choose to rent an instrument for the first few months of instruction.

Music in the Norman Public Schools is known across the nation for its high degree of excellence. Your participation in this program will be a rewarding experience, and I hope you will want to become a part of it.

Sincerely,

Supervisor of Music

- -

If you plan to enroll in beginning string music classes this Fall, please fill out this form, detach it from the above letter, and bring it with you to one of the consultation sessions on September 3rd or September 4th anytime from 7:00 p.m. to 9:00 p.m.

I am interested in learning to play a violin, viola, cello, or bass. My

NAME IS____________________. ADDRESS:____________________

PHONE:_______________ SCHOOL____________________________

5TH GRADE TEACHER____________________________. I participated in

summer beginning string music classes.______________(yes or no)

PARENT'S SIGNATURE:__________________________________

Sample Recruiting Letter
Figure No. 1 (A)

NORTH OLMSTED SCHOOLS
NORTH OLMSTED, OHIO

OFFICE OF THE SUPERINTENDENT

October 13, 1976

Dear Fifth Grade Students and Parents:

The Department of Music is offering beginning classes in violin, viola, cello, string bass, flute, clarinet, saxophone, cornet and trombone to all interested fifth grade students. Classes are thirty minutes in length and are held three times a week during school hours.

Learning to play an instrument and belonging to a school band or orchestra opens up a whole new world of friendship and opportunity. As an instrumentalist, a child is able to take advantage of music performance with bands and orchestras at all levels of school. The opportunities for playing their instrument after leaving school are abundant. Besides numerous scholarship opportunities, there are community orchestras and bands; chamber groups, professional playing in dance groups, symphony orchestras, movie and television orchestras; service bands and orchestras. Music students may participate fully in the academic offerings in school, athletics, and other extra curricular activities.

Students who are interested in learning to play an instrument should bring their parents to one of the following meetings which are held at 7:00 p.m.

Oct. 18 Birch School – at Birch School
Oct. 19 Coe and Maple Schools – at Maple School
Oct. 21 Chestnut and Spruce Schools – at Chestnut School
Oct. 25 Pine School – at Pine School
Oct. 26 Butternut and Forest Schools – Jr. Hi. Auditorium

If there is a conflict on the night of your school's meeting, it is suggested that you come to one of the others. At these meetings the entire music program will be explained. There will also be individual consultation to help you select the best instrument for your child and answer any questions you may have.

Please fill out the enrollment blank below and leave it with one of the music teachers before you leave the meeting.

Fees or tuition are not required to enroll in these classes. However, students must provide their own instrument, book, music stand and pencil. Violinist and violists will need a shoulder pad; cellists and bass players will need an end pin stop; string players will need rosin; brass players will need valve oil or slide lubricant; woodwind players will need cork grease and a swab.

Music in the North Olmsted Schools is noted throughout the United States for its excellence. Your participation in this program will be a rewarding experience. We hope you will want to become a part of it.

Sincerely,

Supervisor of Music

- -

(PLEASE BRING THIS TO THE MEETING AND TURN IT IN WHEN YOU HAVE DECIDED WHICH INSTRUMENT IS BEST FOR YOUR CHILD.)

I am interested in playing:

violin ________ flute ________ cornet ________
viola ________ clarinet ________ trombone ________
cello ________ saxophone ________
string bass ________

NAME ____________________ ADDRESS ____________________

PHONE __________ SCHOOL ______________ TEACHER __________

PARENT'S SIGNATURE: ______________________________

Sample Recruiting Letter
Figure No. 1 (B)

Local Newspaper

Although a fine job of teaching and recruiting is absolutely necessary for the program to be able to sustain itself year after year, it is equally important that people in the community know *what* is being done. The reason that this is so vital is that, after the first year, prospective students and parents are receiving most of their ideas of what the music program is all about from people *other* than the teacher. Therefore, it is an extremely important part of the teacher's job to make sure that the people know what it is that it is desired for them to know. For these reasons, all means of communication available must be used. Probably the most obvious and easiest place to start is with the local newspaper.

A copy of the recruiting letter and an article about the string program should be taken to the school editor (sometimes news editor) of the local newspaper approximately a week ahead of the demonstration concerts for the students. At this time, the editor should be told what is being done and ask him to use this information as a basis for a news release about the recruiting and other activities. It is also good to arrange for a picture from a recruiting demonstration to be presented to the editor for publication either with the article or even at a different time. The editor or reporter should be given a chance to ask questions as this may lead to the development of clever human interest stories about the orchestra program for use later.

Radio and Television Stations

Many television and ratio stations in large towns have public service programs or "spots" that will allow groups to announce coming events. Be sure to find out if there are programs of this type and make use of them if they are available. Also, in smaller towns it may be possible to arrange to be interviewed and explain all about the orchestra program, especially if the people are convinced that something new and exciting is happening.

Who Should Be In The Program?

All should play. The string teacher must plan the presentation of instruments to the students carefully, making sure that it appeals to *all* of the children – boys as well as girls. If the program is not planned carefully, there will be a preponderance of girls. There are many ways to avoid this. Some of these are:

(1) Ask older male students to assist in the demonstration. (If possible, use a boy that is well-adjusted and popular – possibly an athlete.)

(2) Be careful in the presentation not to inadvertently give the impression that more girls than boys play stringed instruments.

(3) Point out that most of the famous concert artists and professional players in the past were men but, of course, this is changing now as more and more women achieve recognition.

(4) Remind them that orchestra does not conflict with football as marching band does.

(5) When the students' hand shapes and sizes are studied, point out that the boys often have the larger hands and are therefore especially suited for the viola, cello and bass that require more size and strength of the hand.

(6) Point out the analogies of music to athletics; both athletics and string playing require a very refined coordination and development of strength.

(7) Be certain that the impression is not given that it would be unusual to have as many boys as girls in the orchestra program. Act as if it is expected that many boys will participate in the orchestra.

Student Recruiting Demonstration

The first and most important rule is to *Be Positive.* Assume that every child starts out wanting to play. The teacher's role is to get the children so excited that they will go home and tell their parents that they want to play. The students *must be* convinced that they *can* play no matter who they are.

It will be necessary to take all of the stringed instruments that will be taught to the demonstration. These instruments should be new and shiny so as to be attractive, and they should be "set up" exactly as the teacher wants the instruments equipped for the class (i.e., four steel strings, adjusters, and patented adjustable pegs). It is best to have both student-size and full-size instruments at this demonstration so the students can see for themselves that smaller instruments are easier to play. This way the *students* will be aware of what kind of instruments their parents should get for them.

During the demonstration, the students should be shown that the stringed instruments can be played pizzicato as well as with the bow. They can be shown how the pitch can be changed by moving from one string to another as well as by putting fingers down onto the string. Some simple tunes can be played for the students and it can be pointed out to them that these tunes are ones that they will be able to perform very soon after they begin playing. If the teacher plays well, the bow should be used – if not, he should play the tunes pizzicato. Don't play a "concerto" type piece for the students as it will not impress them. In fact, it will probably intimidate them! This type of music will sound so difficult to the students that they will be sure that a stringed instrument is too hard to learn. Besides, they probably won't even like this kind of music at this time.

When playing tunes at the demonstration concert, it is best to use television theme songs, commercial tunes, traditional favorites or a current pop tune that the students are sure to know. The teacher should keep a running commentary going while showing them those tunes with such comments as: "This is really fun! *You* can do this! Wow, when you start you can do this yourself! You have just what it takes to do this!"

Never give the students a chance to react negatively. *Never* say: "How many of you want to play an instrument?" This question assumes that some people will not want to play. The teacher must act as if they will *all* play. At the conclusion of the demonstration ask: "How many of you like the sound of the bass best? How many like the sound of the violin best?" The teacher should query each student to determine which instrument be likes best.

BALANCING THE STRING CLASS

One of the biggest problems encountered in the recruiting of the strings is that often the result is a violin class instead of a heterogeneous string class. This happens because the students and parents already know about the violin and many people even have one in their home. Therefore, if the teacher doesn't do something special to avoid this problem, the class will be made up mostly of violin students.

To have balanced string classes (at least one cello, one bass, and one viola to every three violins), the teacher that is doing the recruiting *must* assume some control over the instruments the children (and their parents) select. There are several things that can be done to avoid having nearly everyone choose to play the violin.

Most of the demonstration time should be spent demonstrating the cello, viola, and bass and comparatively little time on the violin. Because the students are most impressed with the first and last instrument they are shown, a good order of presentation of the instruments is probably the viola, violin, bass and cello. This order supposes that the violin and the bass (if there is one available to demonstrate and play) are relatively more familiar and therefore more attractive.

Explain to the children (and then later to their parents) that in order to have an orchestra, *all* of the stringed instruments are necessary and so it is imperative that people start on viola, cello and bass as well as on the violin. Some points that should be stressed both at the student demonstration and then again later at the parents meeting follow.

SCHOLARSHIP AVAILABILIY

Parents are especially very interested to hear that most colleges and universities have scholarships available for people who play the string instruments well (particularly for viola, cello and the string bass players). Many times it is not even necessary to major in music to receive a scholarship to play in a college orchestra. It should be emphasized that scholarships on the viola, cello and bass are even easier to secure than those on violin due to the fact that there is less competition on these instruments.

INDIVIDUAL PREFERENCES

It should be pointed out to the students especially, that just as they all look and think differently, so are the instruments all different. Explain to them that it is very important for each one to choose the instrument that appeals to him the most. It is a good idea to include a statement some place in the presentation such as: "Be sure to pick the instrument that is really *You!* Wouldn't it be a funny looking orchestra with all the same instruments in it?"

PHYSICAL CHARACTERISTICS

Looking at Body Size – The choice of what instrument to play is much simplified by the fact that there are physical characteristics that definitely make one instrument better for each student than any other would be. One of these is obviously size. Not only will a very large person find it easier to handle the larger instruments (viola, cello, or bass) than a small person will, but he will find it harder to play a violin than a smaller person will (especially when he grows up and achieves full size).

Looking at Hand Size – Because hands vary in shape, as well as in size, there can be a natural advantage to choosing one instrument as opposed to any other. Experience has shown that cello and bass players of long standing have developed a larger than average stretch between the first and second fingers of their left hands because of the way they are forced to use their hands when playing an extension (cello) and half steps (bass). Cello players also develop a larger than average spread between their third and fourth fingers. Experience has also shown that about a third of all children already have fingers that are spaced this way. So, it can be readily seen that if a large child with hands shaped this way chooses the cello or bass, much time and frustration can be saved because his hand already can do what it would otherwise have to be laboriously trained to do. On the other hand, a smaller hand without the larger spacing between the first and second fingers would be best to recruit for violin. A large hand of the same basic shape as the violin, perhaps on a larger person, would be a good choice for the viola. To take advantage of this information, a procedure similar to the following is suggested.

At some point, not too far into the student demonstration, the teacher should ask all of the students to hold up their left hands with the fingers spread as far apart as possible. The teacher could announce that God gave everybody in the room a hand specially suited to playing one of the stringed instruments and they are going to be told now which kind of hand that they have. (See Figures Nos. 2, 3, 4, and 5 for sample drawings of an ideal hand for each instrument.)

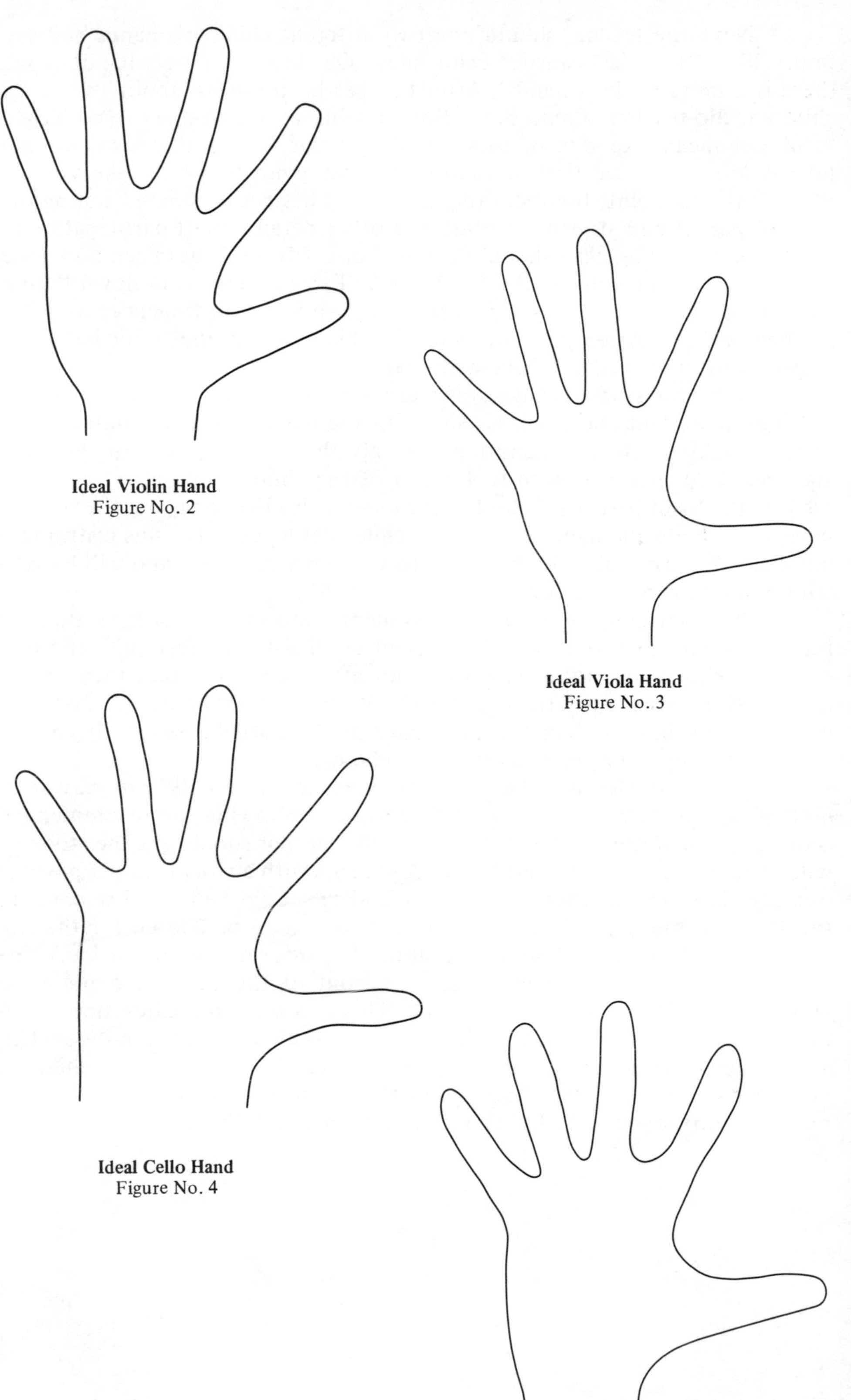

Ideal Violin Hand
Figure No. 2

Ideal Viola Hand
Figure No. 3

Ideal Cello Hand
Figure No. 4

Ideal Bass Hand
Figure No. 5

Next the teacher should point to different children's hands and say things like: "I see a beautiful cello hand! Oh, there is a viola hand! Wow, there is a fantastic bass hand!" After this has been said to about five or six children, the teacher should say: "Boy, it looks as if *each* one of you have a hand just meant for one of these! Let's get this written down so *you* can take it *home* and see if your family all have hands that look like yours."

At this point, the recruiting letter that has been prepared stating the time of parent and student meeting and other details about participation in the beginning string class should be passed out. After this has been done, the children should be told by the teacher to: "Put your left hand down flat on the back of the letter that was passed out and spread your fingers apart as far as they will go. After you have spread it big, trace around your hand and fingers with the pencil you have with you."

After the students have drawn around their hands, the teacher should go to each student and mark his slip with the name of the instrument most suitable, taking into consideration not only the shape but size of the hand and the child that goes with it. Interest of the child should also be considered. If the hand best fits violin but the child is dead-set on cello, the teacher must re-evaluate the hand and tell the child that he can play this instrument but that he must realize he will have to start on a small one and will have to stretch the fingers a great deal.

It is amazing, but true, that students who may never have thought for one second of playing *any* instrument at all will now feel quite an interest in a cello, viola, string bass or violin after being told that they have a hand just for that specific instrument. It might also be mentioned that parents really like the fact that the child's physical attributes have been considered in helping the child to arrive at a choice.

The next step is to show the students that *any child can play right now if he will just do what he is told to do.* Following the recommended order of presentation of the instruments, the teacher should ask the students with viola hands to raise their hands. A student with a viola hand (if possible one the classroom teacher has said is a leader) should be invited to come to the front of the room. The correct size viola should be chosen for the student. (See Pages 29–32 in this chapter for information on sizing.) The teacher should "size" the instrument in front of the other students while explaining to them what is being done. This is good as it creates more interest in playing and also makes them feel that they are "in the know." This also makes it harder for a parent or a music dealer to later give the child the incorrect size because the child *knows* that he should be fitted for the correct one. Furthermore, he has an idea of how it should be done.

The actual conversation between the student and the teacher at this point should be a light-hearted, "fun-type" exchange. A general outline of how this might go is as follows. The teacher should, however, feel free to improvise and to let his own personality show.

Teacher: "What is your name?"

Student: "Tom Stephenson."

Teacher: "Students, I would like to introduce Tom to you. He is going to play his first viola recital today just for you."

Class: (snicker, snicker)

Teacher: "Now class you should not laugh because this is a very serious occasion and we do not want to make him nervous. Isn't that right Tom?"

Student: "Yes."

Teacher: "Tom, have you ever had a viola lesson before?"

Student: "No."

Teacher: "Class, just to prove that ANYONE can learn to play a stringed instrument if they will only follow my directions, I am going to teach Tom to play a song right here in this very room, this very day, in front of your very own eyes!" "Now I am going to put the viola under Tom's chin and put his right hand into position to play pizzicato. Next, I will show him where his index finger (first finger) will need to be placed on the string tightly to make a different note from just a string alone."

While all of the above is being done, the class will probably get noisy. At this point the teacher should turn to the class and with great mock seriousness say:

Teacher: "Tom is about to play his first solo and I want all of you to raise your right hand and repeat after me the following: I promise"

Class: "I promise"

Teacher: "That I will listen quietly"

Class: "That I will listen quietly"

Teacher: "To everything that Tom plays"

Class: "To everything that Tom plays"

Teacher: "And no matter what it sounds like"

Class: "And no matter what it sounds like"

Teacher: "I will not laugh and "

Class: "I will not laugh and"

Teacher: "I will applaud enthusiastically"

Class: "I will applaud enthusiastically"

Teacher: "When he is finished."

Class: "When he is finished."

If the above is done in the right spirit, they will know that they are being "put-on", but they will enjoy it nevertheless.

The teacher should then turn back to Tom and at the same time say to the class:

Teacher: "See if you can tell what this song is."

Point to the D string and tell Tom to pluck it twice. Then point to the A string and tell him to pluck it twice.

Push his first finger down on the A string and have him pluck it twice. Pull his finger up and have him pluck again once.

At this point, if the tune has been recognizable, the class should be asked to give him applause. The teacher can then say:

Teacher: "Now that you know it, let's do it all the way through again. (Student plays again.) "Are you sure that you haven't played the viola before?"

Student: "No."

Teacher: "Wow, was that ever good! Wasn't it class?"

Class: "Yell."

This same basic idea should be repeated for all the instruments with a boy and girl trying each one. The reaction from the class will be that they will all want to come up and try to play. At this point, the teacher should say:

Teacher: "We don't have time to let everyone of you do this today, however, if you make sure that you and your parents come to the meeting that we have told you about in the letter you have drawn your hand on, you will *all* get a chance to try the instruments to be sure which one is best for you. We will help convince Mom and Dad that you should play, too."

At that, the teacher should prepare to leave the class telling the students that he will see them at the meeting.

The Parents Meeting

There are several things that must happen for the meeting with the parents and their children to be a success. First, both the students and the parents must be at the meeting. The parents need to be there so that they can learn about the program and know what equipment their children will need. The children *must* be there so that they can be fitted for the proper sized instrument.

As this may be the last time the teacher will see some of the parents, they must be told *all* of the things that they need to know to avoid having them be the cause of the child's failure at playing. They will need to hear about such things as are mentioned in the paragraphs that follow.

Does the fact that the child does not want to practice mean that the child does not like music? The teacher's answer is of course: "No! This is normal – practically *no* child really likes to practice. Besides, if the class is properly taught at least three times a week, practice outside of class is really not necessary at first."

How do I know my child has enough talent to merit his spending the time and me spending the money necessary for lessons? The teacher should answer: "Everybody has some talent – some more, some less. The most important factor is not the talent but the willingness of the child to work at what they are told to do. Almost anybody (95% or more) with the proper physical equipment can and will learn to play if they can follow directions and are taught properly."

How do I know if my child is doing well? The answer is: "If the child is happy in the class, he is probably doing well. In the event that the child is having real problems, you will be called and consulted with. If you just want to know how he or she is doing, please call me at school and I will be happy to tell you."

Parents should also be told that they *should not attempt to evaluate the child's progress,* because the only basis of comparison they have as parents are professional players they have heard on the radio, the television, or in concert. They should understand that their child is not going to, and should not be expected to sound like a professional player. Also, it is necessary to warn them at all costs to avoid such remarks as: "Are you going to practice in here again? My, that sounds awful – sounds like a dog fight! Where are the chickens?" etc. All of these remarks, even when intended to be humorous, are certain to give the result that is not wanted – the child will probably quit!

How do I know my child won't lose interest? He is enthusiastic about a lot of things – after we let him get involved he loses interest! The teacher's answer is: "You *don't* know. However, experience has shown that if the child is properly taught in a class, and is being supported at home, the success rate is more than 90%. Your child deserves a chance to find out if he can succeed and this may be the opportunity to change this pattern of quitting things he starts. The odds are very much in favor of your child staying in the program and being successful. Being supportive means that you must not only tell the child that you approve and like what he is doing, but you must be careful to take time to listen and compliment him even when you may not be especially impressed or interested."

Concerts are a culmination of the classroom work and in the nature of a test. Parents should be made to understand *now* that attendance should not be considered optional. They should also understand that it is a real motivation for the child to be able to play for his parents at the concerts. Another point is that it is really the only chance for the parent to know what the child is doing because his practicing at home does not convey a true picture of what is really happening at school. They can sound terrible alone and fantastic in the group!

The Importance of Proper Adjustments and Accessories to Student Instruments

For the teacher to be able to function at maximum efficiency (i.e., accomplish the most in the least amount of time), it is necessary that the instruments be equipped and adjusted properly. This must be explained to the parents at the meeting so that they can be sure to have their child come to class the first day with his instrument properly equipped and adjusted.

If the teacher will use instruments borrowed from the local music dealer, equipped and adjusted properly for the student demonstration, the students will observe what they are like and will want the same kind. This will make it easier for them to get the proper instruments.

Strings and Pegs

All beginning instruments (including the so-called "attic" instruments) *must* be equipped with four steel strings, and (except for the bass) with four adjusters and patented adjustable pegs. Make sure that these pegs are made of wood and not plastic (plastic is apt to break apart). The teacher should also be certain that the tension adjustment mechanism works by squeezing one side of the peg box and not by expanding inside the hole (this can eventually cause the whole peg box to break apart). Neither should the peg work by squeezing the two sides of the peg box together (this can eventually cause the peg box to collapse). Adjustable pegs are necessary to allow the teacher to teach the students to tune their own instruments at the earliest possible moment. But, they must work properly and not damage the instruments. For violas and cellos adjustable pegs are especially necessary.

The strings for the students' instruments must be of the proper size (length), i.e., *never use full-sized strings on small-sized instruments.* If a string is used that is too large for the instrument, the string will have to be tuned so loosely (to compensate for the lack of length) that the string will not respond properly. Only chrome wound steel strings are available in the various sizes whereas gut wound strings are not. Therefore, steel strings *must* be used on any instrument that is not full-sized. The authors also strongly recommend that chrome steel strings be used even on full-sized beginners' instruments as the steel strings stay in tune better between lessons. Insist on the proper size string for the best sound and playing ease!

Tailgut

The tailgut must be the right length so that the tailpiece is resting on the saddle – not pulled back towards the bridge. (See the drawings in Figure No. 6 showing correct and incorrect adjustment of the tailgut.)

Wrong

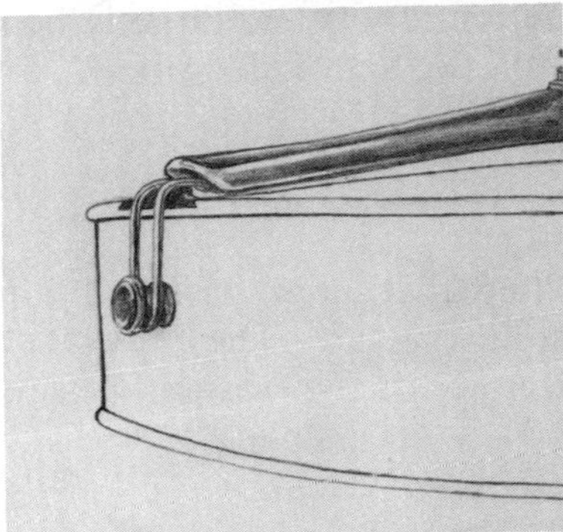

Right

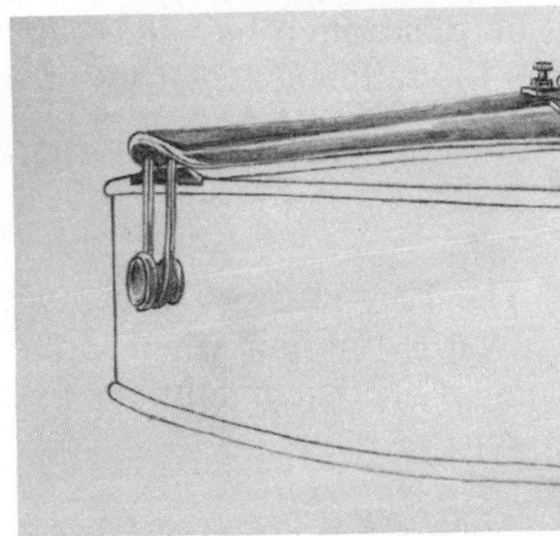

Tailgut Adjustments
Figure No. 6

Bridge

The bridge should be high enough so that the strings don't buzz but not so high that they are difficult to push down with the fingers when played. The bridge should be placed on the instrument in a vertical position excactly between the notches in the inside of the "F" holes. (See Figure No. 7.)

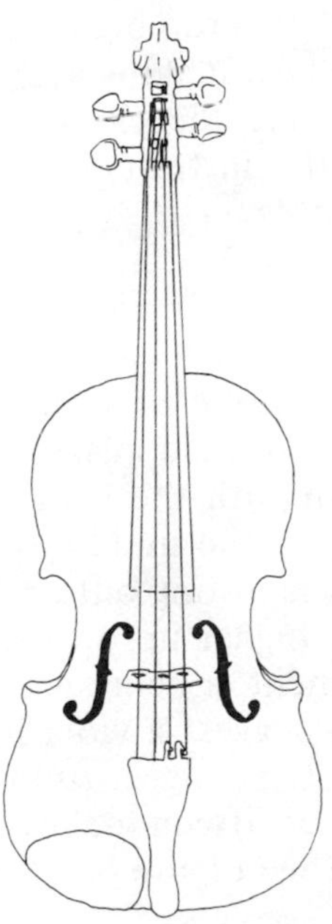

Correct Placement of Bridge
Figure No. 7

Soundpost

The soundpost must be *in* the instrument in the vertical position. It should be positioned half the diameter of the soundpost and directly behind (towards the tailpiece) the foot of the bridge on the high string side.

Bow

The bow must be straight when looking at it lengthwise and curved down towards the hair when looking at it from the side. The hairs must be clean and of sufficient number to extend clear across the frog and be several layers deep.

Fitting the Instrument to the Child

One of the most common reasons for children to discontinue studying stringed instruments is that the instrument is *not* the right size for them. Playing on the wrong size instrument (too large) is very uncomfortable and at times very painful for them. Many times the student will give some other reason for wanting to quit (because often they themselves are not aware of what is wrong) but in reality, experience has found that an improperly fitted instrument is often the real reason.

The reason that a too large instrument is uncomfortable is very obvious – it hurts for a child to stretch his hand and fingers into the position necessary to play an instrument that has been designed for use by an adult. To convince the parents of this, ask them to hold their left arm straight out for about three minutes in the position that the child's arm assumes when he is playing a violin or viola that is too big for him. Then, ask the parents to hold their arm out with the elbow making a "V" as it would be if they were playing a smaller instrument like the child needs. They will immediately understand why the size of the instrument can make a difference in the success or failure of the student.

Violin and Viola

Choosing the right sized violin or viola for the string student can be done quite easily. The teacher should place the instrument upside down under the outstretched left arm with the palm of the hand facing down. If the bottom of the scroll fits into the middle of the palm the instrument is just the right size. If the scroll is resting out on the fingers, it is too big. If it is on the heel of the palm or higher up on the arm, the instrument is too small unless a full-sized instrument is being used. If a full-sized violin is too small, then it might be well to suggest a viola instead. If a full-sized viola is small, then the teacher should try a bigger full-sized viola. Violas are considered full-sized when they are over fifteen inches long. They come in 15, 15½, 16, 16½ and 17 inch lengths. (See Figure No. 8 for photographs on sizing of the violin and viola.)

Too Large

Too Small

Correct Size

Sizing the Violin and Viola
Figure No. 8

Cello and Bass

When the teacher is fitting the cello and the bass there are three main factors that must be considered. They are listed in order of importance and are:

(1) The fingers must be able to reach comfortably the basic intervals that must be played early on the cello and bass. For the cellist, this is a minor third and the bassist a major second. The teacher should place tapes on the instruments in the proper places for these intervals and check to see if the students' fingers can reach this far.

(2) The position of the scroll in relationship to the student's head must also be considered. The lower peg should be about even with, or slightly above the left ear. It will be higher for the bass than for the cello if the instrument is the right size and height.

(3) The position of the instrument's bowing area (area between the fingerboard and bridge) relative to the length of the bow arm when the cello or bass is held in playing position by the student. On the cello this will be correct if the student's knees can grasp the cello right below the middle bout (the indented part in the middle of the cello) and at the same time the lower peg is slightly above the left ear and the endpin is firmly anchored to the floor. The bass fits the child (or vice versa – more likely, the child fits the bass) when the lower peg is slightly above the left ear and when the player is leaning slightly forward, the right hand and arm should easily put the bow into the bowing area of the bass (see Figure No. 9 for correct positioning of the cello and bass).

Cello

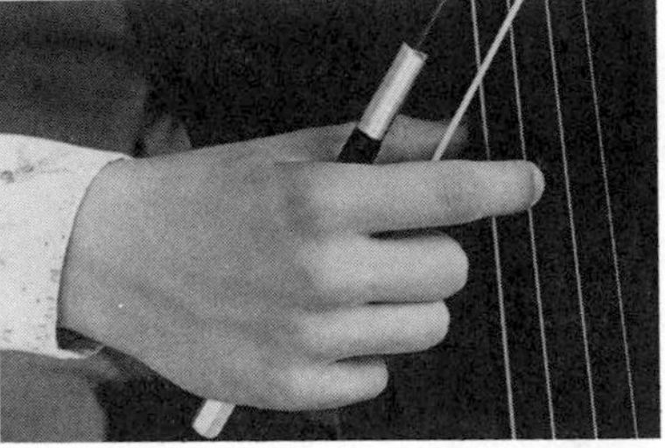

Bass

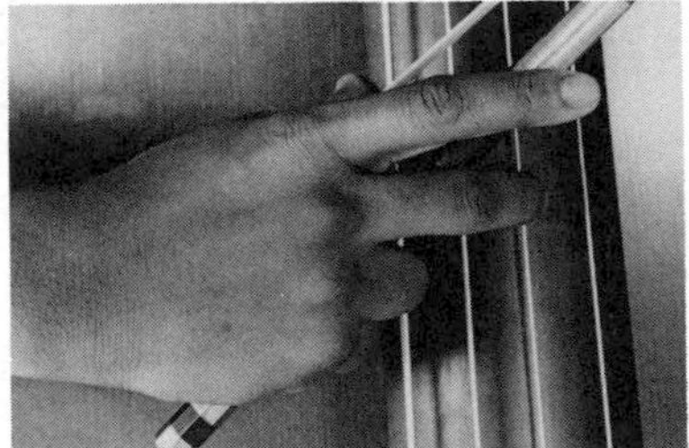

Correct Positioning of the Cello and Bass
Figure No. 9

Follow-Up

Recruiting and Class Balancing

At times the teacher will go through all of the previously mentioned procedures, activities, etc., and when the first day of class arrives the class might be either too small and/or unbalanced (less than eight students and/or no violas and cellos). What then? Do not despair, much still can be done.

First, talk to the classroom teacher, music teacher and the principal. Get a list of students that they feel have potential and have not elected to play an instrument. Talk to the students who are enrolled and ask who their friends are who are not playing. Also ask them if there were students who wanted to play but for some reason didn't start. Make a quick tour of the rooms that were previously recruited and find out if there are students who wanted to start but somehow didn't.

The next step is to talk to all of these students and encourage them to play. Explain to them that they should be playing. The teacher should now make use of the list of telephone numbers secured from the classroom teachers and start calling the parents. *Remember:* The teacher need not accept either a small class and/or incomplete instrumentation as the above suggestions have worked successfully many times in the past.

SECONDARY LEVEL RECRUITING

Rather than accept incomplete or unsatisfactory instrumentation if dropouts or "move outs" leave the orchestra with holes in some of the sections, recruiting can be done quite profitably by the director on the secondary level.

Some places the director might look for students on this level are:

(1) General music classes.

(2) Band or choir students that may be considering music as a career.

(3) Friends of the present string players.

(4) Piano or guitar players.

(5) On the junior high level, especially in the seventh and eighth grades, the teacher can go to the study halls and ask for volunteers. Most students are bored in study halls and welcome a chance to do something else – *anything else!* It should be mentioned, however, that recruiting *totally* inexperienced students from study halls is probably not a good idea past the seventh or eighth grade as the students already playing will probably be too far along for people with no musical experience to be able to catch up. Students with a musical background, however, can learn fast enough to be contributing members (before graduation) of even a quite advanced orchestra when they start as late as the tenth grade. Many times these late starters will be some of the orchestra's most enthusiastic and best players. So, the teacher should be sure to not overlook this source of new talent.

Part Two

Teaching an Orchestra Program

Concept-Directed Teaching 3

INTRODUCTION

What is a concept-directed approach to the development of a comprehensive instrumental music program? How does it differ from just teaching the facts? Too often in the past teaching has consisted of the mere passing out of facts to the students. This certainly is a part of teaching, as concepts cannot be applied without having a grasp of basic facts about what it is that is to be done. Vocabulary, nomenclature, fingerings, names of notes, etc., are all basically a matter of learning facts. But even here, there are sometimes underlying principles that can be ascertained and passed on to the students to help them integrate apparently unrelated facts.

It is important to teach concepts and when and how to apply them instead of just presenting instruction. Merely presenting instruction as to what to do, means that every time something new comes up, the student must return to the teacher to find out how to do the next step. By teaching the principles involved, the students soon progress to the point that each one can figure things out for himself, thus freeing the teacher to take the group on to new concepts and skills. The teacher then becomes necessary *only* to teach new facts and to introduce new concepts. Eventually, ideally, the teacher makes himself unnecessary as the student is able to function on his own.

The principles that follow must be applied daily from the earliest beginning class to the most advanced orchestra – obviously, some more at times than others. In the chapters that follow, the authors will attempt to show how the procedures they advocate relate to as well as apply these principles. The teacher should do *nothing* that is not consistent with *some* defined principle.

TEACHING EFFICIENCY – THE NAME OF THE GAME!

As has been stated in the introductory paragraphs, *everything* that is done in a classroom should be done for a reason. The most important reason anything should be done is to enable the teacher to teach the *maximum* amount in the *least* amount of time.

This use of time in the most efficient manner is probably one of the biggest differences between an average, or below average teacher, and a really good teacher. Even a relatively poor teacher probably can do a good job if he is given enough time. However, time is the one thing that there never seems to be enough of.

To teach the maximum amount in the least amount of time requires that many things be considered. Not only must the teacher consider techniques of teaching subject matter, but also the effect that the teaching is having on the students psychologically and socially. This is true because, although some will make a career of music, for most students, the main purpose of the music program must be to enrich their lives.

If the purpose of the great majority of students in the program is not kept firmly in mind, large numbers of students will be lost. The students are human beings, and no matter how much they are learning, or how well the group plays, *if they do not like what they are doing* and *don't have a feeling of accomplishment, they will drop out.* Students dropping out of the program represent the most gross inefficiency of all.

Understanding then, that to be an efficient teacher includes not only the teaching of music but the developing of self-sufficient, independent and enthusiastic music students that stay in the music program, there is just one overriding consideration: TEACHING EFFICIENCY (with many subsidiary teaching concepts to make the goal of utmost teaching efficiency possible).

Responsibility of the Teacher

Unfortunately perhaps, there is *no end* to the teacher's responsibility for *everything* that does or does not happen in the classroom. To assume anything else puts the teacher at the mercy of circumstances that he cannot control. To assume that the teacher *cannot* control everything *does* provide the teacher with good excuses for not accomplishing what should be accomplished, but it also *removes* the possibility of seeking solutions to problems.

Fulfilling Teacher Responsibilities

Necessary Teacher Attitudes

To help the teacher realize both the importance and scope of the responsibilities that a good teacher must assume, a listing of some necessary teacher attitudes that will facilitate good teaching follows:

At any level, *the teacher must be prepared to teach anything that he expects the students to know.* To help the teacher to be able to do this, there are two very important things that the teacher must remember. One, constantly *re-teach* all the things that have been previously taught until they are thoroughly learned. Even though something has been presented to the students once or twice (and supposedly learned at the time), it may not remain a part of them if it is not frequently reviewed with them by the teacher. Two, before presenting new material, the teacher must make sure that the students really know *everything* that has been taught up to that point. If the students don't know everything up to the point where the new material is being presented, of course they will not understand the new material. So, the teacher will have to expect to "re-teach" at that point before going on to the new material.

The *students must be constantly watched* to make sure that they are able to do what the teacher expects them to do. If they aren't doing it, it *hasn't been taught and the teacher must try another approach.* The teacher does not dare ignore the fact that the students are not getting it and go on to something else!

The teacher must constantly be aware of every student's problems even though he is working with a group. Although he is teaching a class, the teacher must realize that it can never be forgotten that a class is made up of *individuals.* Individuals cannot be allowed to have problems without being helped by the teacher.

Since learning takes place constantly, *the teacher needs to make sure that everything is being done correctly at all times. Remember:* The students will learn the wrong things just as easily as they will learn the right things (perhaps easier).

If the teacher wants the students to feel that what he (the teacher) is doing is important, then all of his actions must convince them that he feels what he is doing is important. (Don't miss class, come late, waste class time repairing instruments, doing clerical work, or talking off the subject.)

The teacher must realize that *students will never do more* than the teacher asks them to do (although they will often do less). The problem usually is that the teacher doesn't ask for enough from them so the class never really achieves its full potential. The *limitations* to the *students' achievements* are usually in the *teacher's mind* rather than inherent in the students' abilities. It is important that the teacher projects the feeling that he feels that the students can do just about anything, once he has given them the proper tools to work with.

The teacher must be aware when preparing a group for a concert or contest, that he will need to have the group "over-learn" the music to insure that they can come through under pressure. The teacher cannot just teach something once, barely to the point of comprehension, and then expect the students to do it right again the next time. *Remember:* Playing it right once is not enough – they must be asked to play it correctly two or even three times "in a row!"

Teaching Techniques

FROM THE KNOWN TO THE UNKNOWN

The teacher should always move from the known to the unknown when presenting new materials. The new problem should be related to the familiar things that the students have been doing. First, they should be shown *all* of the things that are familiar in the new problem and then next the new and different part of the problem that is being presented.

ONE THING AT A TIME

A very basic principle of good teaching is that the teacher must present new materials in such a manner that the child faces only *one* new problem at a time. This is important at all levels, but is especially important with very young beginners.

Isolate Problems – At times, even in the best written method books, the child is faced with more than one new problem at a time; and, if the teacher does not realize this he will not understand why the child is having trouble. Considerable experience and ingenuity are required on the part of the teacher to be able to see these spots, isolate the problem(s) and then present them one at a time. When rehearsing an orchestra on the secondary level, the same thing must be done – isolate the problem and then work on it (i.e., rhythm, style, notes, intonation). *Never* try to work on all the problems at once!

Don't Complicate – Especially on the beginning level, the teacher must be careful not to burden the students with many things they don't need to know to be able to play the music. As they get older, it will become necessary more and more to explain the concepts and principles at some length so that the students can generalize for themselves and apply them to future problems. Beginning students, however, should only be told what they need to know to play the music as, at their maturity level, playing is what they expect to do.

The Spiral Approach – All of the aspects of music that the student is going to need to know as a mature high school player, need to be introduced as soon as possible. In the first year, the child should be introduced to such concepts as balance, style, rhythm, phrasing, intonation, tempo, following a director, etc. On the elementary level, however, it will be necessary for the teacher to break these concepts down into small components so that the young students can understand them on their own level. Then, the teacher should present these small portions one at a time and teach them more and more until ultimately the most difficult of concepts can be mastered.

THE WAY AS WELL AS THE HOW

One of the most important goals of teaching is to have the things that have already been taught carry over into the things that are going to be done in the future. For this "carry-over" to occur, the child must realize that the new problem is similar in some respects to a problem that he has already solved.

Teach Independence – The student will not learn independence without help from the teacher. Many, if not most, children do not think in terms of generalities unless they are taught to think this way. This can be taught quite easily by presenting materials to them as concepts and not merely as directions to do something. Never just say: "Do this" or "Do that" rather say, "Whenever you see this in the music do that" or "Do this because." If they are taught the "why" and the "when" of what they are to do, they will learn to make decisions for themselves and be able to function as their own teacher.

Repetition With A Purpose – In the process of teaching skills on any level, repetition and drill are an unavoidable necessity. To keep repetition to a minimum and to insure the likelihood of students learning from it, *repetition must have a purpose and the students must know what it is.* There are two very strong reasons for this. First, psychologists have long known that repetition without a purpose is ineffective. Second, if the students understand what they are trying to do, they will not be resentful when they are asked to repeat or drill on something, as they will understand that it is necessary because they have not yet learned what needs to be learned. If they are not aware of the reason that they are repeating something, they are very likely to feel *either* that the teacher is being arbitrary or is punishing them.

Student Attitudes

Playing an instrument well is an inherently frustrating activity because it involves the coordination of so many physical and mental processes. When many instrumentalists are combined into an orchestra, the problems and possibilities for things to go wrong increase astronomically. When these problems are then compounded by a teacher who insists on everything being done in a certain way, and all together, it is easily seen that the morale of an instrumental group has to be a prime consideration.

There are two fundamentally different ways of handling the problem of keeping a good morale in a group. Many people avoid the problem of having frustrations develop by making few if any demands on the players. This, of course, results in the teacher having groups that play poorly, learn little, have no real pride, and thus he will usually lose more than his share of the better students. (The better students have so many demands made on their time that they cannot afford to spend their time for several years in a class that does not really make them feel that they are getting something that they can't do without.)

The other way for the teacher to handle the frustration the students may acquire from trying to do a fundamentally impossible task, is for the students to recognize that *it is* an extremely difficult task but that it *can be done*. And, when it is done, it will really be an accomplishment worth working for. To put it another way, a good teacher finds ways to make the frustration seem tolerable and worthwhile to the students because the reward is so great.

SUCCESS IS THE GREATEST MOTIVATOR

The greatest motivator of all is success. Therefore, the entire instrumental experience must be structured in such a way that *failure is impossible and success is inevitable* for anyone in the group who is willing to try to follow the directions and be reasonably involved (at least during the time they are in class).

Insuring the feeling of success can be done in many ways. Two of the most important ways are: One, the problems that are to be solved must be broken down into small enough parts so that they can be solved in a period or less; two, the teacher must know how to help the students solve their problems. Given these two basics, the following attitudes consistently presented by the teacher, will pretty much insure that the students will work for achievement merely for the sake of achieving.

Always "Better" – NEVER "Perfect" – Every time a part is rehearsed, the director should comment (unless it obviously is not so): "That was better, now let's try it again and work on . . ." *Always notice their improvement* and then point out what is still left to do. There must be a preponderance of positive comments to the students, although at times the comments will have to be negative if only to make the positive comments more meaningful to them.

Praise Each Student For His Own Improvement – In any large group, there has to be many different levels of ability and achievement. When the director is praising students for their improvement, it is absolutely necessary that he does not expect the poorer students to achieve at the same level as the best students. Conversely, the best students should not be praised for achievement adequate only for a poorer student. Psychologically it is probably better to praise the students of lesser ability *before* the best students are praised.

Every Student Should Be Working On His Own Level – This can be done during a rehearsal or class by the director praising the poorer student perhaps for getting the rhythm right, then for getting the rhythm and the notes, then the rhythm, the notes and the bowing, etc. The better student, however, would be *expected* to do these things right in the beginning and so he would be praised for such things as phrasing, intonation, expression, style, etc. It is important that *everyone* be praised when they succeed, and succeed they must, but, they must always be striving towards the next goal, which must be set for them by the director.

Pace the Class Fast Enough To Challenge But Not Fast Enough To Frustrate – This is especially important with a beginning class where they are all close to the same ability level.

Students Should Practice Only Materials That They Know – Again, especially with beginning students, *do not* send them home to practice material that has not been gone over in class and explained to the point that they understand thoroughly what they are to do. To let the student practice on music he doesn't understand is to risk that the student will learn things incorrectly and then it will be necessary to unlearn and relearn. Not only is this inefficient but it allows unnecessary failures.

SELF-MOTIVATION

Because the teacher must constantly be aware of the students' needs to be in a situation structured to insure success and obviate failure, the teacher (as soon as possible) must teach the students to want to do what has to be done because they have decided that *they* (the students) want to do it right. They must develop a *pride* in themselves and the group that will not allow them to do a "less than their best" job.

The above-mentioned attitude does not just happen, it must be carefully nurtured and taught over a period of several years. It *starts* with the students being convinced that the teacher cares very much that they do everything right, and furthermore, that the teacher will be watching them to make sure that they are doing it correctly. Soon, each student will conclude: "If what *I do* is important, then *I am* important and what I do matters to me, too."

Each Student Must Accept Responsibility For Himself – At this point, the students should begin to accept some of the responsibility for their own progress, but the teacher must *remember* it all starts with the teacher showing that he really cares.

Help Students Achieve Their Goals – To foster the attitude in the students that they must *do what is right because it is right* and *not because of fear of punishment*, it must be made very clear to them that the teacher's job is to help them to be as good as they can be, and not to catch them doing something wrong.

Criticize The Students' Errors, NOT Them – To help the students to understand and truly believe that the teacher's only reason for correcting the students is to help them and not to punish them, it is very important that the students understand that a criticism of what they are doing is *not* a criticism of them personally.

When the students feel that the teacher is criticizing them, rather than their playing, they become resentful towards the teacher. Often, instead of the student feeling responsible for his learning and that the teacher is helping him, it becomes the student *against* the teacher and he feels that the teacher is *making* him (the student) do what needs to be done. Avoid this situation at all costs.

Perfection Is The Unattainable Goal – The students *must* be convinced that nothing less than perfection is good enough to allow them to stop trying to improve, but, at the same time, to avoid hopeless frustration, they must realize that through no fault of their own they will never be completely able to achieve it. Therefore, they must learn that although perfection must be the goal, at any point along the way, *success is measured in terms of improvement.* Perfection is the goal but they must feel that success is knowing that they are improving every day.

Students Help Each Other – Fortunately, although the teacher must be responsible for all that happens in the class, there are things that do happen by themselves – *the students learn many things from each other.* They not only learn about playing from each other but their attitudes are especially affected by the interaction with the other students. The teacher must be aware of this fact and try to use it advantageously. This can be done in several ways. For example: the teacher can comment about things that are being done well by the students or, the students can be seated in such a way that the best students play first so that their example can be seen and heard before the others take their turn at playing.

MAINTAINING INTEREST

There is another vital consideration in the motivating of students. It is very hard to do anything with the students if they are not paying any attention to what is being said. The reason that this kind of situation often develops is very basic. If the students are not kept busy and involved in what is happening, they will think of other things to do. (Their creativity in this area may astound the teacher.) The best discipline of all for a class is the discipline of being busy trying to accomplish something together as a group.

All Students Involved All of the Time – Keeping the class involved can be done very easily in a beginning class situation by the use of the various drill routines that this book advocates. On the secondary level, in the full orchestra situation, it is more difficult to do this, but it can be accomplished most of the time by carefully planning rehearsals so that individual and small group problems are worked on in sectionals rather than when everyone is there.

Talking too much is often a problem for teachers as they always seem to have so much "wisdom" to impart that it is sometimes difficult for them *not* to impart all of it at one time. It must be realized that many times it is better for the teacher to have the group play before *all* of the problem things have been completely discussed, and then, come back again later to those problem spots and discuss them further – thus *talking less at any given time.* It may not be what is being said or how it is being said that is causing the lack of attention on the part of the students, but rather that they just get tired of sitting without being active. It should be realized that when the students' attention span is exceeded, *no one* can keep their interest! On the other hand, the director must be warned that many teachers are so worried about boring the children that they don't cover the materials thoroughly enough, because often they (the teachers) are bored and so assume the students are bored, too. But, this is usually not the case!

Colleague Attitudes

There is one more area of teacher responsibility that dare not be overlooked or everything else that is done will be to no avail. That is, that the classroom teachers and the elementary school principals must be convinced that what is being done in the instrumental music classes is really worthwhile. Classroom teachers are always going to be unhappy about students leaving their classes, but, if they can be convinced that what is being done when they leave their classes is really worthwhile, most of them will support the music teacher and what he is doing.

Even more important, from their point of view, is that the music teacher realizes the importance of what the classroom teachers are doing and the inconvenience that the music students cause them by leaving their classes. This is most important in maintaining good relations with the classroom teachers. It should also be kept in mind that no matter what the music teacher says about that which he is doing, what outsiders see impresses them the most. *Actions speak louder than words!* The classroom teachers and principals will never be convinced of the importance of what the instrumental music teacher is doing if he misses classes, comes late, dismisses class early, or if they hear reports from the students that nothing was done in the string class.

The Beginning String Class 4

INTRODUCTION

The most important year in the instrumentalist's musical life is the beginning year as it is during this time that the basic foundation will be laid for all the years that follow. How this year is handled has a profound effect on whether the student will continue or not, and even more important what kind of musician the student is to become. A common mistake made by many administrators is to place the least competent and/or least experienced teacher at the beginning level, thinking this is where he can hurt the least. Students seldom recuperate from a poor start, and if they do, both they and the teacher find it very difficult and discouraging.

Because the start is so crucial, the explanation of how to teach the first few lessons will be extremely detailed to help the beginning teacher to avoid skipping any step that could cause failure if not covered thoroughly. This extreme detail might seem unnecessary, but it is really imperative that all these steps be taken. Any step skipped will probably result in problems in the future. Although it seems like there are so many things to be done that the class will never "move", in actual practice, these steps can be done in three or four class periods.

WHAT KIND OF CLASS?

A Large Class

It once was felt by most music educators that it was far superior to teach string beginners on a "one to one" basis – the "old conservatory" approach. Their thinking was that there was so much to be learned that each student needed constant individual help (True!), which is only possible in a very small, like-instrument situation (False!). The authors have found that *all* of the students will do better in ensemble playing when taught in a large-group situation of eight or more. The average students will make about the same progress as they would in a small group and the poor students will do much better. The best students, taught in a large class situation meeting at least three days a week may not develop as much technique, but considering all aspects of playing, will be equal or slightly ahead of those taught privately (with the same or an equally qualified teacher).

From the administrative point of view, teaching many students at once is a much more efficient use of time than teaching a few students. Obviously, the cost per student is less when teaching ten students at a time rather than four students. Also, the teacher can teach more students per day or meet the same number of students more often. For example, in three periods a week, a teacher can meet three groups of four *once* a week or one group of twelve *three* times a week. With today's emphasis on cost and accountability, this is an important consideration. Most administrators would also rather schedule one large group at a time rather than several small groups at different times.

Following is a list of some of the reasons the authors feel large classes properly taught are generally superior to small ones:

(1) No student feels scared or worries that he will have to play alone and be embarrassed.

(2) Students learn from each other. The example of the fast achievers will motivate all.

(3) It is more fun to be in a large group.

(4) It is easier to build feeling of team spirit.

(5) The discipline of a large performance group is understood from the beginning.

(6) The motivation of class accomplishment makes it unnecessary for the teacher to tell individual students how they compare with the rest of the students – they know!

(7) One large class, rather than several small ones, makes it seem to younger students as if there are more students involved – that everyone is participating. This is important when it comes to recruiting future students.

(8) A large class (minimum of eight) can and will develop its own momentum (the larger the class the more the momentum).

(9) Teaching the skills of ensemble playing obviously will be easier when students are in an ensemble situation all the time.

A Heterogeneous Class

There are many reasons why the heterogeneous (mixed) instruments string class is the best way to develop a fine orchestra program. Among them are:

(1) The students need to be in an orchestral situation (with all the family of stringed instruments) from the very beginning so that they realize immediately what an orchestra really is.

(2) The heterogeneous class helps them to realize immediately that all instruments are equally important to the orchestra.

(3) If taught correctly, the students will find a mixed class more interesting and more fun than being in a like-instrument class.

(4) A class of mixed instruments will sound much fuller and more mature at earlier stages because of the complete ranges of string sound.

(5) The heterogeneous class, because it can be larger, is more efficient both financially and in use of the teacher's time.

(6) As soon as students progress to the point of being able to play harmonized parts, it will be easy to rehearse as an orchestra without causing any schedule changes.

PRELIMINARIES TO TEACHING

The elementary string class should begin no later than five minutes after the students arrive in the room where the class is to be held.

Preparation of Room

The teacher should arrive early enough to be able to make sure the chairs are set up for the class. If possible, it should be the responsibility of the school custodian to take care of this task, but it will be necessary in the beginning to show him the correct set-up. It is a good idea to give the custodian a drawing of the desired seating. Remember, it pays to cultivate the friendship of the custodian as his support and cooperation will be extremely valuable. A little praise can bring many dividends later. If custodial help is not available, then it is the teacher's daily responsibility to make sure everything is ready for class.

It must be mentioned that the type of chairs chosen for class is an important consideration in developing correct playing positions. Each student, while sitting forward on the front edge of the chair, must be able to touch both feet on the floor. Slick-finished chairs or chairs that slope backwards promote poor playing positions, because the students will slide back in them. The chair seat *must* be parallel to the floor (see Figure No. 1).

This (rather than) This

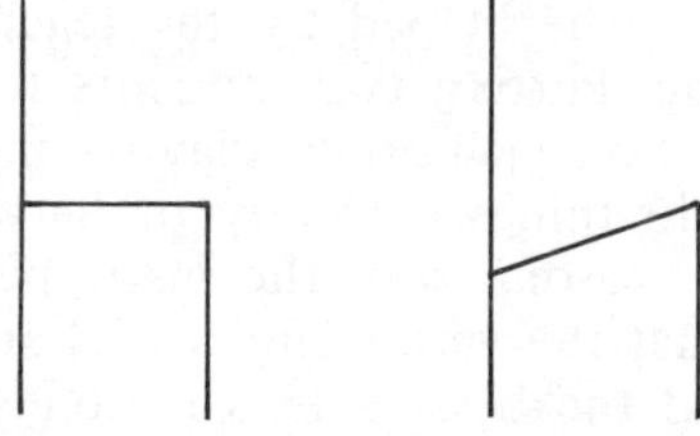

Chairs
(Figure No. 1)

Cello players, especially, must have chairs of correct height and shape and frequently will need higher chairs than the other students. With today's stackable chairs, the height can be adjusted by using more than one chair.

Stools of the correct height might be a good answer to the chair problem, as with stools, the students cannot lean back. Bass players definitely need stools if they are going to rehearse more than thirty minutes. Stools also facilitate holding the basses more securely.

Seating the Class

Good teaching of any instrument involves watching students constantly to see that correct posture and holding positions are established and maintained. The students should be seated so the teacher can move continually from student to student, observing and correcting them from either side, as the class continues to play. For this reason, it is recommended that chairs be placed in rows rather than the conventional semi-circle formation (see Figure No. 2).

Row I	Row II	Row III	Row IV	Row V	Row VI
*x	x	x	x	x	x
**o	o	o	o	o	o
x	x	x	x	x	x
o	o	o	o	o	o
x	x	x	x	x	x
o	o	o	o	o	o
x	x	x	x	x	x
o	o	o	o	o	o
x	x	x	x	x	x
o	o	o	o	o	o
Vln.	*Vln.*	*Vln.*	*Cello*	*Vla.*	*Bass*

***x student**
****o music stand**

Recommended String Class Seating
(Figure No. 2)

This seating makes the above objectives possible and offers other teaching advantages. *Note: In order to provide an aisle on both sides of each student, each student must have his own stand and music.*

The most important advantages gained from row seating in the string class is that all students can be helped by the teacher and will also have plenty of room for bowing. Putting two students to a stand makes it too easy for students to depend on each other. Playing one on a stand, a student feels as if he had better do things correctly or he will be seen and heard.

There are specific reasons why the instruments are placed in this unusual manner. Notice that the violins and violas are separated from each other as are the cellos and the basses. This is done so the violas will feel their own identity as a section of importance and not as if they are simply "over-grown" violins. Likewise the basses are separated from the cellos so that they also can develop a feeling of identity. The second reason for the separation is that all students are far enough apart to be able to hear themselves individually for better intonation and tone quality. It can be seen that this seating arrangement fosters the feeling that *every* instrument is of equal importance. This is crucial in holding violists and especially bassists, in the string program.

This string-class seating arrangement is a teaching device that should be used even in later years whenever a new technical problem is being taught to the strings. It is very helpful even with secondary school orchestras when such skills as vibrato, shifting to positions, advanced fingerings, bowings, or tone work, are to be worked on extensively. Whenever students are to be conducted, the conventional orchestra seating should be used. This seating is a string-class seating and not a performance or orchestra seating! The importance of this seating arrangement cannot be over-stated as many of the teaching procedures that will be advocated later in this book will depend on the use of it.

Tuning the Class

In keeping with the philosophy that all of the class period should be spent learning to play, it will be best if the instruments are tuned ahead of time and placed on the chairs (for the first year only). This is feasible provided students put them in the room where the class is held each day and that the room is free ten to fifteen minutes ahead of class so the teacher may tune them. This situation is, of course, ideal but the teacher must realize that if such an optimum situation is not requested at the beginning there is little chance of getting it. Valuable class time must be used for learning to play – not for peripheral activities.

In summary, tuning should take up very little time. Don't accept instruments in your class that are in such poor condition that they can't be tuned quickly. The teacher should not be a repairman! The teacher will have to do the tuning during most of the first year but remember, use no more than five minutes for each class daily.

Class Tuning Procedure

Tuning should take as little time as possible, especially if the teacher must tune after the students arrive. The class must be organized so that it can help the teacher to spend every minute teaching. The following student behavior rules have proven effective in doing this:

(1) Come into class quickly and quietly.

(2) Get instrument out and take seat.

(3) Place case under chair so the teacher can move through the class without tripping.

(4) Be quiet while waiting for the teacher to tune instrument (no playing or talking).

(5) Put stand in place while quietly waiting.

(6) Get out music, rosin, shoulder pad, cello end-pin stops, etc.

(7) Sit quietly and wait for class to begin.

The following suggestions will make it possible for a teacher to tune everything in five minutes (with practice), provided the students are quiet when in the room.

(1) Tune pizzicato (it is much faster than with the bow).

(2) Only tune the strings that will be used in class that day.

(3) Move quickly from student to student.

(4) Require every student to have chrome-steel strings (they stay in tune longer) and all except the string basses need four adjusters (tuners).

(5) All instruments, except string bass, must have well-fitted pegs, or even better, satisfactory patented adjustable pegs.

The teacher must realize the importance of using the correct concert "A" each day in tuning for three important reasons:

(1) If there are students that have perfect pitch they should be hearing the correct tone to avoid future frustration.

(2) Others can and will learn the relative "feel" of the correct pitch if they hear the same one everyday.

(3) The instruments don't have the right tone quality unless tuned to the correct pitch. Therefore, it is strongly recommended that a tuning bar or a piano kept at the correct pitch be used.

ORDER OF PRESENTATION OF PROBLEMS

Obviously, there are many things that must be taught to the beginning string player. The order in which these problems are presented has a great bearing on the success or failure of the student in learning to play. Therefore, the problems will be presented in the order that the authors feel gives the greatest probability of success. Some method books will allow you to follow this order of introducing the problems more easily than others. But, it will be the prerogative of the teacher to decide whether the advantages in this order of presentation are greater than the advantages found in method books not adhering to this order and then to choose the method book accordingly. We will follow the order of the presentation of materials found in the Muller-Rusch string series by J. Frederick Muller and Harold Rusch, a widely used string class method.

PROJECTED GOALS

The schedule of projected goals that will be outlined year by year is predicated upon the assumption that the students will begin in the fifth grade with a minimum of three half-hour sessions a week. If the students are started earlier than the fifth grade, the progress that can be expected is considerably less for the first year. This is because the students are less mature at this age and thus normally unable to learn at as fast a pace as fifth grade students.

A WORD ABOUT HOME PRACTICE AND GRADING

Home Practice

A word needs to be said about the teacher's attitude toward home practice. Individual home practice is desirable and a good thing to encourage the students to do. However, the emphasis should be on the students' being able to play the music properly rather than trying to "check-up" on each student to see whether he has practiced a specific number of hours a week. What the director needs to realize is that it is not the number of hours practiced that counts but rather whether the student is able to do what is expected of him.

In a well-run class, some students will need to practice very little while others may need to spend a great deal of time outside of class practicing. It is better to demand that the students play the music to the teacher's satisfaction rather than to simply demand a specific number of hours to be practiced.

Grading

Grading has two main purposes. One, to let the students and the parents know how they are doing and two, to *motivate* the students to do their best (possibly more important). This means that to give all high grades or all low grades is self-defeating. If all the students know they are going to be given high grades many will feel it is pointless to work because they will get a high grade anyhow. On the other hand, if they feel that no matter how hard they work the teacher will not recognize it with a higher grade, they will feel: "why try?" This means that the ideal grading system will be structured in such a way that it rewards accomplishment and improvement, and discourages indifference and failure.

THE FIRST LESSON

Introduction

The first lesson is the single most important one in the life of the instrumentalist, because it sets both the psychological tone and musical foundation for all those that will follow. It is of utmost importance that the new students leave the first class knowing that it is going to be fun, and that something important will be learned each day.

It is recommended that students actually experience in their first class some of the problems as well as some of the satisfactions of playing in a musical group. To do this, the teacher must be sure to have them at least produce a few organized musical sounds on the instruments. However, before students actually are taught to play, the teacher must tell them how to take care of their new instruments.

Care of Instruments

The students need to be told *immediately* how to take care of their new instruments so as to avoid mishaps that will cause them to have to miss class. While telling them of the "do's and don'ts" of correct care, it is easy, and a good idea, to include the nomenclature for the parts of the instrument that are necessary to understand both for proper maintenance and for correct playing of the instruments. It is sometimes fun to make a game out of seeing how quickly students can point to the various parts of their instruments while selected students take turns in calling them out.

At this first class, the teacher needs to check to see that all students have the proper sized instruments with correct adjustment and accessories. If not, the teacher must immediately call the parents and let them know that it is going to be difficult for the child to succeed with the handicap of an instrument that is not the right size or improperly equipped. Don't "bug" the students about these things as they may think that this means they aren't liked by the teacher. Sometimes parents don't pay attention to the child when they mention these things at home. For these reasons, getting a name and address list with correct home telephone numbers of the students is invaluable.

The main points of properly caring for an instrument that will need to be mentioned to the students on the first day are as follows:

(1) Find a safe place to store their instrument where it is out of the way of younger children and *never* where it is too hot or cold (away from heaters, air conditioners and *not* in a hot or cold car).

(2) Be sure the instrument is kept in the case when it is not being played so that it cannot get damaged or dirty.

(3) Don't drop or slide the case as the instrument can be damaged even though it is inside the case.

(4) Keep the instrument clean – free of rosin, dust and fingerprints. A soft cloth will be needed to wipe off the instrument each time after use. Wipe the rosin off the strings, fingerboard, and main body of the instrument.

(5) Polish should only be used on the main body of the instrument. Only a commercial violin polish or a liquid lemon oil polish *applied with a cloth* should be used.

(6) Don't tamper with the pegs as broken strings will probably be the result.

(7) Explain that the bridge is being held up by the strings and that when the tension of the strings is lessened the bridge will fall down. *Don't ever glue the bridge in place!*

(8) Tell the students about the soundpost and that it is necessary for complete tone. Explain that if the strings are loosened it may fall down, and that if it does fall down, be sure to save it. Students have been known to think that a "stick" has fallen inside and shake it out and throw it away.

(9) Be very careful with the bow – always protecting it so it doesn't get broken. Don't use the bow as a sword or leave it where someone can sit on it.

Students may also need to be told how to "sack and unsack" their cellos and the correct way to carry them. If the students are furnishing their own folding music stands, as is strongly recommended, it will be necessary to show them how to set them up and take them down as well as put them into the canvas carrying cases.

LEARNING TO PLAY

In order to present the new materials in small, one-step-at-a-time pieces, the following order of presentation will be used to prepare the students for using the bow, fingering and reading music at the same time:

(1) Learning rhythm fundamentals (clap).

(2) Positioning instruments.

(3) Learning open strings pizzicato (rote).

(4) Preparing to follow a printed line (teacher points to notes on the board).

(5) Learning to follow a printed line (book).

(6) Learning to finger notes pizzicato (rote).

(7) Playing fingered notes while reading from the book.

(8) Learning to bow open strings (rote).

(9) Bowing open strings while reading notes.

(10) Bowing and fingering together (rote).

(11) Bowing and fingering together while reading notes.

When all of the above steps have been mastered, the students should be able to successfully combine bowing, fingering and reading of music. It will be necessary, however, on new tunes in the early lessons especially, to start with step Number 6 and follow through the rest of the steps. If there are rhythmic problems, it may be necessary to also do step Number 1. Do not be mislead by the apparent brightness of your class and try to skip any of the above steps. If this is done, the results of this haste may haunt the teacher the rest of the time that these students are in the orchestra program.

Learning Rhythm Fundamentals

Step 1

Introduction

It is best to begin with the introduction of rhythm fundamentals so that *every* student will be actively involved the first day of class even though they may not all have their instruments. A second reason is that the understanding of rhythm is perhaps the most important of all the fundamentals the teacher will have to teach the beginners. The teacher must realize, however, that the students will not feel this way and probably will not worry very much about rhythm unless they are constantly reminded about it. *Remember:* Rhythm doesn't come naturally to the students – it must be very carefully taught.

Another thing that the teacher must make sure the students understand is that everything that is done in class will be done as a group. "Togetherness" must become the motto for all the group endeavors if the class is to accomplish as much as it really should. This applies first in teaching the group to start and stop together. *Never* allow students to play individually or practice spots alone in class unless the teacher specifically requests it. Tell the students that they can practice by themselves at home but class time will be used only for group practice. The teacher will need to adhere to this rule strictly if the class time is to be used as efficiently as possible.

Learning To Keep A Steady Beat

The first step toward being able to play together is to be able to keep a steady beat (meter). The teacher, after counting an introductory measure of "1-2-3-4," should have the students tap their feet and count aloud with him. Do this at various tempos until they can do it easily. Watch their feet to be sure they go both down and up evenly on each beat. Some children will have to be helped to hold their foot down until the teacher says "up." To help them to do this the teacher must say: "1-up, 2-up, 3-up, etc."

Next, put quarter notes on the board to show them what they look like in written form. Explain that each quarter note gets one count (or beat) and there are four counts in each measure.

Tell them that a count is the same thing as a tap. It also is a good idea to put arrows up and down underneath some quarter notes to show the students the motion of the feet on a quarter note (see Figure No. 3).

Quarter Note = Down-Up of Foot
Figure No. 3

The next step is to have them clap quarter notes while tapping their feet. Watch their feet carefully *now* as many will have trouble keeping the foot moving in the steady down-up fashion necessary. If they have this problem, have them discontinue the clapping and continue to tap their feet (one new thing at a time). When they can do this automatically then try adding the clapping again.

The students will also need to be taught that they are *never* to start playing until the teacher has given them an introductory measure telling them the speed (or tempo) at which they are to begin. Explain that it is impossible for them to know what tempo to play until they hear the teacher count.

Recognizing Different Rhythms

At this point, the teacher needs to introduce the basic rhythm patterns that the students will need for the first lesson. So, look at the book that will be used and find the basic rhythm patterns that are to be presented in the first lesson, and put them on the board. Draw the notes only rhythmically (not on the staff) as for the first few lessons the students should not be involved with more than one step of music reading at a time. The beginner is busy worrying about how to do the rhythms and should not be asked to read notes as well. One new thing at a time!

Examples of basic rhythm patterns the students should clap while tapping their feet are shown in Figure No. 4.

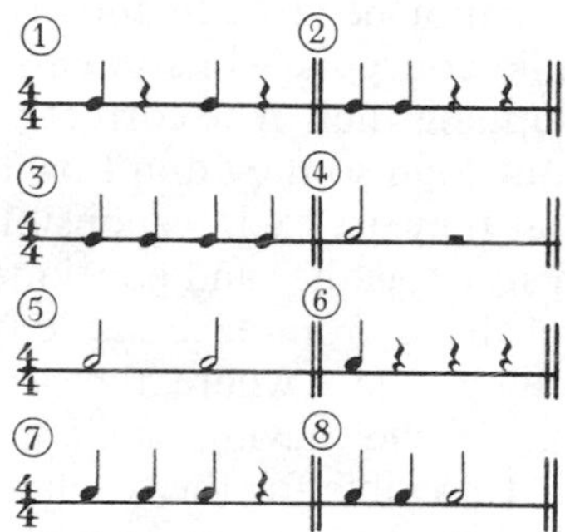

Rhythmic Patterns To Clap
Figure No. 4

These rhythm patterns (various combinations of quarter notes, quarter rests, half notes, and half rests) probably are the most that a beginner should be asked to learn at first.

If not carefully taught, young students will treat rests as if they are not there. For this reason, it is best to ask all beginning students to say the word "rest" out loud during each rest. By doing this, they are physically involved and won't be so apt to overlook them and to play during the rests. For consistency, and also to allow the teacher to know that the student is looking at the right location in the music, the students should be taught to say "half-rests" and "half-notes" in such a way that they cannot be confused with two quarter notes or two quarter rests. One way to do this is to say them as shown in Figure No. 5.

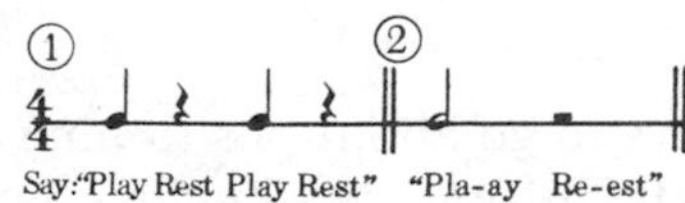

Counting Half Rests and Half Notes
Figure No. 5

In spite of the problems that rests cause, it is absolutely necessary that a book with rests be used so the children learn to handle them as early as possible in their musical career. Besides this, rests can be a real teaching aid, because they allow the teacher to have time to give directions to the students. Rests also help the students to find their places when lost.

In order to allow the development of the "self-propelling" class, which will be discussed in greater detail later, it is vital that every student understand that he is individually responsible for keeping a steady, continuous beat.

Summary of Rhythm Fundamentals

The importance of giving a strong foundation in rhythm fundamentals to the beginning class cannot be stressed too strongly. Constantly keep in mind three basic ryhthmic concepts: (1) students should be able to keep a steady beat (meter) by tapping their feet correctly while playing, (2) students should say all rests out loud so they don't overlook them, and (3) students should understand that they are each responsible for keeping the meter steady so that the class can stay together and continue to play.

By insisting on the above from each student, the teacher will soon have created a "self-propelling" class where the group is able to continue playing steadily without the teacher having to clap, count, or sing while the class plays. This will make it possible for the teacher to then spend the valuable class time helping individuals to learn to do each new step.

Positioning Instruments

Step No. 2

Introduction

Before anything else, the students must be taught how to position their instruments correctly. The teacher must understand that this is most fundamental and that there is no way students can play and progress satisfactorily unless the basic positions are correct. Making sure that the positions are correct will take up a great deal of the teacher's time as students will need to be corrected constantly (even at secondary level). The teacher can never relax and quit worrying about this.

Accepting poor positions is a "cop-out" and indicates a weak and/or inattentive teacher. The students *will* do it right – but only if it is insisted upon and they know that the teacher won't give up until it is correct. If it looks right, it will probably sound right. It is very difficult, if not impossible, to have it sound right when it looks wrong. The teacher's job, of course, is to know what is right and then insist upon it.

Violin and Viola

There are many ways to go about positioning the violin and the viola and it really makes very little difference which method is used as long as the end result is correct. With whatever method the teacher decides to use, remember that it should be used consistently the same way each time so that the students get used to an established routine and can remember it.

It is also good to always *show* as well as tell how to hold the instrument. The teacher will need to carry an instrument to class to be used for this purpose. It is not a good idea to use students' instruments for demonstration purposes as this deprives one of them from performing it with the teacher.

A good way of positioning the violin and viola for the student is as follows:

(1) The student is asked to assume an erect position and hold the instrument out to the left side of his body with the left hand and fist cupped around the main body of the instrument (high string side) with the strings facing away from the player.

(2) Have the student turn the instrument over so that the tailpiece end is up (towards the ceiling) and the scroll is down (towards the floor).

(3) Check to make sure the head is looking over the left shoulder and towards the instrument.

(4) Have the student bring the instrument towards the face and place it on the shoulder with the side of the face (jaw, not chin) resting on the chinrest. The student should still be holding on to the main body of the instrument. Have the student turn (from the waist up) towards the right so that the scroll of the instrument is pointing towards their music stand (or where it will be when they start using it).

For now, this is all that needs to be shown to them as the playing that will be done in the first lesson will not involve the left hand.

Some points that must be checked carefully to insure proper holding position are:

(1) The elbow should be well under the instrument.

(2) The instrument should be horizontal or even elevated a little. This may seem somewhat exaggerated but a higher position at first is important to help combat the student's natural tendency to slump. Slumping not only looks bad but causes them to bow over the fingerboard where producing a good tone is impossible.

(3) The jaw, rather than the chin, should be on the chinrest.

(4) The head should be erect and not bending either forward or sideways (see Figure No. 6 for correct holding position of the Violin and Viola).

Correct Holding Position of Violin and Viola
Figure No. 6

SHOULDER PADS

It is imperative that the students be able to hold their instruments horizontally without supporting them with the left hand or "hunching" the shoulder into an unnatural or uncomfortable position. Being able to hold the instrument without left hand support becomes especially necessary when students are ready to begin learning to shift and vibrato. For the great majority of students, this means that they will have to use some sort of a shoulder pad to fill up the extra space that naturally occurs between the bottom of the instrument and the shoulder.

What Kind of Pad? No matter what type of shoulder pad the teacher decides to use, make certain that it is the correct height and shape for each student. Many commercial pads come in several heights (low, medium, and high) and in many styles. Be sure the pads recommended are large enough to fit across the back of the instrument from side to side and that they will collapse to fit into their cases so they don't lose them. If expense prohibits purchase of patented pads, then a satisfactory substitute can be made from *soft* household or cosmetic sponges. These sponges come in many shapes and thicknesses making it possible to find the correct size and height for each student. They can be easily secured to the instrument by using two or three rubber bands looped together.

A shoulder pad has two main purposes – first, for the comfort of the students so they don't get sore (even if they don't need height), and second, to fill up the extra space between the body and the instrument so the weight of the instrument isn't being held by the left hand and/or a hunched up shoulder. Require *all* students to use some form of shoulder pad. *Warning:* The teacher will have to check continually to make sure the students remember to use them once they have them. They are prone to forget to use them after the newness wears off!

CHIN RESTS

The teacher will need to check each student's instrument to make sure that the chinrest is not uncomfortable and/or causing an unnatural head position. If a student complains several times that he is uncomfortable (or it is noticed that his head is in an unnatural position) then the teacher will need to advise the parents that they should take him to the nearest music dealer where they can try different chinrests on the instrument until one is found that is comfortable. If a local music dealer is not available then the teacher will need to have a supply of chinrests in various sizes and shapes to try on the students' instruments. The students should be as comfortable as possible. Being uncomfortable is often the main reason that students want to quit. Don't allow this to happen in your class!

Cello

The correct chair is crucial to correct positioning of the cello to the cellist. If the chair is too high, the cellist cannot comfortably touch his feet to the floor. The young cellist will often try to solve this problem by putting the feet on the rungs of the chair. If the chair is too low, the students' legs will be crowded and in the way of the bow forcing the player to pull his legs back behind the chair legs to keep them out of the way. The best chair for the cellist is one that has a seat that is *horizontal* to the floor. A horizontal seat does not promote sliding back against the back of the seat and into an improper playing position.

The cellists must sit squarely on the front edge of the chair with the top half of the body leaning slightly forward and the feet flat on the floor (usually one ahead and one slightly behind). Next, place the extended end pin in the floor directly in front of the player and let the cello lean back toward the player at about a 45 degree angle with the floor. The cello will rest on the breast bone (in the center of the chest). Place both knees firmly against the sides of the cello. If the endpin is the correct height (most are not long enough) the knees will be *below* the points rather than in the cut-out section. If the cellist is sitting correctly and holding the cello firmly enough with the knees, it will be difficult for anyone to take the cello away.

After both the knees and the angle of the cello are positioned, make sure the scroll is above the left shoulder (not resting on it) and the lowest peg slightly above and behind the left ear. If the cello is at the correct angle and it is still impossible to place the knees below the bouts with the neck of the instrument above the shoulder, then either the endpin is still at an incorrect height, or the cello is the wrong size and the student may have to try either a larger or smaller one. If the cello is way up in the air, or the knees are in the cut-out section, or both, then the cello is too large. If the scroll is near the shoulder, the knees are in the way when the end-pin is fully extended, and the angle of the cello is correct, then the cello is too small.

The teacher should realize that there will be some people that physically cannot fit all of these requirements. If this happens, get the cello closest to the correct size for the student and make minor adjustments – compromising a little on both ends. Try to make it possible to bow without having to raise the left arm too high above the left ear.

In summary, make sure the following main points of cello position are correct:

(1) Feet flat on the floor.

(2) Cello directly in front of the player.

(3) Cello at a 45 degree angle with the floor (neither resting on the should nor too straight up and down).

(4) Knees gripping firmly below the points.

(5) Scroll above and behind the left ear (see Figure No. 7).

Correct Cello Position
Figure No. 7

END-PIN RESTS (STOPS)

It is necessary for secure playing that both cellists and bassists have the end-pins securely anchored to the floor so that their instruments cannot slip. Just as violinists and violists need shoulder pads for comfort and security, so do cellists and bassists need a device to aid them in holding the endpin securely. Some commonly used devices that work effectively are: (1) black, round rubber stops (four inches diameter); (2) peg board sheets; (3) carpet remnants; and (4) T-shaped wooden boards (Cello only).

Many schools solve the endpin problem for cellos by having the industrial arts department make "cello" boards. If making these, it is preferable to use two boards (1 x 4) and put them together like a "T". Be sure the boards are long enough to extend at *least* three feet in front of the chair.

Boards that are too short force the cello in too close to the player and cause the cello to be at the wrong angle to be played easily. Holes will need to be bored about two inches apart (only half-way through) so the cellists has lots of choices of where to place the end-pin. Cello boards can also be made of a single piece of wood, but even when attached to the back legs of the chair, they are not as satisfactory as the T-type. They are not as stable. *Remember:* cellists cannot play with the end-pin slipping around.

String Bass

Beginning bass players should be taught *first* to play standing as they need to know how to stand and play (even if they will play seated) in case their stools should not be available. As bass players graduate to groups where rehearsals are longer than a thirty minute period, stools definitely should be provided (either by the school or the players) as this is too long to expect them to stand. If it is possible to provide stools from the beginning, different height stools will be needed to allow for the rapid growth of the students at this age.

STANDING PLAYING POSITION

The player should stand with his feet about a foot apart with the left foot forward and the right foot back. The weight of the body will be mainly upon the right foot. Bring the neck of the instrument back towards the player and rest the *corner* of the back and side of the bass in the groin area of the body. Try to find the place where the bass will as nearly as possible stand by itself without having to be held up by the left hand. The bass will be sloping back towards the body. The neck and head of the player should be very close to the neck of the instrument (almost touching) to be able to maintain good left hand finger position. The scroll will be behind and slightly above the player's head.

Next, bring the left hand up into position for playing first position. If the hand is too high above the head, then lower the endpin and/or slant the bass toward the student until the left arm is only a few inches above the left ear. If the hand is still too high then a smaller instrument may be necessary. If the instrument is too small, the bass will be straight up and down and/or the left arm lower than the left ear (see Figure No. 8).

As with the cello, it may be impossible to always fit the player to the bass. It is easy to make the adjustment if the bass is too big by lowering the endpin, standing the player on a box, and/or changing the angle of the bass (bass sloping back even more towards the player) or a combination of all three. The player should be able to bow half-way between the fingerboard and bridge without having to straighten the arm into an *uncomfortable* position. An even more important consideration is to be sure that the player can spread his fingers enough to play the finger pattern of first finger to fourth finger without too much difficulty.

As with the cello, it is impossible to play the string bass properly without the end-pin being securely anchored to the floor (many position problems are caused by the student trying to compensate for a slipping end-pin).

Correct Bass Standing Position
Figure No. 8

Correct Orchestral Sitting Position
Figure No. 9

Orchestral Sitting Position

Since orchestral players, rather than solo players, are being trained in the class, the students will need to be taught carefully how to correctly sit and play. Poor sitting position can greatly hamper technical progress.

An easy way to teach young players the importance of sitting squarely on the front edge of their chairs with feet touching the floor is to tell them that they must be able to get up quickly without shifting their weight forward. An activity they enjoy is for the teacher to frequently shout the words "Up" or "Bingo" or any other selected code word to see how fast the class can get up.

The main points of correct sitting position for orchestral players are: (1) sit forward on front edge of the chair; (2) feet touching the floor; (3) back not touching the back of the chair; (4) be ready to get up at all times. "The weight is over your feet, *not* on your seat," (see Figure No. 9).

LEARNING OPEN STRINGS PIZZICATO (ROTE)

(Step No. 3)

Why Start Pizzicato?

To be consistent with the principle of presenting *only* one new thing at a time, the teacher must either start with the bow and use only open strings or play pizzicato and use fingers.

If the student is started with the bow and asked to finger as well, he is being asked to do two new difficult things at once. This is frustrating and discouraging and usually the end result is that neither the left or right hand will be correct. It is practically impossible to solve the problems caused by this mistake and it is often the cause of students getting discouraged and wanting to discontinue lessons. Some teachers attempt to solve this problem by starting with the bow and bowing only on open strings until the correct bow arm motion is established. It is felt that this is better than trying to do both bowing and fingering at once (one thing at a time), but the disadvantage is that the students will be bored because it is so long before they can actually play any tunes (Mom and Dad are bored, too).

Another disadvantage to starting with the bow (rather than pizzicato) is that it is an extremely difficult coordination for a beginning student. Therefore, the authors' choice is to play *pizzicato first* thus teaching them to use the left hand fingers so they will be able to play tunes successfully right away.

PLAYING PIZZICATO

To teach students to play pizzicato, ask them to put their instruments into playing position. Violins and violas hold on to the main body of the instruments with the left hand on the high string side. Cellos and basses rest their left hands on the shoulder on the high string side. Next, ask *all* students to hold up their right arms and show their right thumbs. Check to be sure they show the right one (not the left). Then, ask only the violinists and violists to place the tip of their thumbs near the end of the fingerboard on the high string side of the instrument (see Figure No. 10). Cellos and basses will put their thumbs on the fingerboard about six or eight inches from the end (see Figure No. 11). The teacher will need to use an instrument and show them just how and where the thumb goes on the fingerboard. Ask them to do the same (the teacher will need to check to be sure they are right).

Next ask them to stick up their index fingers (second finger for the bass). Tell them that this is the finger that will do the picking or plucking (called *pizzicato)* and that the thumb's purpose is to hold the place on the fingerboard. The teacher should then show them by plucking on his instrument that they must pizzicato with the fat part (pad) of the finger and not the fingernail. Explain that it must be done this way to have a good sound (or tone). Show them the difference in a good and bad tone (the sound made with the fat part of the finger makes a good tone and the one made with the fingernail makes a bad tone). Let them know that they are always going to be expected to produce a good tone by plucking the string the correct way. (See Figure 10 and 11 for the correct pizzicato positions for the violin, viola, cello, and bass.)

Another skill that must be taught that influences the quality of the tone is how to pull the string. Make sure that the string is pulled a little to the side and then up, rather than straight up. If the string is plucked correctly, a clear resonant tone should result (rather than a dull, "thud" type tone). Students also need to be taught to pluck the string with a brisk motion, rather than a slow, lazy motion to produce a clear tone.

Remember: It is very important from the very first class, that the students are conscious of a good tone so they can learn to discriminate differences in the quality of tones that they produce.

(A)

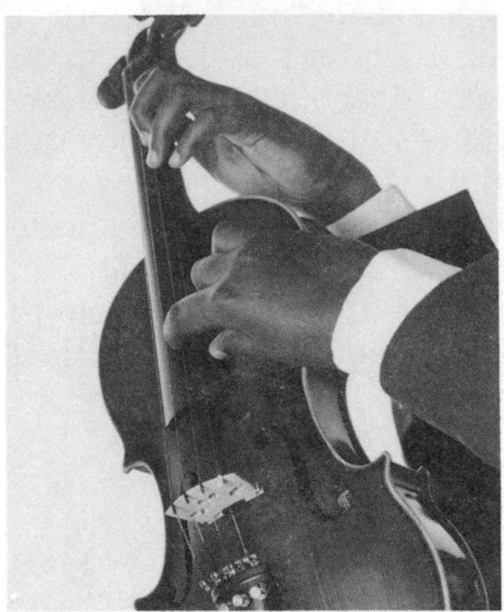

(B)

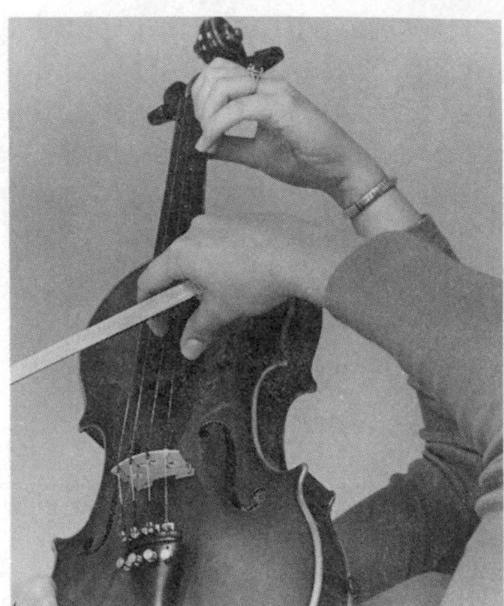

Correct Violin and Viola Pizzicato Position
Figure No. 10

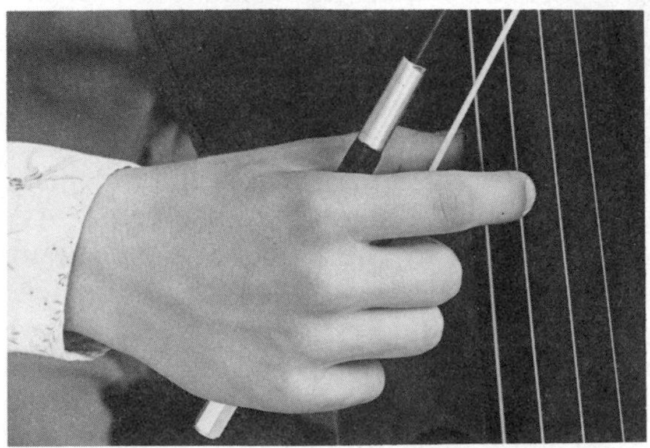

Cello

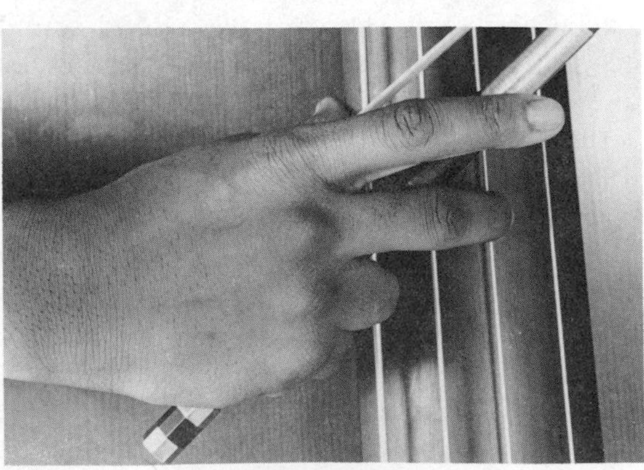

Bass

Correct Cello and Bass Pizzicato Position
Figure No. 11

Learning Open Strings – The teacher should play some open "D" string pizzicato notes on his instrument and ask the students if they can find a string on their instrument that sounds the same. Don't show them where their "D's" are (except as a last resort) as the students need to learn to find the right string by listening. Development of the ear starts now and must continue increasingly as the class moves along. Have them find all the other strings in the same manner that they found the D string. Once the majority of the class can locate the different strings, introduce playing the open strings in different rhythms.

Learning Different Rhythm Patterns – The next step will be to teach the students to find their open strings and play different rhythm patterns on them by mimicking the teacher. *Remember:* Don't at this time tell the students what strings to play on – have them find the strings by ear. As they are shown a new note (string) the teacher should also sing the note's letter name so that the students can be started towards learning note names. Encourage them to sing the note, too, as this will be used a great deal later, and will make them more aware of what strings are higher or lower than others (they will sing if the teacher does). In teaching the following recommended rhythmic patterns, the teacher should play the pattern first, then ask the class to echo it.

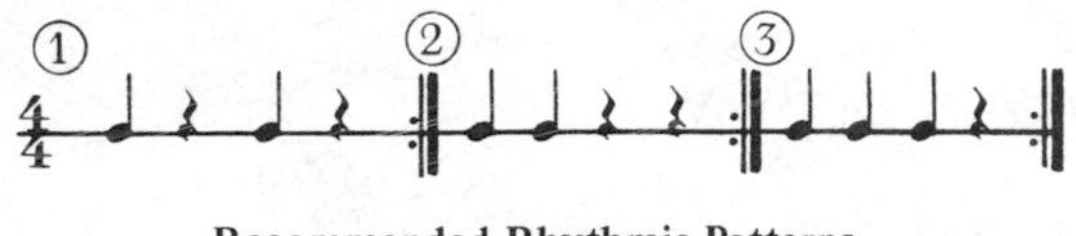

Recommended Rhythmic Patterns
Figure No. 12

Continue to play a rhythm pattern until most of them are able to do it. The students should understand from the very beginning that they will always be working for perfection and that *each* person is expected to play correctly. This makes them feel individually important and helps to build the pride necessary for a fine group.

After one rhythm pattern has been mastered on all the strings, move to another pattern without stopping and talking about it. Once they know all the strings, try mixing up the strings (Ex.: D rest A rest; D D rest rest A A rest rest; etc.). After every new pattern or string is introduced, go back and play one or more of the strings learned earlier before going on to make sure they are remembering the old as well as learning the new.

It should also be understood that most mistakes with beginners will be corrected by *repetition* as it is simply a matter of their needing to "go over" the new area until it is mastered. *Remember:* Only stop and talk when it appears after several chances that they just simply do not understand and probably won't get it by themselves. Keep "teacher-talking" to a minimum as it can waste much valuable class time. They learn by doing!

After students have mastered the recommended patterns, it is fun to ask them to play two D's and two A's with no rest in between and ask, "What does that sound like?" They will answer: "Twinkle, Twinkle Little Star." Ask them if they would like to try to play more of it. Hopefully, they will say, "Yes" and the teacher can then show them how to put their first finger down by rote on the A string (making a new note, B). Then, let them play DDAABBA-rest, rest several times. They will be very excited to be able to play this little bit of a tune they have heard before.

Preparation for Following A Written Line
(Step No. 4)

The teacher should now put all of the rhythm patterns that were learned by rote on the board. This is necessary to teach the students how to follow something written and to play at the same time. The teacher should point to the various examples and ask them to play in tempo with the pointing. Skip around from one example to another until the students cannot be mixed up. When most of them get to this point, then the teacher can be assured that they know the strings well enough to start reading from a printed page while playing.

Steps Number 1 through 4 can all be covered in one class period if all the students have their instruments and books and are ready to go. If not, it may take two periods.

If the Muller-Rusch series is to be used, the group would now be ready to go to Lesson I. If not, it will be necessary to continue by introducing by rote the fundamentals outlined in Steps Number 1 and 2 until such time as the students know enough to be able to go to Lesson I of whatever book the teacher plans to use.

THE SECOND LESSON

Introduction

To avoid being redundant when getting into the "how to" portions of this text, a few remarks will be made about some faults that are frequently seen in the teaching of string classes, particularly at the elementary level.

The teacher must move constantly from student to student during the class in order to be able to observe and correct the mistakes that most likely will be happening all the time. When standing in one place, it is impossible to help *all* of the students.

The teacher, if possible, should demonstrate each new step on an instrument so the students can see how it is done. *Don't play* while the students are playing! It is impossible for the teacher to hear the students or make the physical corrections necessary while playing an instrument.

It should be realized that the piano should be treated as a reward and used *only after* the class has learned something well. When the piano is being played it is impossible for the students to hear themselves so that they can correct any faulty intonation. Also, the teacher can neither see nor hear the students' mistakes while playing the piano.

It must be remembered that it is best to avoid saying (or singing) fingerings, especially in a mixed instrument class, where fingerings are different (as it would prove confusing). It is much better to use letter names of notes, besides, much drill is needed on these.

Learning To Follow A Printed Line In The Book
(Step No. 5)

Remember that if the Muller-Rusch series is not used, there are still six more steps (Numbers 5-10) that must be mastered before the child is ready to simultaneously read music on the staff, use the bow and finger with the left hand.

To teach the students to read from a printed line in the book, ask them to put their index fingers on the beginning of the line that is to be learned. Give the students the meter of the line and ask them to tap their feet in this tempo. Next, ask them to follow the notes on the page as the teacher plays the line. Watch their fingers to be sure that they follow the line correctly. It will be necessary to help some of them. Also, watch to see that their feet continue to tap in the correct down-up fashion as learned earlier.

The next step will be to ask the students to sing the letter names of notes with the teacher as they continue to tap their feet and point to the notes and rests. It is still absolutely imperative that all rests be said out loud.

After the students can follow the printed line, keep a steady beat, and sing the names of the notes and say the rests, ask them to put their instruments into playing position as they are now ready to play the line *pizzicato.* (The teacher should always give one-measure of preparation in the desired tempo before the students play.) Be sure their feet start tapping with the counting. Expect them to play the lines perfectly but don't stop if they don't. Say "Repeat the line" in the rests at the end of the line and keep playing it again and again until it is played correctly. *Remember:* Most mistakes can be corrected during repetition.

Whenever the line is played correctly, move on to the next line without stopping. The teacher *must* continue to move around the room to see if there are students that need help. It may be necessary to point to the place in the book for some students needing additional help in following the printed line. *Warning:* Don't allow students to look anywhere other than the book! Many will try to "fake it" or memorize it rather than looking at the book. They must learn now the importance of looking at a printed line or they will be in serious trouble later.

Some students may need help holding their instruments correctly, tapping their feet, playing pizzico correctly, or playing on the beat, etc. The teacher must see that all of these things are done correctly before moving on. It may be necessary to correct the same child many times on the same problem. If the teacher moves often enough to them, they will "get the message" that the teacher isn't going to give up until they do everything right. They must feel as if the teacher is totally uncompromising. It is of utmost importance that the opinion formed of the teacher from the very first lesson be the one that the teacher wants them to have for the remainder of the time they will be in the music program. If the wrong one is formed, it will be very difficult for the teacher to change it as they learn to anticipate certain behaviors from the teacher just as the teacher does from them.

It is also very important that the teacher sing the letter names of notes and encourage the students to do so also. Keep "bugging" them about saying the rests out loud and keeping a steady beat with their feet. This is extremely important as eventually the entire responsibility for keeping the class going rhythmically must be placed on the students, rather than the teacher.

After the students have played about two lines, it will be necessary to stop and let them rest as they will tire very easily at first. If the violins and violas grow tired of holding their instruments in playing position, the teacher may wish to let them play the pizzicato lines in guitar position. Don't be too sympathetic about them getting tired as it will make it difficult for the teacher to be able to get anything done with them complaining at the slightest little bit of fatigue. Explain to them that *even* an athlete gets tired at first when learning a new skill!

While the students are resting, the teacher should look ahead at the next line they are to play. Talk about any new problems that may occur. For instance if half notes are new, point out the half notes and be sure they understand that they get two taps of the foot. Ask them what string they will play on and, "Is it a higher or lower sounding note?" Next, sing the new line in tempo (with letter names) while again pointing to the printed line with the index finger and tapping the foot. If the line is a difficult one (Ex: involves changing strings), let them first pretend they are playing it pizzicato (with instruments in playing position and merely pointing to the strings).

After the first three or four lines have been played, there will probably be a line that will give the students quite a bit of trouble. It will now become obvious that if the teacher continues to insist that most students play the line perfectly, some additional drill is going to be necessary.

Merely repeating a line (or passage) over and over has several drawbacks and often doesn't solve the real problem of what is actually wrong. Some obvious disadvantages to all repeating a line over and over are:

(1) When everyone is playing the students can't hear themselves individually.

(2) The teacher can't always tell which students are having problems.

(3) The better students are not really located and recognized.

(4) The continual repetition can be monotonous.

(5) The problem may not correct itself without some kind of change that will shift the focus to the real problem.

The authors feel there is a more efficient way to fix problems than the whole group constantly repeating a line over and over. The drill routine that will follow is offered as a way to avoid many, if not all, of the problems mentioned above. We will frequently refer to this method of correcting problems throughout the book as the "Drill Routine," so whenever the words "Drill Routine" are used, the teacher will follow the steps that follow.

The Drill Routine

Introduction

The "Drill Routine" is a class procedure that will be used throughout this book whenever repetition seems to be necessary for the group to learn a new skill. With beginners, it must be realized that some form of drill will be necessary most of the time. The authors feel that the drill method offered here is a more efficient and dependable way of correcting and solving problems than the conventional method of either constant repetition or constant stopping of the class. It will give maximum results, in less time, *if* the teacher handles it correctly.

The idea for this basic "Drill Routine" was originated by Dr. Joseph Maddy and T. P. Giddings for use at the National Music Camp at Interlochen, Michigan. J. Frederick Muller refined some of these procedures and used them in his workshops with the Muller-Rusch String Series. The authors of this book, while using the "Drill Routine" in the classroom at all levels, in turn adapted and added details until it assumes the form it has today.

The philosophy of teaching developed by Joseph Maddy and T. P. Giddings says, in part, that every student must be purposefully occupied for every minute of class time. This kind of class situation makes for faster and more dependable progress, because it may not be assumed that students supposedly listening and learning as others play are really learning anything themselves. Most often they become bored, do not really pay attention, and are very likely to create disturbances.

The method presented here has been used for many years with great success by many fine teachers and by this time is virtually "fool-proof", if used as described. It has withstood the "test of time," and deviations from it will probably lead to a loss of teaching efficiency. This "Drill Routine" Method is in very widespread use and is producing outstanding string programs all over the United States and Canada.

Since this routine consists of small groups playing while others are involved tapping feet, singing letter names of notes, bowing in the air, etc., the recommended row seating mentioned earlier is necessary to achieve the best results (see Seating Chart on Page 6). If the teacher is tempted to be a creative person (hopefully he is), this is not the best place to be creative. Remember, row seating should be used.

Drill Routine Procedure

It is best to use one whole line of music as a drill portion (at least while still learning to follow a printed line), because students will find this easier than smaller portions. However, if the teacher is using a method book that is not set up so the lines for each instrument end in the same place, then it will be necessary to go from either letter to letter or number to number. Or, if the book has no numbers or letters, teach students to observe eight bar phrase segments.

The procedure is as follows:

(1) The whole class plays the line (while tapping their feet and saying any rests out loud).

(2) Without stopping, the line is repeated and played alone by Row 1. While Row 1 plays the line, the rest of the class sings letter names of notes, says the rests, and continues to tap its feet steadily while watching the music. music.

(3) Without stopping, the whole class repeats the line playing together.

(4) Next, repeat with Row 2 playing alone while the rest of the class keeps the beat steady by tapping its feet or singing names of notes, etc.

(5) Everyone again repeats the line playing.

(6) Row 3 then should play alone while the others tap feet, sing notes, say rests, etc. as before.

(7) The entire class plays the line again.

Continue this procedure until every row has had its chance to play alone.

After going through these steps, the line will have been played through many times with corrections while performing, and the teacher can be pretty well assured that the entire class will have mastered it well enough to go on. In the beginning, almost every line will need to be drilled out with the above steps before all can play it satisfactorily. Do not attempt to save time here because it will hurt the group later on.

Until this routine has been used for a week or so, the teacher will have to continually tell the group what and when to play as well as to encourage them to tap their feet and to sing letter names of notes and to say the rests. From the beginning, the teacher should be working towards having the responsibility for keeping the class going assumed by the students. When this is accomplished, the *"Self-propelling" Class* will become a fact. This will make it possible for the teacher to spend the majority of the class time moving in and out of the rows, checking and correcting each student individually and making sure that everything is being done correctly. It can be seen that with this routine it is possible to give more individual help than is given with classes taught in a manner where the teacher must stop the class to correct individuals.

With the *"Self-propelling" Class,* the teacher should watch each row as it plays alone, and wait to make any corrections of those students until it is time for the entire group to play together again. Waiting to correct a student until the class again plays together spares the child from his embarrassment at others realizing that he is having problems. In fact, most students won't even realize who was helped during a class period!

Another reason it is recommended that the teacher wait to correct an individual until his row has finished playing, is that the teacher will not be disturbing the row that is already "on the spot." Experience has shown that it is also a good idea, when physically correcting a student, to also *tell him* what needs to be changed so he will understand what needs to be done the next time.

When teaching the students to use this routine, the teacher can expect considerable inertia and passive resistance from the students. Consequently, the students at first will need to be pushed to keep the routine going. *Remember:* The class should not be allowed to stop unless most of the group is lost and it is obvious that they really don't know what is happening. After a few weeks, they will be able to keep track of which row's turn it is to play. This must happen so that the teacher is free to do the job he is there to do – teach!

If at any time during the drill routine the line is played satisfactorily by most of the students, the teacher should (without stopping the class) move the class on to the next line. It has been found that students will not mind repetition if it has a purpose and they know what it is. But, having to repeat something, just to be repeating, (especially after it is correct) really "bugs" them and makes them think the teacher is just being nasty. The students *must feel confident* that whenever a line is played satisfactorily, they will be able to move on to the next line. If drill is not handled in this way, they will soon quit trying to do it right the first time, as they know that they probably will have to play it again anyway.

For the first eight or nine lessons, every line played will probably need extensive drill, and the teacher will need to tell the class at the end of each line (also during any rests in the line) the things they still need to correct. It should also be realized that, at first, the most the teacher should try to cover is two or three lines before letting the students stop to rest.

A Word of Caution: This drill routine guarantees learning. The teacher must realize that it will teach the wrong thing just as easily as it will the right thing, especially if the teacher is careless and doesn't watch every student every minute. This drill routine will not take the place of good teaching because the teacher must still know correct position, bow techniques, etc., and then make sure that things are done in the correct manner.

SUMMARY OF THE "DRILL ROUTINE"

The "Drill Routine" presented here allows the teacher to be able to cover more material in a class period than teaching in the traditional way where the teacher tells the students what they are doing wrong at the end of each line before beginning to play again. Moving from line to line and only stopping when almost everyone is lost or having trouble, should make it possible (even in the first few lessons) to cover at least a half a lesson in each class period. It should be possible to cover a whole lesson during each class period after the students have progressed a little.

The "Drill Routine" also makes it possible to be able to move from lesson to lesson without reviewing. Not having to review makes the students feel as if they are really progressing. Also, they don't get the idea that they are going to have another chance to learn today's lesson; therefore, they feel they are compelled to learn it today. This keeps the class from getting "bogged" down. It should also be mentioned that well-written method books are constructed so that extraneous review is not necessary because the review is built into the sequence.

Remember: Review should not be necessary, except in very unusual cases, and if it is, it is the teacher's fault rather than the students! If review is necessary, one or more of the following teaching errors have been made:

(1) More than one new thing at a time has been taught.

(2) The class has been moved on to new material too soon.

(3) A step was skipped.

Possibly the most important advantage of this "Drill Routine" is that it allows more time for individual help than is possible with the traditional way of teaching. Even students that never study privately will learn to play at a very high level as they are never allowed to do anything wrong because they receive constant individual help. It may seem that the teacher wouldn't have enough time in a large class to give enough individual attention to achieve real quality with all the students. However, it will be found that after moving to the same student to fix the same thing several times during a class period, all the teacher needs to do is move towards that student and he probably will remember to fix the thing that has been constantly corrected.

Learning To Finger Notes Pizzicato (Rote)
(Step No. 6)

By now, the students should be able to hold their instruments correctly, know the open strings, play pizzicato with a good sound, have a clear understanding of the rhythm fundamentals introduced so far, and be able to follow some type of pre music-reading symbols. In addition, they should be fairly well-acquainted with the "Drill Routine" sequence.

The beginning class is now ready to start using their left hands to play some fingered notes by rote (Step Number 6). Before showing the students how to finger notes, the teacher must show the students the proper position of the left hand for each instrument.

Left Hand Position

VIOLIN AND VIOLA

On the violin and viola, the neck of the instrument should be placed inside the hand and between the thumb and index finger. The index finger can rest against the neck of the instrument in the early stages. *Important:* Be sure that the neck does not rest in the crotch between the thumb and index finger (there should be enough space so that one can take the other hand and run the index finger through the space that is left underneath the neck of the instrument.) The teacher can tell the students that there must be a "peek-hole".

Ideally, the wrist and lower arm should make a straight line (without a break). This is an extremely important point as there is no way students can learn to play with the wrist bent in towards the body.

Last, the teacher needs to check to make sure the elbow is underneath the instrument and *not* out towards the G string (C string on the viola) side as beginning students are prone to do. Also, the instrument should be horizontal to the floor and the head erect and correctly placed on the chin-rest (see Figure No. 13).

Correct Left Hand Position (Violin and Viola)
Figure No. 13

CELLO AND BASS

The left arm on the cello and bass must also be in a straight line (with no break anywhere from the elbow to the fingers). The elbow should be very little lower than the fingers when the hand is in playing position. Students will tend to drop their elbows so it will be necessary to constantly remind them to keep them up. It is certainly better to have the elbow *too* high than too low, although in reality, this probably won't happen!

The placement of the left thumb is often wrong. It should always be placed *underneath the second finger,* not the first finger! Students cannot make the necessary stretches between fingers with the thumb in the wrong place. A good idea is to place a round bandaid or a strip of masking tape on the back side of the neck of the instrument to show the correct thumb placement (see Figures No. 14 and 15 for correct left hand position of the cello and bass respectively).

(A)

(B)

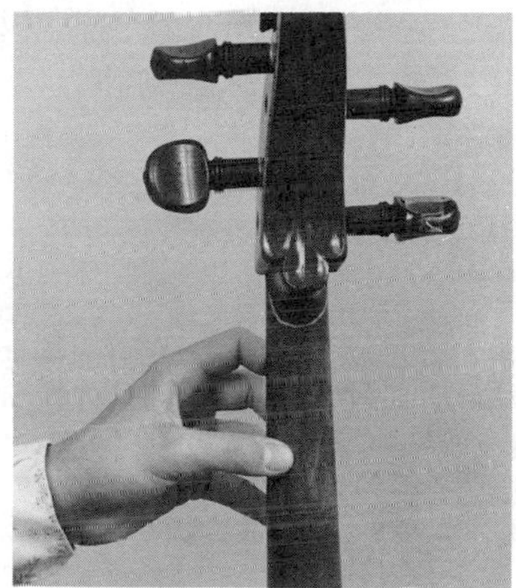

Correct Left Hand Position (Cello)
Figure No. 14

A

(B)

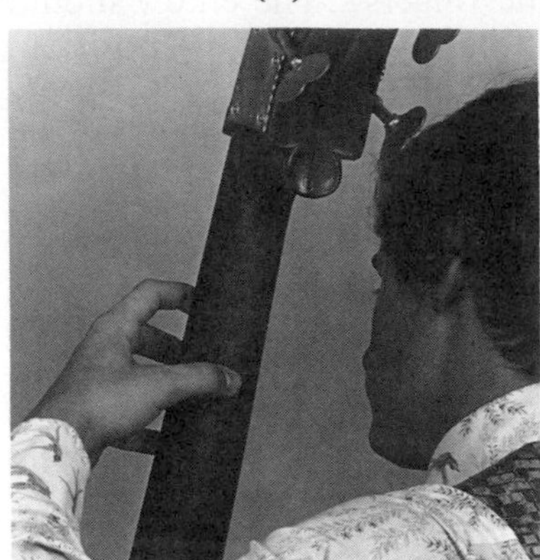

Correct Left Hand Position (Bass)
Figure No. 15

Preparation for Using First Finger

First, the teacher will need to tell the class how the fingers are numbered. Explain that the index finger is called first finger, the middle finger is called second, the ring finger is called third, and the little finger is called fourth. Since some students may play piano, they need to know that the string players thumb isn't numbered as it is for the piano.

Next, the students need to be told that the finger must press the string down tightly enough on the fingerboard so that the pitch can be changed from the open string pitch to the higher pitch. Show them how to play D and E pizzicato (open and first finger). Ask them: "Can you hear the difference in the sound when the first finger is put down on the D string? Does it sound higher or lower?" Hopefully, they will be able to tell the difference. If they can't, try making the difference more obvious by playing the open D string and F-sharp (or higher if necessary), until they can tell that the two tones sound different. It has been found that at first they can hear large pitch differences more easily than small pitch differences. Once they can do this, the teacher should play D and E pizzicato again and say: "I am playing D and E. D is played with no fingers, or the open string, and E is played with the first finger." Tell them that every note they learn to play will have a letter name and that they will be expected to remember its name as well as how to play it.

Then the teacher should play D and E again and ask them to sing with him. Have them sing it several times until most can match the pitches with their voices. Once they can do this, the teacher should say: "Now, this is how D and E should always sound. Memorize their sounds."

Play D and E again and do it wrong (extremely high) and say: "Is that right?" They should answer: "No, it is wrong." Then ask: "What is wrong with it?" Hopefully, they will say that it sounds too high. Then the teacher should say: "Well, what am I doing wrong?" And they should answer: "Your finger is up too far towards the bridge," or maybe just: "The finger is in the wrong place." If they can't tell what is wrong with it, exaggerate it even a little more by playing D and G with the first finger until they can hear that difference.

Next, place the first finger down on E and gradually move the pitch up, while continuing to play pizzicato. Ask them: "What is happening to the notes?" They should answer: "They are getting higher." The teacher says: "Yes, when the fingers press the string down closer to the bridge, the notes get higher. What do you suppose happens if I would go the other direction with my finger?" They should say: "The notes will get lower." If they don't understand, repeat the whole procedure again.

After this, the teacher should ask the students if they have noticed that whenever the string was pressed down, it was done with the tip of the finger rather than the flat part. Explain that this is because it takes strength to press the string firmly against the fingerboard and that more strength is possible using the tips of the fingers rather than the flat part. Tell them that they will always be expected to curve their fingers and play on the tips. *Warning:* Do not let them play with long fingernails as it is impossible to play correctly this way!

Locating First Finger

TO MARK OR NOT TO MARK?

Now that the students know how E sounds, the next step will be to let them see if they can find their E's. This brings up the sensitive issue of whether it is all right to place any kind of marks on the instruments to help the students know where to place their fingers.

The authors realize that "to mark or not to mark" is an extremely controversial subject that is certain to cause raised eyebrows and fortissimo voices whenever discussed. The authors feel strongly that the marking of the instrument (at the beginning) is an absolute necessity for maximum progress when teaching *large* groups to play stringed instruments. Because we feel so strongly about our position, and realize that other people also feel this way about theirs, we are going to attempt to convince all that our position is at least well thought out and works well.

The fingerboard should be marked where the fingers are to be placed (at least at first) because the alternative is to teach the students to find the finger location entirely be ear. This is a dangerous concept because students with really good ears will *never* be able to place the fingers accurately because they learn right away that it doesn't really matter where the fingers are put, because if the note is missed, it can always be changed. A much more useful and certainly more accurate concept is to ask them to place the fingers with reference to the physical relationship of one note to the next or one finger to the next. If it doesn't *sound* right then, they are taught from the very first day that it is to be changed. It should be realized that the initial finger placement should be a physical response (kinesthetic) rather than an aural response. Otherwise, the result is a constant play the note, see if it is right, and then "fix it" process. Therefore, to be sure that the students don't end up with a "seek and ye shall find" (maybe!) attitude towards playing a stringed instrument, it is recommended that the marked fingerboard be used in developing an attitude that all good string players have found to be useful. This attitude is that the performer knows how far it is to the next note by the "feel" that he has learned through practice. Good string players *do not* start with the idea that: "If I miss it, I will change" (although they will, of course, if necessary).

Many critics of marking the fingerboards say that the students think that all they have to do is to put the finger down on the mark and that the notes will be correct. They feel that this method will lead to out of tune playing. Our answer is: "No, it will not – the students should be taught from the very first lesson that the mark on the fingerboard is only a place to begin – an approximate position to help them get a "feel" of where the fingers if it sounds wrong – no matter where the marks are, and they understand the concept of moving the fingers to adjust pitch from the very first day. Aside from the logic of both positions, experience has demonstrated to the authors (who have done it both ways) that "in-tune" playing results faster and more surely when fingerboards are marked.
strated to the authors (who have done it both ways) that "in-tune" playing results faster and more surely when fingerboards are marked.

Another aspect to be considered is that, especially on cello and bass, the "eye" should have a great deal to do with the placement of the fingers. The idea of looking at the fingers may be surprising and many will say that it is not advisable. The reason that this frightens some people is that they feel that looking at the fingers will cause the student to lose his place in the music (true at first!). However, our experience has shown that the students will learn very quickly to look back and forth and not get lost, and that the real advantage is that looking helps them to learn exactly where the fingers go more quickly. After "eye-spacing" is developed, it is easier to develop the "feel" of how far it is from one tone to the next. It should not be felt that this is merely a crutch for beginners, because the finest professionals can be frequently observed looking at their hands when preparing for a difficult entrance. No professional would hesitate for a moment to look at his hand if it would help him to avoid a mistake.

Before ending our discussion of the pros and cons of placing marks on the fingerboard to help students in the beginning stages, we would like to mention several other reasons why it is a positive aid rather than a harmful crutch. Marking on the fingerboard:

(1) Helps to get the beginning class "off the ground" more rapidly and gives the students a psychological lift because of the obvious, early progress thus lessening the drop-out rate.

(2) Makes for better teaching efficiency because the teacher, at a glance, can tell visually which students need a reminder to check their hand positions.

(3) Helps greatly with the large class situation advocated in this book because the teacher cannot possibly tell by "ear" which students need help as it it impossible to hear each student's pitch while all are playing.

(4) Makes for better intonation right away and thus keeps the better students from giving up in disgust. (In many classes those that have acute ears simply give up because they hear so much wrong around them that they figure: "Why try – it sounds terrible anyway."

(5) Because of the improved intonation, the students are more aware of how it should sound when they are right and therefore can be expected to play more in tune.

We believe that the ear will compromise and begin to accept faulty intonation unless the teacher keeps pointing it out and insisting that it be changed. In the final analysis, however, whether the fingerboards are marked or not is not the important question, but rather it is whether the children are being taught to play in tune. It is rather obvious from the foregoing paragraphs, that the authors feel that "in-tune" playing can best be taught by marking the fingerboards.

How To Mark – If the authors' arguments seem to be sufficiently strong, and it is decided to mark the fingerboard to help the students, time should not be taken from class to do this. Class time should be reserved for student participation and learning.

When marking the fingerboards, the first finger for *every* instrument definitely should be marked, even if no other one is, so that the students learn where "home base" is. For the violin and viola, the teacher can either mark the position of the second finger-high and have them place third finger next to second finger-high, or mark the first and third finger and tell the students to play high second finger close to the third finger, or second finger-low close to the first finger. For the cello, mark the third and fourth finger as well as the first finger. For the bass, mark the second and fourth finger as well as the first finger. As was mentioned earlier, marking the thumb for the cello and bass helps to establish the kinesthetic concept of left hand position.

Playing First Finger E By Rote

After the students' instruments have been marked for first finger, it is now time to let them try to find their E's. The teacher should ask the students to listen and watch as he plays a series of four quarter note D's followed by four quarter note E's (pizzicato) followed by four quarter rests. Then, the students should be asked to sing letter names of notes with the teacher as he plays. After this, the students can be asked to imitate what the teacher has been playing. The importance of using rests now becomes obvious – they give the teacher time to tell the students what they need to correct. The teacher needs to remember to always give a preparatory measure so the students can start tapping their feet before beginning to play.

While the students are playing D's and E's by rote, the teacher will need to see that every student has established his hand position correctly and is placing his first finger in the correct place. This is a good place to make use of the Drill Routine introduced earlier, as it allows the teacher to move around and make sure each student is doing things correctly. At this point be sure that all are holding their instruments properly as well as playing on the tips of the fingers with the fingers curved and in the right place. The students will probably need to be reminded of how the Drill Routine goes.

If the students are having trouble putting their first fingers in the correct place, the teacher may want to let the violins and violas put their instruments into a guitar position allowing them to see their left hands more easily. Be sure that correct left hand positions are still expected. *Warning:* This is only a temporary aid and should not be used for any length of time (one or two lessons).

The teacher must listen very carefully to make sure that the class is not allowed to rush the tempo. If this happens, and the teacher does not stop it at once, it will become worst and will be almost impossible to correct. Don't accept rushing – just don't let it get started. Students will rush if the teacher allows them to.

Another thing that the teacher must realize early is that students will only do as much as the teacher expects of them – never more. Many times the problem is that the teacher simply doesn't expect enough! Students will probably never do more than asked of them – usually they will do less! Therefore, in order for the class to progress, the teacher must keep asking the students to do more and more. Once the teacher is satisfied, the students are prone to stop trying to improve. The more they do, the more the teacher must ask for!

Besides making sure that the students are learning to keep a steady tempo, the teacher needs to be certain that they are also singing letter names of notes. Now that they are playing fingered notes, have all students finger the notes on their instruments while the other rows are playing alone. It is very important that students are never allowed to sit idly.

After the teacher has made sure that all of the students can find their E's, it is a good idea to have them try several other rote D and E exercises. Some suggestions for exercises using all quarter notes or quarter rests are:

(1) D D E E r r r r
(2) D D r r E E r r
(3) D r E r
(4) D E r r
(5) D E D E r r r r

Playing F-Sharp By Rote

If the book that is being used introduces F-sharp at the same time that it introduces E, then the teacher must go ahead and teach them by rote before the students are allowed to open up their books and attempt to follow these new notes on a printed page. All new notes should be introduced away from the book regardless of how the book chooses to introduce them. The students must have a chance to find the notes visually first, as they cannot see their books and fingers at the same time! *Remember:* Always, only one thing at a time!

Since the fingerings for F-sharp are not the same for all instruments, the teacher must explain the fingering for each one. The violins and violas play F-sharp with two fingers, the cellos with three, and the string basses with four. The teacher will need to tell the students that whenever they put down more than one finger, the fingering will be considered wrong if only one finger plays it. The students should be taught that if the note needs to be played with the second finger (F-sharp violin and viola, and F-natural bass) that it will be called a two-finger note because both fingers must be down. A note that needs to be played with the third finger (G violin and viola, and F-sharp cello) will be called a three-finger note. Likewise, on a three-finger note, three fingers must play the note and on a four-finger note, four fingers will play. This is very important, because this is the only way that students can develop a "feel" for how far it is from note to note and to develop correct intonation.

BEGINNING RULES OF FINGERING

Rule No. 1: A fingering is only considered correct when all possible fingers play it. *Rule No. 2:* Once a finger has been played, it should be left down until it has to be picked up, because it must play another note or it is necessary to go to a lower note on the same string.

The teacher will find that the students will have difficulty stretching their fingers enough to play F-sharp in tune. The students need now to be told only that sharps raise notes (makes them sound higher – to stretch or move their fingers towards the bridge), and that the space or interval between E and F-sharp must be big enough. The teacher should tell them that it is preferable to play F-sharp too high rather than too low. It will probably be necessary to ask them to sing E to F-sharp as the teacher plays to be sure they know how it is to sound. Then, as done earlier on D and E, the teacher should play it incorrectly and ask the students if it is right (play it too low). The teacher can say things like: "Doesn't that sound awful? Let's hope that yours doesn't sound like the one I just played! Raise your hands when you think it sounds right."

Before asking the students to play their F-sharps, the teacher should also show them the correct fingering on each instrument while making comments about correct left hand position. Say such things as: "Violins and violas, notice where my elbow is. See my straight wrist. Cellos and basses, notice that my arm is raised and in a nice, straight line, etc."

Now the group should be ready to try some rote D's, E's, and F-sharps. An exercise that uses all quarter notes and quarter rests might be as follows:

D D D D r r r r E E E E r r r r F# F# F# F# r r r r E E E E
r r r r D D D D r r r r

Be sure to teach the students to say the rests out loud and to use the time the rests provide to get their fingers ready for the next note. The students should also be taught to readjust their fingers during the rests whenever they are found to be in the wrong place. The teacher should let the students know that they are expected to try to be their own teacher. By expecting them to constantly think about what needs to be done to play correctly, they will be prevented from daydreaming and playing by "guess." Students are prone to not really think unless the teacher constantly finds ways of keeping them totally involved and catches them whenever they are not concentrating.

Some other suggested rote exercises that can be used to be sure students are correctly playing D, E, and F-sharp before having them read notes from a book are shown in the following quarter note and quarter rest examples:

(1) D D r r E E r r F# F# r r E E r r D D r r

(2) D D E E r r r r E E F# F# r r r r F# F# E E r r r r E E D D r r r r

(3) D E D E r r r r E F# E F# r r r r F# E F# E r r r r E D E D r r r r

(4) D E r r E F# r r F# E r r E D r r

The teacher should always refer to notes by their letter names rather than the fingering because: (1) the fingerings are printed in most books so the students really don't need them; (2) it is vitally important that students know notes by their letter names (unless a teacher refers to note names instead of fingerings they will only learn the fingerings); and (3) there are at least three different sets of fingerings used in the heterogeneous class (violin and viola, cello, and bass) and it is very confusing for students to hear one fingering and have to play another one. Always say or sing letter names of notes, rather than fingerings so students will have constant reinforcement on letter names.

CELLO AND BASS

A special word needs to be said about cello and bass left hand fingering and position. Playing only an open string and first finger is "death" to the hand position of a beginning cellist or bassist as it contributes negatively to the correct hand position that is already difficult to establish. It is absolutely necessary (no matter how it may be presented in the method book) to make sure that all four fingers are put down on the cello and bass almost immediately so that the hand position is correctly established. Be sure that all the fingers are spread apart and at a 90 degree (right) angle to the strings. A 45 degree angle (like violin and viola) is often seen and it must not be tolerated! Asking the students to rotate their hands towards the bridge usually helps correct this problem. The arm, wrist and hand must be in a straight line with the hand rotated towards the bridge. The thumb must always be underneath the second finger! In addition, the teacher must make sure that the students' fingers are curved and playing on the tips (rather than the flat of the fingers).

THE THIRD LESSON

Playing E and F-Sharp From The Book

Now that the students have located E's and F-sharp's and have played several rote exercises using these fingers, they are ready to play these notes from their books.

As before, the teacher will need to make sure their fingers are placed correctly – in the right place, curved and on the tips, and with firm pressure. Also, the teacher will need to continue checking the students' basic sitting and holding positions so that no bad habits develop.

Summary of Class Teaching Fundamentals

The teacher needs to remember daily to give the class enough repetition (use the "Drill Routine") so that the students can develop the correct physical coordination necessary to be able to play the material as perfectly as possible. Starting and stopping the class unnecessarily needs to be avoided unless most of the students are lost or don't understand what they are trying to do. This can be done more easily if all new or difficult things in the lesson are introduced, talked about, and tried by rote before an attempt is made to play the lines from the book.

It is best to try to move from line to line without stopping (except in case of student fatigue). In the first few lessons, the goal should be to play at least two or three lines before stopping to rest. Later on, a reasonable amount to cover would be about half a lesson. After the students have been allowed to rest, the balance of the lesson should be covered (if possible) before the class ends. This may be impossible for the first few lessons but it is certainly a *reasonable* goal for later on.

Another important goal that the teacher must continually work towards is to have the class accept the responsibility for playing steadily until the teacher finds it necessary to stop them. This "self-propelling" class can become accomplished sooner if the students tap their feet, sing names of notes, and say all rests out loud as they play. When this happens, the teacher is free to spend the class time helping with individual problems. *Remember:* To accomplish maximum results with the class, *every* student needs to be occupied in some active aspect of learning to play throughout the entire class.

As soon as a line or lesson is learned, the class should move on to the next one. *Remember;* The teacher has done a poor job of teaching the material if it is necessary to review. Don't blame the students if this happens!

After a lesson has been completed, the students find it fun to play the lesson straight through, moving from line to line without stopping. Being able to do this gives the students a great sense of pride and accomplishment because lines that they remembered as being difficult before now will seem easy. This is often their first contact with the idea that the "price of success" is hard work, but that hard work does pay off in accomplishment.

USE OF PIANO

It is also fun to "treat" the students by the teacher accompanying the class on the piano. *Note:* The piano should *only* be used as a reward for learning the lesson because it is impossible for the teacher to see and hear the students if the piano is constantly being played.

HOME PRACTICE

If the students are scheduled for at least three lessons a week, it may be just as well if they do not practice at home between lessons because poor practice is probably worse than no practice at all. When they are practicing by themselves, especially at first, the chances are that the instruments will be out of tune, they will not remember to tap their feet, read the notes out loud, play in tune and do all the other things the teacher wants. Also, if the class is scheduled at least three days a week, the teacher can be assured that during this time everything is being done correctly and that they are being moved forward at a reasonable rate of speed.

Another reason that home practice may not be a good idea, especially at first, is that the parents will hear some things that may cause them to form bad opinions about the child's progress which they may pass on to the child and other parents. It is probably better that they don't hear the child until the habits that the teacher wants to establish are firmly implanted.

Later on, if students do practice outside of class, they should always practice the material that has been presented and learned at their last lesson (reinforcement). The next lesson should be a presentation of new materials which in turn are then practiced at home *after* the students have learned them thoroughly in class. If the teacher is encouraging the students to practice at home, they should be told to practice the material played in class that day in the same way it was done in class (sing, play several times, etc.).

Never tell students that they have to practice a certain amount of time. Time is an eternity to them and so it is much better for them psychologically if they are asked to practice every line of the assignment a certain number of times rather than a specific amount of time. The authors believe that the same rules should apply to young musicians that apply to those in a professional group. No one tells a professional musician that they have to practice – if they need to, they practice; if they don't need to, they don't. The only thing a conductor asks of a fine orchestra is that the musicians be able to play the music to his satisfaction. How much time, or how little time it takes to do this is an individual thing. So, likewise, in a school music class, the students should be individually responsible for being able to play the assigned music well enough to satisfy the teacher. Some students will have to practice a great deal – others will not. This kind of thinking is usually readily accepted by most students as being fair, and they can understand that, if they don't know their music, this is reason to practice it.

THE NEXT FEW LESSONS

The teacher should continue teaching the students how to finger and play (pizzicato) additional notes until they can play all the notes possible in the key of D on the D and A strings (a one-octave scale). Be sure to stress the difference in placement of fingers for half-steps and whole steps. This means insisting that the students carefully form a large enough whole step between E and F-sharp and B and C-sharp and a small enough half step between C-sharp and D and F-sharp and G. *Remember:* The teacher must ask the students to exaggerate the size of the whole step and minimize the size of the half-step. This means that the students' finger positions will need to be checked continually by the teacher. A teacher cannot assume that anything is being done right by the students unless it is both visually and aurally checked.

Learning To Bow

Introduction

After the students have played for five or six periods they will probably start "bugging" the teacher to use the bow. It is then appropriate to go ahead and introduce how to hold the bow and to work on it a little each day. At this point, start spending about five minutes of every class period preparing them for the use of the bow. *Warning:* Under *no* circumstances should they be allowed to use the bow before the left hand finger positions are set.

Care of the Bow

The students will need to be taught immediately how to take care of their bows so as to avoid accidents with them. The important points that students need to learn are:

(1) Always protect the bow as it is fragile and can break easily. Don't use it as a sword or leave it where someone may sit on it.

(2) Keep the bow hairs clean. Don't touch the hairs with the fingers as the slightest bit of oil from the skin will make the bow hairs slip on the string.

(3) Loosen the bow when not playing so that it won't warp from being left tight.

(4) Don't tighten the bow too tight or it may break. It also makes proper bowing more difficult (approximately four turns for violin and viola, six for cell, and eight for bass are good numbers to teach beginners).

It is also important that they know the various parts of their bows and have some understanding of the mechanics of them, so that when the teacher refers to parts of the bow, the students know which part is being talked about. Most method books will have a drawing of the parts of the bow in it and it will be easy to use this as a guide to show them the parts of the bow they need to know. The teacher should ask them to point to these parts on their bows as they are called out.

Holding the Bow

PUTTING THE FINGERS ON A PENCIL

It is easiest to teach the correct bow grip by asking the students to first place their fingers on a pencil rather than a bow. The pencil is much easier to control and it makes it much easier to see how the fingers are to be placed. Also, students need to be taught early the importance of having a pencil for rehearsals and this insures them having one.

Violin and Viola – The violin and viola bow grip will be taught alike. The steps towards learning the proper bow grip are:

(1) Have the students turn their right hands over so that their palms face up.

(2) Have them curve their fingers up until the thumb and the middle finger form an "O" when they touch.

(3) Next, have them place their curved thumb against the inside of the highest knuckle (first knuckle of the middle finger). Point out that their hands now look as they *must* look when they are placed on the pencils.

(4) Have them pull their thumbs away from their fingers so that the pencil can be inserted.

(5) Have them place their pencils between their thumb and fingers so that it rests on the tip of the little finger and angles across the fingers to a spot between the first and second knuckle of the index finger.

(6) Place the thumb so that it is opposite the middle finger and curved into the "O" position mentioned in (2).

(7) Have them turn their hands over and the correct bow grip should be established (see Figure No. 16).

Positioning the Bow Grip On A Pencil
(Violin and Viola)
Figure No. 16

Cello and Bass – The cello and bass bow grip will be taught alike although there will be a larger spread of the hand on the bass bow because of its larger size. It is assumed that the French bow will be used and taught to all students as it is felt that it is the basic bow that is best for beginners to start on. Also, when teaching heterogeneous classes, it is better to only have to teach two basic bow grips. Later on, if a bass student becomes quite advanced and studies privately, he may want to learn the German bow grip but it should not be taught in a heterogeneous string class.

The steps to use for learning to hold the cello and bass bow are:

(1) Have the students hold their pencils parallel to the floor with their left hands.

(2) Have them raise their right elbows until their forearms slant down and their hands are in a relaxed hanging position.

(3) Have them curve their hand and fingers as if they were to have balls placed in their hands (make sure that their thumbs are curved).

(4) Have them insert the pencils between the curved fingers and the thumb.

(5) Ask them to let all of their fingers (except the thumb) fall down *over* the pencil with the tips of the two middle fingers even and lower than the first and fourth finger. The pencil will be between the first and second knuckle of the middle two fingers. The first knuckle of the index finger and the little finger will lay on the pencil.

(6) Ask them to place their curved thumb on the pencil opposite and between the second and third fingers (see Figure No. 17 for correct positioning of the bow grip on pencil).

Once all of the students have been taught how to correctly position their fingers on their pencils, the teacher should have them do it several times, telling them that they need to memorize how it looks and feels when it is right. Once they can do this correctly, several times in a row, they are probably ready at the next lesson to start placing their fingers on the bow. Going from the pencils to the bows is simply a matter of doing on the bow what has already been learned on the pencil.

Cello

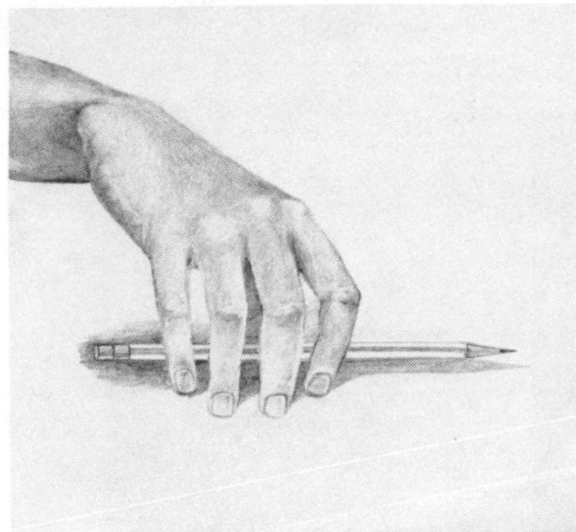

Bass

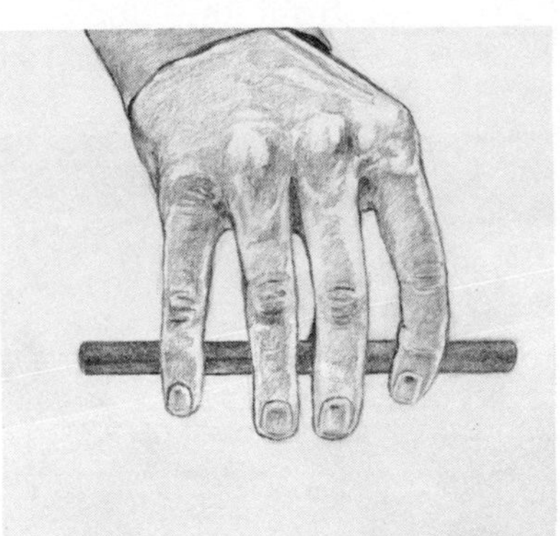

Positioning the Bow Grip On A Pencil
(Cello and Bass)
Figure No. 17

PUTTING THE FINGERS ON THE BOW

Violin and Viola – The teacher should follow steps 1 through 7 as given earlier to establish the basic grip on the violin and viola bow. Check to make sure the following things have been done correctly:

(1) Thumb on the bow stick curved.

(2) Little finger on top of the bow and close to the other fingers.

(3) Hand leaning on the side of the index finger and slanting towards the tip end of the bow.

(4) The middle fingers handing slightly over the bow stick and down onto the frog somewhat.

(5) The bow running between the first and second knuckle of the index finger.

(6) All fingers curved and rounded and fairly close together (see Figure No. 18).

Cello and Bass – By following steps 1 through 7 for positioning the fingers on a pencil, the teacher should be able to establish the basic grip on the cello and bass bow. Check to make sure the following things have been done correctly:

(1) Little finger in the middle of the frog.

(2) Fourth finger (ring) on the ferrule.

(3) Third finger resting on the side of the hair.

(4) Second finger (index) resting slightly on the left side at the first knuckle.

(5) Thumb high and curved and placed close to the frog on the bow stick.

(6) The fingers should be curved and spaced apart evenly.

(7) The arm, wrist, hand, and fingers should be suspended from the elbow joint down without a break anywhere (see Figure No. 19).

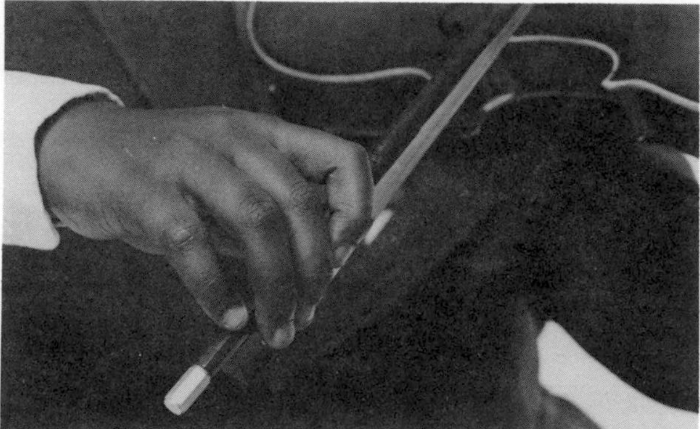

Front

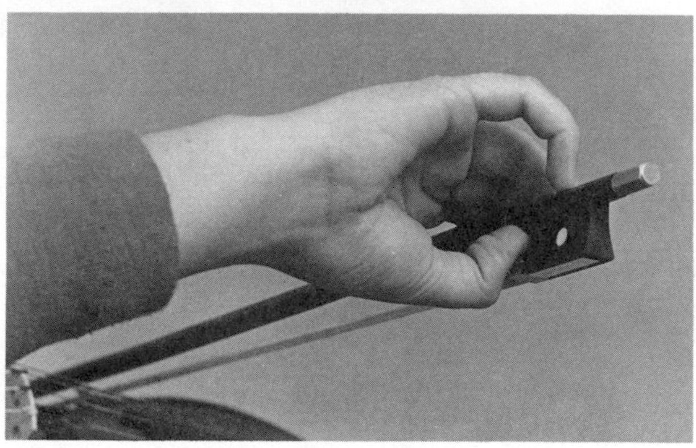

Back

Positioning Fingers On The Bow
(Violin and Viola)
Figure No. 18

Cello

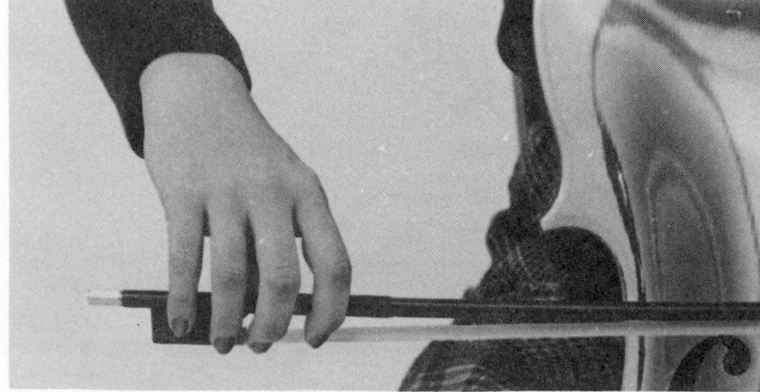

Front

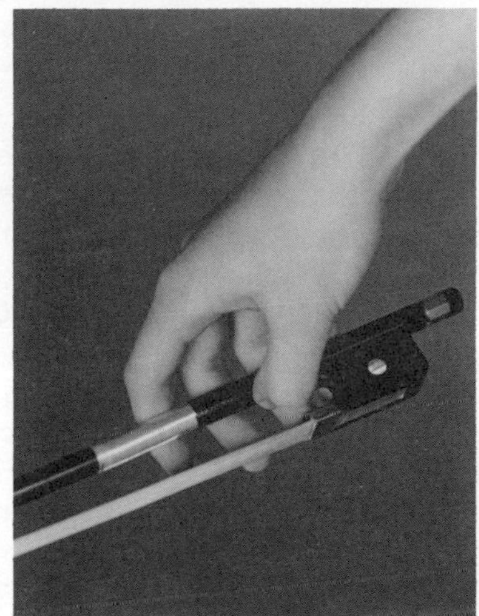

Back

Bass

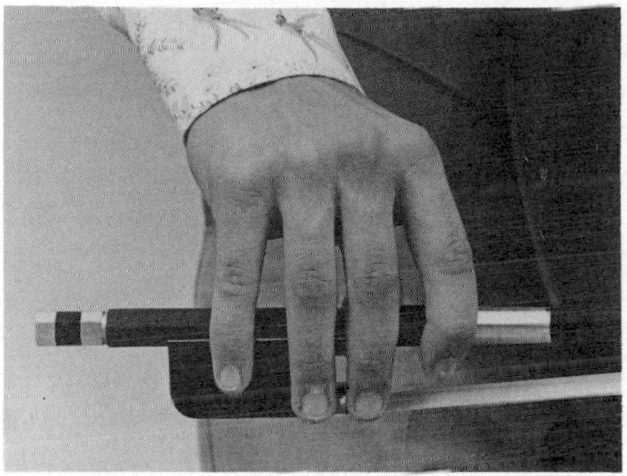

Front

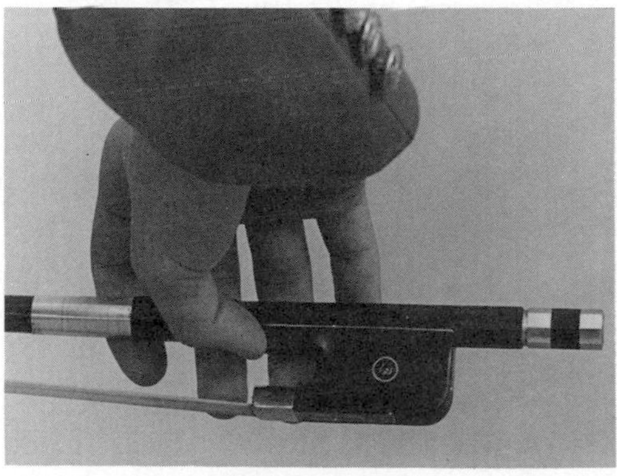

Back

Positioning Fingers on the Bow
(Cello and Bass)
Figure No. 19

Bowing

USING THE ROSIN

Putting Rosin on the Bow – Now that the students have learned how to hold their bows, it is time to teach them about putting rosin on the bows, because they will soon be beginning to bow on their instruments.

All violin, viola, and cello students should have a fresh cake of clear, light-colored rosin. This light-colored rosin, which is recommended for beginners, is harder and dryer than the rosin that will be used later when they have learned to control the bow better. Because this rosin does not grip the string as much, it is easier to control the bow and thus more desirable until good bow control is established. The light-colored rosin usually comes in an oblong box and it is wise to specify this kind, because the oblong, wooden trough can be used to great advantage when the teacher is introducing bowing.

Bass students will need a special rosin made just for the bass bow. This rosin is darker colored and softer than the one recommended for violin, viola, and cello. Because it is softer and stickier, it grips the larger strings more easily and must be used to produce a good bass tone. *Warning:* Violin, viola, and cello rosin won't work! Bass rosin comes graded by numbers with the smallest number being the softest and the largest number the hardest. Which number to use is determined by the climatic conditions of the area where it is to be used. Most players will need Number 2 or 3.

A daily routine of rosining the bow as a class needs to be established in the first few weeks and reviewed from time to time later. This teaches the students the importance of rosining the bow each time they play. It also helps them to learn the correct way to put rosin on the bow.

It is best to teach the students to put rosin on their bows by stroking the bow firmly on the rosin while holding their fingers on the bow with the correct bow grip. The procedure to use to put rosin on the bow (except for bass) is:

(1) Hold the rosin in the left hand.

(2) Put the fingers on the bow as if going to play.

(3) Place all the bow hairs flat on the rosin at the frog end of the bow.

(4) Move the bow slowly from the frog to tip and then tip to frog while being sure that the bow is pushed firmly into the rosin.

(5) Move the bow up and down (violin, viola, and cello only) about twenty times or until the bow has an ample amount of rosin on it.

Don't let the students "scrub" at both ends of the bow or make a few, hurried light strokes across the rosin – neither does a good job of getting sufficient rosin on the entire bow.

To rosin bass bows, the teacher must teach the students that they will only use down bow strokes. Because the bass rosin is softer and stickier, the hairs will dig in and stick to the rosin and can pull the hairs out if rosin is applied in the usual down and up fashion. *Note:* If a "squeak" is heard while putting rosin on the bow, it means that the bow is still in need of rosin. When the squeak disappears, the bow has enough rosin.

It is a good idea to teach the students the terms "Down" and "Up" bow as these motions are done on the rosin. Ask all students to hold their rosin so they can move their bows as if it were on the instruments. Since the bass bow is only rosined down bow, ask them to actually rosin the down bow and pretend to make the up bow stroke by holding the bow an inch or so above the rosin.

The students should be told that for now they will always begin playing with a down bow and that it starts at the frog end of the bow. It should also be explained that the down bow straightens the arm and that the up bow bends the arm into a V-shape (with the exception of the string bass which is more of a whole arm motion).

Developing the Correct Bow Stroke – Many of the fundamentals of correct bowing can be established while the students are learning to rosin their bows. Learning to pull and push the bow correctly on the rosin greatly facilitates and expedites the learning of bowing on the instrument later. Some of the most important areas of bowing that should be pointed out to the students while they bow on the rosin are:

The bow should always follow a straight line (parallel with the sides of the box of rosin). This is called "straight" bowing. The teacher should show the students both straight and crooked bowing so the students really understand the difference.

There must be flexibility of the hand on the bow while bowing. The teacher should tell the students that the wrist should lead a little on the up bow and drop very slightly on the down bow (this is more evident on the violin and viola).

The arm straightens on the down bow and bends back up into a "V" on the up bow (except for the string bass). An exercise that helps students to learn to do this is to have them grasp the right arm (just above the elbow) with the left hand so that the upper arm cannot move. Then, have them pretend that they are bowing several consecutive down and up bows. Be sure that the wrist pushes towards the nose a bit on the up bow and drops a little on the down bow (violins and violas). After this can be done fairly successfully, the students should be asked to try to do the same thing on the rosin.

The teacher will need to check each student very carefully as he bows on the rosin to see how far he can pull the down bow without pulling it crooked. This point should be marked on the bow stick with masking tape. Then, the students should be told that they should always start bowing at the frog and pull the bow down to the marked place. Likewise, they should understand that every up bow should end back up at the frog.

Learning Rhythm Patterns – An efficient way to prepare students for bowing work is to bow the rhythm patterns that are to be used next while rosining the bow. In this way, the basic physical motions can be learned on the rosin before they attempt to play these rhythms on their instruments. *Remember:* Good teaching is to present only one thing at a time and a good way to do this is to always master any new skill by rote first. If this concept is followed, the students will usually be successful and will seldom feel the discouragement of failure.

The teacher should next look in the book to be used and find the first bowing lesson. The rhythm patterns that are found there should then be practiced on the rosin. Some basic rhythms that will be included in most books in the early lessons are shown in Figure No. 20. Because the authors feel so strongly that beginning students should start bowing with quarter notes, the examples given will pre-suppose that the books used will approach first bowing with quarter notes.

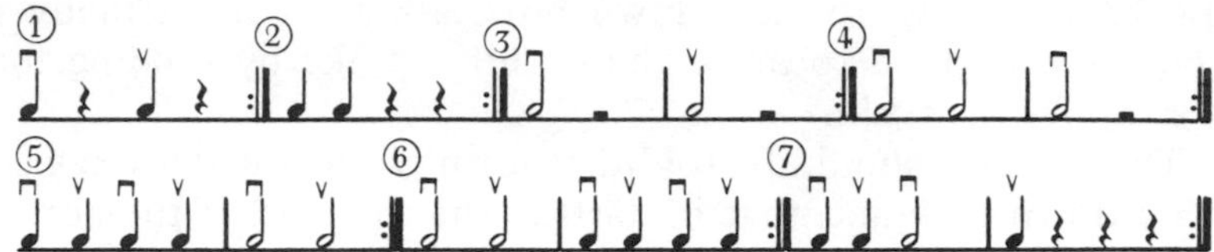

Rhythmic Patterns to Practice On The Rosin
Figure No. 20

At this time, the concept of down bow and up bow should be introduced along with the signs used to indicate them. Another concept that should be introduced at this time is that normal bowing procedure is always down, up, down, up, etc. unless the composer or arranger indicates otherwise in the music.

The students should also be taught at first that it is very important that quarter notes use the whole bow (as marked on their bows with masking tape) so as to be able to establish a free, relaxed bow stroke that is necessary for a full, resonant tone.

The students must be taught that a whole bow must be used on each bow stroke to get a full, resonant tone. However, because of the difference in the size in the diameter of the strings of the different instruments, the bow speeds cannot be the same on all instruments. The bigger the string the slower the bow must travel. Because of this, the larger instruments must pull the bow slower and less bow will have to be used than for the smaller instruments. Therefore, when the violin and viola beginners are told to use the whole bow, a whole bow for them will be most of the bow. For cello, only two-thirds of the bow will be used, and on bass, about half of the bow will be sufficient.

Next, the students need to be told that half notes should also use a full bow. Show them some half notes (on the rosin) and ask them what they observed about the speed the bow was pulled. Say such things as: "Was the bow moving faster or slower on the half note?" Someone should be able to answer that the bow moved slower on the half notes. After complimenting that student, the teacher should explain to them that to give the half note a whole bow, the bow must travel half as fast as it did for quarter notes. Likewise, when even longer notes occur, a full bow will still be used. Because the bow will be going even slower, there will be some loss of tone at first. The teacher should not worry about this now, because as the students progress, they will learn how to avoid this loss of tone on longer notes by adding pressure. *Warning:* At this point, the students should not be taught to add bow pressure as it will result in a "screechy", "crunchy" tone because of their lack of bow control.

The teacher should next have them play Nos. 1-4 of Figure No. 20 on their cakes of rosin. Be sure that they are still remembering to tap their feet while doing this. Point out again that there must be two toe taps on a half note. It also is good for the teacher to say aloud the direction of the bow so that students will be getting familiar with these terms and can bow in the right direction.

Once they can successfully manipulate the bow on Nos. 1-4 they are ready to try mixing up quarter notes and half notes shown in Nos. 5-7 of Figure No. 20. After this has been done, the teacher should go back and continue working on left hand finger patterns (pizzicato) and tell them that at the next class they will play the rhythms learned on the rosin on their own instruments.

ON THE STRING ROTE BOWING

At the next lesson, the students should be ready to do some rote bowing on their instruments (provided they were able to successfully do at least the first four rhythm patterns in Figure No. 20 on their cakes of rosin). It might be a good idea to go through these patterns (at least the ones that will be used that day) daily as well as the routine of tightening the bows together and rosining them the correct number of strokes.

It should be remembered that the students will tire easily from bowing at first, so the majority of class time still will need to be spent continuing to master the left hand finger patterns (pizzicato). Five or ten minutes is probably enough time to spend on bowing for the first few lessons.

Before the students are ready to bow on their instruments there are some additional things about bowing that need to be shown to them. It is best to use an instrument to demonstrate these things.

Bow placement for the violin and viola is half-way between the fingerboard and the bridge. For the cello, the bow should be placed a little below the mid-point between the fingerboard and the bridge. For the bass, the bow should be placed about two-thirds of the way down between the fingerboard and bridge. *Remember:* Playing close enough to the bridge is imperative if the beginners are to have a clear, solid tone. Telling them once won't be enough – the teacher will have to constantly remind them where to bow and then make sure that they do it.

Place the bow flat on the string so that all the hairs make contact with the string. The bow must be pulled "straight" as it was on the rosin. Explain to them that if they are bowing straight, the bow will make a square corner (or right angle) to the strings and the bow will be parallel to the bridge. Drawing a picture showing both the right and wrong angle of bowing (see Figure No. 21) will help them to understand this important aspect of bowing. It is also good to demonstrate this on an instrument (see Figure 21).

The teacher will find that most young violinists and violists will need to be told to pull the bow out – away from themselves a bit on the down bow to make sure that the bow continues to cross the string at a right angle. The violin and viola students must realize that their arms are straight out in front of them at the end of the down bow. The teacher should tell them: "A down bow is really an *out* bow." The cellists and bassists will only need to pull out away from themselves on their highest string.

The students must be careful to use the designated amount of bow (to the tape) for a full bow. To do this, it will be necessary for them to start playing at the frog and plan the bow so they end up at the mark on the bow stick.

The students' wrists and arms should be flexible as they were before when they played on the rosin (the teacher should demonstrate this).

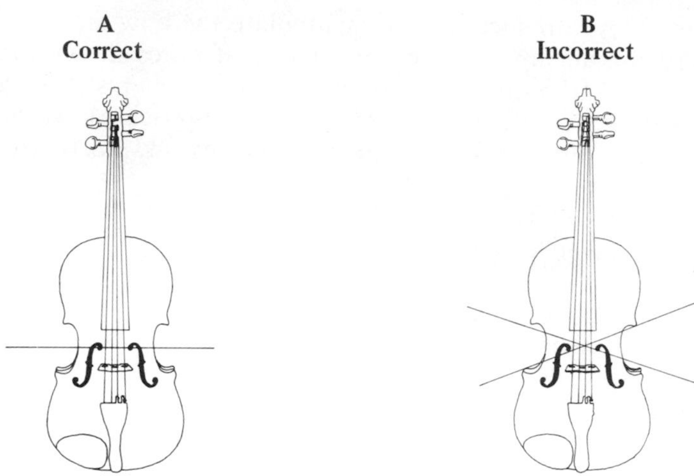

Correct and Incorrect Bowing
Figure No. 21

Bowing Quarter Notes – First the teacher should have the students play a quarter note, quarter rest rhythm pattern over and over by rote. To do this it will be necessary to do some preliminary steps as follows: Have all students place their bows on their D strings (making sure all bows are placed as explained above). Next, the teacher should count aloud one measure of preparation and ask the students to start tapping their feet on the first beat of this measure. On the second measure of tapping, they should begin to play the quarter note, quarter rest rhythm pattern. Have them play this until most are getting it or are beginning to tire. Whenever they tire, the teacher should stop the class and let them rest.

The importance of checking students individually and making necessary changes in the bow arms cannot be overstated. Once the group can stay together and understand what they are doing well enough to play independently of the teacher, it is time for the teacher to start moving from student to student making corrections in their bowing. It will seem as if there is nothing right and everything is wrong. Don't be alarmed! This may be true at first but the teacher should remember that with constant correction of students by the teacher, it will not be too long before they will show a great deal of improvement. Once improvement is evident, be sure that it isn't taken for granted that everything is alright, because the minute the teacher stops constantly checking the students individually, they will stop being careful and will slip into careless playing habits. The students need to think that it will be horrible if they don't do things right! This may seem a little extreme to the teacher, but unless the students are convinced that it is of utmost importance that things be done right they will not try as hard. The teacher needs to constantly "bug" them about every detail. Eventually, they give up and do things correctly if the teacher is insistent enough. They can and will form good playing habits but only if convinced that they have no other alternative!

It is also important that the teacher remember that positive reinforcement needs to be given along with constructive criticism. The teacher might say something like: "That was really good – now let's try doing this, too." By handling it this way they understand that they are improving but still have more to learn.

Using the Drill Routine – To allow the teacher enough time to be able to make the adjustments that will be needed with each student, it will be necessary to use the drill routine described earlier. The teacher may find that the group will find it difficult to stay together and that there will be a tendency to rush. This problem can be solved by being sure that they are both tapping their feet and saying the word "rest" for the full value of the quarter note. The rushing must be stopped now or they will rush tempos in performing groups later. *Remember:* Don't allow rushing! A trick that is effective in stopping rushing is to say to them: "Shame on you, you rushed! Now because you have rushed, we will have to play it even slower." (Of course, they will hate this.) Have them play it slower once, then say: "Now wasn't that a drag?" Of course they will say, yes. Then say: "Well then, don't rush or we will have to go even slower." This usually solves the problem (at least for awhile).

After the class has learned to bow, the "Drill Routine" will work as before except that when the rows play alone they will bow (rather than play pizzicato). The rows that are not playing will sing the letter names of notes and pretend that they are bowing (bow above the string an inch or so – this is usually called either "bowing in the air" or "practice bowing").

The teacher should use the "Drill Routine" on all the rhythmic patterns given in Figure No. 20 over a period of several class periods. At first, the students will need to rest a little bit after completing each one. After all patterns have been done on one string, the teacher may wish to do them on all the strings or combinations of strings. When the students tire from bowing it is a good idea to change to some left hand pizzicato work. Once all the rhythm patterns are fairly well mastered, the students should be ready to start reading the same rhythm patterns from the book.

Combining Bowing of the Open Strings and Music Reading

By this time, the students should be aware of the importance of good instrument holding positions and be fairly consistent at maintaining them. They also should be able to finger and play pizzicato all the notes in the key of D on the A and D strings, and handle some rote bowing with good positions on the open strings. When the students have reached this point, they are finally ready to attempt combining the reading of music and some open string bowing.

BOARD DRILL ON READING OPEN STRING NOTES

In the beginning, much stress will need to be placed on the position of notes on the staff. This is best done by the teacher putting the open strings notes that will be used in the first lesson on the board and talking about what line or space these notes are placed on or in. The teacher should say such things as: "Violins, your A is in the second space; violas, your A is in the space above the staff; cellos, your A is on the top line; and basses, yours is in the first space." Likewise, point out where the D's are and so on.

READING OPEN STRING NOTES FROM THE BOOK

After this has been done, the teacher should ask the students to open up their books to the first lesson where there are open string notes written on the staff. Ask them to look at the first line and see if they can recognize the notes that were just put on the board. Next, ask them to follow the first line by pointing to the notes and saying the letter names in rhythm as they tap their feet. When they can follow the notes and keep the rhythm, the teacher should ask them to *sing the notes* while pointing with the fingers and tapping the feet. The singing helps to give a pitch center for the class and helps them to begin to understand the relationship between higher and lower notes on the staff and higher and lower sounding notes.

It is recommended that only note and rest values of one and two beats be used with this first combining of bowing and music reading so that the students are free to concentrate mainly on these new areas.

BOWING IN THE AIR

The next step is to ask the students to put their instruments up into playing position and place their bows an inch or so above the strings and make the motions of drawing the bow as if to play the line that they have been singing. The teacher must watch them carefully to make sure that their eyes follow the printed line. Unless the students are told not to, they will try to memorize the line and play it without looking. If the teacher allows this to happen, it will make it *more* difficult for them to learn to read notes later. The "bowing in the air" gives the teacher a chance to make sure that the students are using full bows and that the bows are going in the right direction, etc. If there are rests in the line of music, the teacher should make sure that the students say them out loud in the appropriate places as they continue to sing the names of notes and tap their feet.

After most of the class has developed the coordination to pull the bow in rhythm above the string, they are ready to do it on their instruments. The first line should be repeated until all can keep their place in the music. This is a good time to use the drill routine. As individual rows (groups) play, the other students should sing and bow in the air. The teacher should move around the room constantly and straighten out any crooked bows (guiding bow arms until they get the "feel" and look of bowing correctly and straight). The students will also need to be reminded continually to use full bows.

If the lesson uses both quarter notes and half notes, be sure that the students are reminded that the bow speed is different for the different note values – half as fast on half notes as quarter notes.

If at any time the students seem confused and play on the wrong strings, the teacher may want to stop the class and ask them to do the line an easier way – either pizzicato or "bow in the air" until they connect the notes seen visually on the staff with the correct string. Or, if it seems that they are not sure what notes they are looking at, it may be necessary to go back and explain where each note is placed on the staff as well as sing and point to the notes again.

The teacher must be certain to not spend the entire class period playing only open strings, as the students will be very bored with it. It is much better whenever the students begin to tire for the teacher to go back and play some lessons learned earlier using pizzicato, perhaps moving from line to line without stopping. A faster tempo than was used before is fun for them, as they can see readily how much they have improved since they played it last.

Combining Bowing, Fingering and Music Reading

Since music reading is the last major new step that has been introduced, it is good for the teacher to continue to have the class sing the line before attempting to play it. Any new notes that are introduced must be talked about in relationship to those already known as well as their placement on the staff (whether on a line or in a space and in which line or space). Most well-written books will have a section or chart at the top of each page that explains any new notes or problems. The teacher must be sure to point these out to the students and take a few minutes to study them with the class when they occur.

Since the philosophy of the authors is to introduce only one new thing at a time, the teacher must remember not to ask the students to read, bow and finger simultaneously until each new problem has been mastered by itself. Following this philosophy, the teacher should first have the students sing the names of the notes in rhythm, and then, ask the students to play the line pizzicato until the fingering seems fairly automatic. After they have done this, the bow may be added. If the bow is added and the students still cannot play the music satisfactorily, then the teacher may want to have them follow the line and "bow in the air." After all of these steps have been done, the students should be able to successfully combine reading, fingering, and bowing.

It should be realized that expecting a young group to sight-read a line without any preparation from the teacher is asking for trouble, because it is most likely that they will break down and will have to start over. Doing this to a group of students is definitely poor teaching and should not happen, as it causes the students to feel like failures. *Remember:* The students can always feel successful *if* the teacher plans carefully and only expects them to do one new thing at a time.

The "Drill Routine" will be needed on almost all of the lines in the beginning lessons and it is important that the teacher does *not* move on to new lines until almost all of the students can play the line they are on fairly well.

BOW MARKINGS

The teacher will need to be sure that the class understands the symbols for (⊓) and up (V) bow. They should already know the terminology and these symbols if the teacher used the words and signs earlier when they were learning to bow by rote. Another symbol that will be found in most beginning books is the common (ʾ) above a rest or at the end of a phrase. The students should know that the comma means to lift the bow and place the bow back on the string at the frog end.

KEEPING THE FINGERS DOWN

As soon as the students have learned to put down more than one finger, the teacher must make sure that they keep all fingers that have been used down on any given string until they are needed somewhere else. It is imperative that the teacher insist upon this to develop fundamental habits that will enable the students to play in tune as they progress to more difficult music. The students need to learn to "feel" from one note to the next, because they must know if the next note is a half-step or a whole step away – then make noticeable differences in the spacing.

The teacher must insist upon good intonation and this means seeing to it that the students are accurate about where they are putting their fingers (spaced correctly), and then insisting that they keep them down once they are played. Many books indicate in the music when the students are to keep their fingers down. The teacher should point these markings out to the students and insist that they be observed.

FINISHING THE FIRST YEAR

Depending on how many days a week the class has met and the thoroughness of the teacher, by about the third month of playing, the group should have developed fairly good bow arms and have correct left hand position and finger placement. If this has been accomplished, the group will now begin to move along faster and sound fairly mature. This is usually about the time the students have learned to play all the first position notes in the Key of D on the A and D strings.

The Importance of Good Intonation

Now that the students can play a one-octave D Major scale, the teacher needs to insist even more strongly that the class play in-tune. By now, the students should be expected to understand where the whole and half steps are in a scale and should be asked to mark them in their books (if the book used doesn't mark them) as shown in Figure No. 22.

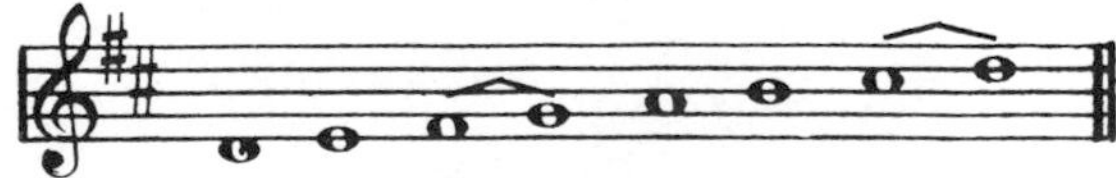

The Marking of Half Steps
Figure No. 22

If the teacher constantly says such things as: "A whole step is a large interval and a half-step is a small interval, so be sure that you make a big difference in the size of the two when you play them," the students will eventually realize the importance of knowing this. They should also be reminded to watch their hands as they play to be sure that they don't let their fingers slip out of place. *Students will not play in tune unless they are made to.* The teacher must insist on good intonation and not give up until it is accomplished. Young string players can play in tune contrary to what many people think. It is just a matter of insisting that it be done. It is much easier to cure intonation problems while the students are playing simple, unison tunes than to have to try to solve these problems when the students are playing harmonized music.

The Importance of A Good, Resonant Tone

Full Bow Is Necessary

By the time the students can play a one-octave D scale starting on the D string, they should have developed a free, resonant tone that comes from using a relaxed, free-flowing "full bow" (as designated for each instrument). If every student in the class is taught and then made to do this, even a beginning class can have a very mature, large sound. The *Resonant Tone* is the most basic tone and must be developed first.

Teaching the Full Bow Concept

In order to insure that the students start each down bow stroke at the frog and end at the tip of the bow, there are several insights that will help the teacher to make the students realize how to do it properly.

First of all, when the students start at the frog, they are going to feel a little uncomfortable. They will tell the teacher that they feel "scrunched" up and crowded. The teacher's reply should be: "Good. If you don't feel this way at first, then you probably are not starting the down bow where you should."

Second, on the up bow, in order to completely get back to the frog, it will seem to them as if the up bow is faster than the down bow. In reality, of course, it isn't – but it does seem this way (to them) because the up bow stroke requires more energy due to gravity and the crowded, "scrunchy" feeling that occurs when they are playing close to the frog. It is helpful for the teacher to go around and physically move the students' arms to help them to develop the "feel" for using full bows – especially on the up bow.

Changes in Bow Speed

The students must also clearly understand that the bow must change speeds for different note values – a faster stroke on quarter notes, half as fast on half notes, and a fourth as fast on whole notes. They must be very carefully trained and then constantly reminded of this or they will use up all of the bow on the first beat of the long note.

Bow Placement Relative to Fingerboard and Bridge

The last area that needs to be considered that affects the amount of tone the beginning class will have is where they are bowing relative to the fingerboard and bridge. Students must be told where the correct place to bow is on their particular instrument and then be expected to play there so that they can achieve the fullest possible tone. Beginning students should *never* be allowed to play over the fingerboard, because there is no chance for a good tone there. The teacher should check for rosin on the fingerboard as this is a sure sign of bowing in the wrong place.

The Teaching of the Slur

Most beginning books introduce the slur around the time that the students have learned the first position notes on two strings (usually the A and D) and have developed fairly good bow control on some basic easy rhythms (usually half notes and half rests and quarter notes and quarter rests). If approached correctly and the problem isolated, the teaching of the slur can be relatively easy.

The steps recommended to teach the slur are as follows:

(1) Tell the students that learning to play slurs will now make it possible to play *many* notes on a bow instead of just one.

(2) They should be asked to listen while the teacher plays several times (as fast as possible) the open D string to first finger E. Tell them it sounds sort of like a bee buzzing. Have them count and see how many D's and E's they think were played in one long down bow stroke.

(3) Have the students do the same thing (play as many D's and E's as they can in just one down bow). See who can do the most. Do this two or three times until everyone is doing the multiple notes on a bow (have a little contest.

(4) Next, have them play just one open D and first finger E with only one bow (stopping the bow at the tip). Ask the students to lift the bow up and place it again at the frog and do the same thing again.

(5) After they can play two notes in a down bow, try the first exercise shown in Figure No. 23.

(6) After the students can change from a down bow to an up bow with rests in between, the teacher should have them eliminate the rests and play the second exercise shown in Figure No. 23.

Learning How To Slur (Rote Exercises)
Figure No. 23

It is helpful if the teacher says loudly the direction the bow should be travelling so the students can check to see that they are right. Bowing any problem spots in the air will help to solve the problem and also enable the teacher to be heard when giving bow directions. The students *must* understand from now on that if their bow goes the wrong direction it will be considered a mistake.

When the students can slur fairly well on the note exercises given earlier, they should be ready to read from their books. In the event, however, that the rote exercises given in Figure 23 do not apply to the first exercises in the book being used, rote exercises taken from the book should be used before going on to the next step. The teacher should then ask them to open their books to the first lesson in the book on slurring. To insure success, it would be wise for the students to play each line pizzicato so that the left-hand can be "set" first. Then, have them finger and bow the line in the air before they attempt to play the line as written.

The teaching of the slur can be easy if the teacher approaches it positively and correctly. The students *cannot* be expected to sight-read lines containing slurs without some rote preparation beforehand. There will need to be much emphasis on bow direction and the students must be made to feel that it is wrong if they bow the wrong direction. *Group bowing must be uniform* right from the beginning!

The Intense Tone

Start on the G-String

After the beginning students have played about a semester, they should have developed enough bow control so that they can learn to play with even more tone than playing with full bows allows. This new tone is easiest taught whenever the book used introduces the G-string notes. It is on the G-string (the thickest one on the violin) that it is the easiest to recognize that for a full sound, the thicker strings demand a different bow technique.

To produce a good tone on the G string, it will be necessary to make several changes in the way the students are bowing (although they must not forget how to bow for a resonant tone). The tone that will be produced when these changes in bowing are made will be called the *Intense Tone* from now on in this book, as opposed to the basic resonant tone which is produced by a fast-moving, long bow stroke.

To begin to produce an "Intense Tone" that will be much more centered and consequently sound louder, the first and most important change will be to teach the students to play with a slower bow stroke. A slower bow stroke allows the bow hairs to grip the string more solidly (especially if additional bow weight is added). To gain this added weight, the students will be asked (for the time being) to play only in the lower half of the bow which causes more natural weight from the arm on the string. Next, the students should be asked to grip the bows more firmly. While playing in the lower half of the bow and adding bow pressure gives more tone than before, these two changes will probaby not be enough to make an obvious difference in tone (especially with young students). Therefore, a third thing needs to be done: play closer to the bridge.

It is rather difficult, at first, to convince the students that they must both bow closer to the bridge and bow with a slower bow stroke to be able to produce a louder, intense tone. They must also understand that if they play close to the bridge, but do not slow the bow down, a harsh, ugly sound will result. *The bow must be pulled slower when playing close to the bridge!*

The students cannot be told exactly how close to the bridge they should play, as this varies from instrument to instrument. They will need to be encouraged to experiment and find the right place on their instruments. If the students don't play close enough to the bridge and much pressure is added, the tone will be "scratchy" sounding, and this is a cue to the teacher that the student is *not* bowing close enough to the bridge. Likewise, if the bow is placed too close to the bridge, the tone can be raspy, harsh, and un-musical. The teacher should move around the class and help each student to find the place on his instrument where the best "Intense Tone" is produced.

Two other points to be mentioned to the students in regard to producing a louder tone are that they must have well-rosined bows and that they must use a different kind of rosin than they used in the very beginning. About the time that the G-string is introduced, the students should be told to purchase a softer rosin which grips the strings more firmly. This rosin is darker in color than beginners' rosin (nearly black) and usually comes in a round cake rather than a rectangular case.

A good rote exercise to help the teacher to teach this tone is to ask the students to play two quarter note open G's followed by two quarter rests. The teacher should remind the students to see that their bows stay close to the bridge and that they only use the lower half of the bow. Remind them also to keep a firm grasp on the bow. After the students can produce this bigger sound on the open G-string, the teacher may want to try a one-octave G-scale with the same rhythm pattern. The teacher must realize that the sound will be somewhat rough until the students learn to control the bow at a slower speed. The class will need to be reminded to keep trying to play smoothly.

In conclusion, it should be understood that the teaching of an "Intense Tone" is a necessity if the group is ever going to be able to play above a mezzo forte. Many directors erroneously believe that the only way to expand tone (other than using more and more bow) is to ask the students to purchase better instruments. This, of course, does help but it has been the authors' observation that most groups don't produce more than half of the potential tone possible in the instruments that they already have.

Playing near to the bridge is a necessity for a full sound on the G-string on the violin as well as the lower strings on the other instruments, but the teacher should realize that *whenever* a louder sound is desired on any string, the same technique that has been explained here for the G-string can be used to produce additional tone on the other strings as well.

Learning to Play the Keys of G and C

In different books, the keys of G and C are presented at different times. The authors feel that these keys should be presented in the first year – preferably as early as possible so that the students understand that there are two major finger patterns rather than just the one used in the key of D. If changing keys is delayed too long, it will be more difficult for the students to change finger positions, because their hands will be almost permanently set for the key of D.

Key of G

Most books will introduce the C-natural on the A string following the learning of the G-string notes. The students need to be told that there is now no C-sharp in the key signature and that every C that will be played will be lowered a half-step (to C-natural). It should be explained that from now on, they will always need to remember to look at the key signature so they will know whether to play C-sharp or C-natural. To help the students to remember that all C's are now lowered, it is a good idea to ask them to either circle all the C's in the lesson or put a natural sign to the left of them.

Next, the teacher will need to explain to the class how to play C-natural. The violinists and violists should be told (and shown) that now they will use the opposite finger pattern from the one that they have been using. The first and second fingers will now play the half-step (fingers close together), and there will be a whole step (stretch) between the second and third fingers. The students should do this finger pattern away from the instruments at first. Tell them to be sure to exaggerate the large space between their first and second fingers. Students often think they are doing something distinctly, when in reality they are hardly doing it at all. By the teacher asking them to exaggerate these finger spacings, there is at least a good chance it will be done correctly.

After the violinists and violists have been told how to play their C-naturals, the teacher should show the cellists and bassists how to play theirs. The bassists will need to understand that to play their C-natural, they will need to use their second finger instead of the fourth finger. The cellists will use the second finger rather than the third. Cellists will need to be cautioned to place their second fingers close enough to the first finger or this finger will be too high. The bassists will need to be reminded to be careful that the space between first and second finger is large enough. The tendency is to play the second finger flat because of the bass's larger size.

Before the teacher asks the class to play lines from the book, some rote drill using both C-natural and C-sharp should be done. These can be extracted from the music that is going to be used next. Ask the students to make big, obvious differences between these notes. Check to see that the violinists and violists slide their fingers on the string from C-natural to C-sharp and vice-versa. Once the students can find these notes fairly consistently, the class is ready to try playing the exercises using C-naturals that will be found in their books.

Key of C

In most books, the key of C is presented in much the same manner as the key of G. The students will need to understand that the F-natural is on the D-string and will be played exactly the same as the C-natural was played on the A-string. As before, these notes should be found by rote before an attempt is made to play them from the book. It is again advisable to have the students mark the F and C-naturals in their books so they will remember to play them.

LEARNING THE C-STRING (VIOLAS AND CELLOS)

Most books will present the C-string notes to the viola and cello players about this time. It should be made clear to these students that they will use the same pattern on the C-string (in key of C) as they used on the G-string for key of G. The teacher will need to spend some time alone with the violas and cellos letting them find the C-string notes as they are difficult to hear, especially when the entire class is playing. They will also need to be told that since the C-string is the thickest one, some obvious changes in how they finger and bow will need to be made to enable them to produce a solid sound. These changes are: (1) be sure that the left hand *presses very tightly* so as to make solid contact with the string and fingerboard, and (2) be sure to play with a slower bow stroke as well as closer to the bridge ("Intense Tone" technique). They will probably also need to be reminded to be sure that the bow makes a right angle (square corner) to the string. For the violists this means that they will need to pull straight out from their bodies and the cellists will have to pull back more towards their bodies.

C-MAJOR SCALE

After all the students have been taught how to play the new F-natural, the C-scale should be taught (most books will include it). The basses will need to be taught how to slide up a half-step from B to C (on the G-string). They should slide on the fourth finger (whole arm moving as a unit) along the string from one note to the next. Later on, they will be taught the traditional fingering for the C-major scale, but it is best for the teacher at this point to not get too involved in the techniques of shifting. Simply announce to the bass players and the entire class: "Today the basses are going to learn to shift before anyone else does. It is really very simple – you just slide your hand down the string until your fourth finger sounds like C instead of B. There are only two rules you must remember and this goes for the rest of you, too (to class). One, your finger must always stay on the string when you slide your hand. Two, the whole hand must move as a unit with the thumb remaining under the second finger. Don't try to leave it behind!"

Be sure to remind the violinists and cellists that they are to use a slower bow stroke and play closer to the bridge ("Intense Tone" technique) if they are playing the low octave of the C-major scale (starting on open C-string).

Learning the E-String

In most string class methods, the violins and string basses will learn the E-string notes at the same time. Just as the violas and cellos were told to use their slowest bow stroke on their C-strings, the basses will need to do likewise on their E-string since it is their thickest string. Conversely, to produce a clear, full sound on the E-string, the violins will need to pull the bow with a very fast bow stroke since this is their thinnest string. They will need to be constantly reminded to do this. The bow must move the fastest on the thinnest string and slowest on the thickest string. This is true on all instruments.

The violins will need to learn two finger patterns on the E-string to be able to play in the keys learned so far. In the keys of D and G, for the notes F-sharp, G, A, and B, the finger pattern will be first and second fingers close for the half-step between F-sharp and G; second and third fingers stretched for whole-step from G to A; and third and fourth finger stretched for a whole step between A to B. Once the students have learned these notes by rote they should be ready to play from their books. At this time, the violins in particular, need to play a scale using these notes. If the book being used does not have one, have them play a one-octave G-scale with the violins starting on the D-string, the violas and cellos starting on the open G-string, and the basses starting on the E-string.

The second E-string finger pattern that needs to be taught to the violinists is the one needed to play in the key of C for the notes F-natural, G, A, and B. The violinists will need to be taught to slide their first finger from F-sharp (normal first finger position) to F-natural which is played first finger low. After they can find the F-natural, the teacher should have them stretch a whole step (from F-natural to G) with the second finger, then another whole step to A with the third finger and still another whole step to B with the fourth finger.

Since this is a brand new finger pattern for the violinists and a new string for both the violinists and bass players, they will need much drill, just as the violists and cellists needed more drill on the C-string. Use of the "Drill Routine" is strongly suggested on all new and/or difficult lines of this type whenever they occur. As mentioned previously, having the students mark whole steps and half steps is a good teaching technique, especially when there are new finger patterns.

Other Skills To Be Learned In The First Year

There are several other skills that many first-year books will ask the students to learn and some of these will be touched on before presentation of the second year of instruction.

Finger Skills

USE OF THE FOURTH FINGER (VIOLIN AND VIOLA)

Use of the fourth finger for the violin and viola should be introduced sometime during the first year, as using this finger "forces" the student into a correct left hand and arm position. Putting the fourth finger in the correct place demands that the left arm be well under the instrument and that the left hand fingers be curved properly.

The second reason to use the fourth finger as early as possible is that it often helps to avoid awkward changes of strings. A good rule is to require that the students use the fourth finger instead of the open D, A, and E strings whenever the passage does not continue on up onto the next string with fingered notes (see Figure No. 24 for examples of this rule).

When to Use Fourth Finger
Figure No. 24

As one can see by looking at the first example in Figure No. 24, it would be unnecessary to go over to the A-string for just one note, and so it would be easier to use the fourth finger. In the second example, notes other than the A are played, so it would be alright for the students to play the A-string open and then continue on with the other notes on this string.

In the first year, students should be required to use the fourth finger whenever it is appropriate. However, the teacher should be careful about never letting them use an open string once the fourth finger has been taught. An occasional open string is needed by young students to check to see if the intonation is correct. As a beginning adult student participating in a string-class teaching workshop once said: "Happiness is an open string." However, the students will need to be constantly reminded to use the fourth finger in places where the teacher has decided that it should be used. They will try to avoid it!

As has been done before on learning any new skill, the teacher should ask the violinists and violists to drill on some rote exercises to find the correct position for the fourth finger. The rote exercises shown in Figure No. 25 are shown only on the D-string, but the teacher will want to do similar ones on the other strings.

(1) (2)

Rote Exercises for Finding the Fourth Finger
Figure No. 25

Bow Skills

PLAYING MORE THAN TWO QUARTER NOTES IN A SLUR

Because playing multiple notes in a slur is like bowing a long note, the students must realize that they will have to adjust the speed of the bow so that they don't run out of bow while the notes are played.

The students must also understand that slurs make the tone softer because the bow is travelling slower making a large resonant sound impossible. It must also be understood that additional weight needs to be added as well as to move closer to the bridge ("Intense Tone" technique) if a louder tone is desired. Also, they will need to be reminded that they should keep solid contact with both hands while playing slurs.

The teacher will need to encourage the students to work for smoothness, particularly on the bow change. Students have a tendency to change the bow too quickly causing a "jerk." It must be remembered that the slower the bow travels, the slower the speed of the bow change must be.

HOOKED BOWING

Sometime during the first year, the students will need to learn to play two consecutive up bows in order to make a first beat of a measure come out down bow. This technique of two consecutive up bows (or down bows) is used very frequently so that the composer and/or arranger can adjust the bowings for the effects he wants. This type of bowing is referred to by several different names – hooked, linked and detached slur are three of the more common ones. In this book, it will always be referred to as "hooked" bowing. The students will need to understand that it is frequently necessary to "hook" two notes together in an up bow to make the next measure begin with a down bow.

When teaching a beginning class to "hook" two bows together, it is best to do it first by rote on an open string. They will need to be told that there must be a definite stop (a rest) between the two notes (up bow, rest, up bow). After they can do this well, the teacher should put some examples on the board of how the hooked bowing can be notated. It can be notated several different ways but with all of them meaning to play two consecutive up (or down) bows. The students should be taught the names for this kind of bowing as well as how to do it, because they will be asked to do it frequently (see Figure No. 26).

Different Notation for Hooked Bowing
Figure No. 26

As always, first have the students play the "hooked bowings" by rote, then have them open their books to the lesson where this bowing is introduced and proceed in playing the appropriate lines or tunes.

Rhythm Skills

TIME SIGNATURES

The time signatures of 4/4, 3/4 and 2/4 should be understood by the end of the year. The students should understand what both numbers of the signature mean.

Learning about the three time signatures and what they mean is a good chance to learn how these time signatures will be conducted. (See Chapter VII, Part II, for detail on how to teach the students to follow a conductor.)

NOTES OF LONGER VALUES

In addition to the quarter and half notes introduced thus far, most beginning books will probably introduce notes of longer values – dotted halves and whole notes.

Longer note values do require a slower bow stroke and the teacher must be sure that the students learn to move the bow slowly enough that they don't run out of bow before the note has ended. The students must feel that if they run out of bow, it is a mistake – *the note must be held full value.* Some students, however, will pull the bow so slowly that they only use part of the bow. They must realize that this is also wrong as this causes a weak tone.

TEACHING EIGHTH NOTES

Tapping Foot – When teaching eighth notes in 2/4, 3/4, or 4/4 time the teacher must make sure that the teaching of them is tied to the tapping of the foot. First, the students must realize that two eighth notes equal one beat or quarter note. It helps the students to realize the tempo of the eighth notes if the director first taps his foot in a steady down-up fashion while he claps consecutive eighth notes. The students should then be asked how many eighth notes they see and hear on each tap of the foot. Hopefully, they will answer. "Two." The teacher replies: "That's right, one when the foot goes *down* and one when the foot goes *up*." Show them that the foot always taps the meter, not the rhythm, and that it *does not* change when the rhythm does. They are not to tap the eighth note rhythm when they play them! (See Chapter VII, Part II for more detail on teaching eighth notes.)

Understanding the Division of the Bow – To prepare the students to play eighth notes, the teacher should first explain to the students that since eighth notes are faster than quarter notes, there is not time enough to use the whole bow. Since eighth notes are twice as fast as quarter notes, they will use only half as much bow as they used on quarter notes. Eighth notes should never use more than half of the bow. Tell them that they can use the lower half (usually marked L. H.), the upper half (U. H.), or the middle (marked M.) depending on what dynamic level is desired. (Lower half – mf and above, middle – mf and below; upper half – p and below.)

Eighth notes will not be played with a whole arm motion, so the teacher will need to tell the students which part of the bow they should use to play the eighth notes. A common mistake is to have the students use lots of bow all the time for a bigger sound. At any dynamic level or tempo, faster notes (eighths, sixteenths, etc.) must use less bow than longer notes or the bow will "skim" on the top of the string. If it is pulled too fast, the bow hairs can't "grip" and make solid contact with the string. Using lots of bow on fast note values also makes rhythmic precision impossible.

In conclusion, remember to teach the students to use less bow on notes of short duration (never more than half of the bow on eighth notes; one-fourth of the bow on 16th notes; and one-eighth of the bow on 32nd notes).

Rote Playing – Before trying to play the exercises in the book, the students should put their instruments into playing position, tap their feet in the given tempo and pretend that they are playing eighth notes in the air (above the string). When they can make their feet tap the meter (rather than eighth notes) steadily and move their arms in an eighth note pattern, they are ready to do the same on an open string. Once they can play consecutive eighth notes by rote on an open string, they are ready to try reading some simple tunes from their books that use eighth notes.

Orchestra Skills

LEARNING HARMONIZED TUNES

Sometime before the end of the first year, the string class should begin to play some simple rounds and harmonized orchestra tunes. The authors strongly believe, however, that any supplementary music used must apply things that have already been learned in the class method book and not ask them to play new keys, notes, rhythms, etc. that have not been covered in class. If the string series used has a supplementary orchestra book that follows the method book, it is recommended that the teacher use it so that the supplementary material will be coordinated with the method book.

It should also be clearly understood that the authors believe that there should be a minimum of supplementary music used in the first year, as it is most important to finish whatever book the class has been using so that the students will be ready to start a Book II in the second year, a Book III in the third year, and then be ready to play in a full-fledged orchestra with winds in the fourth year.

LEARNING ROUNDS

Teaching the students to play rounds is probably the easiest and most efficient way of getting beginning students to play different rhythms together. Such rounds as Scotland's Burning, Are You Sleeping, etc., are often found in beginning books. If the book doesn't have any rounds, the teacher might want to write some out for the students.

USING THE "DRILL ROUTINE"

The "Drill Routine" presented earlier can be used to great advantage when teaching students to play harmonized materials that have different parts. This is done by having the whole group play a phrase with their bows and then repeating the same phrase with one of the parts played alone with bows while the rest of the class plays pizzicato. For instance, the first violins will use their bows while everyone else plays their part pizzicato. Next, all will repeat the first phrase with their bows. Then, the second violins play the part with their bows while all others play pizzicato. By continuing this procedure, section by section, phrase by phrase, it is possible to teach very young groups a harmonized piece very quickly and efficiently. The reason that this method is more efficient than the traditional way of rehearsing (for very young students) is that it helps them to concentrate on their own part while they are playing with the bow and to pay attention to the other parts when they are playing pizzicato.

Activities of the First Year Class

In the first year, performance should be a very small part of the total activities. There are three reasons why the first year class should not be burdened with very many public performance responsibilities. They are: (1) there is so much material to cover and so many fundamentals to teach that time does not allow the teacher to teach special materials for concerts; (2) the students really are not far enough along to play formal concerts; and (3) something to look forward to should be saved for later.

In the event that a program by the first year students is unavoidable, specially early in the year, it is suggested that a "This Is How We Learn" session using music that the group is playing in the regular class be considered as not only best for the students, but more informative for the parents of the students and prospective students' parents as well. This kind of program would be especially appropriate for P.T.A. concerts.

All-Area or All-City String Festival

It is a good idea, however, to have *one* program each year that includes as many of the beginning students as is possible (near the end of the school year). If this program can include all the beginners from several schools it is even better, because a large group is more impressive to the audience and certainly more fun for the students than a small one.

At this program, the first year students should play four or five unison numbers from their first year class book and possibly one "real piece" that is harmonized and has an accompaniment. This type of concert should include students of two or more grade levels (fifth grade orchestra, sixth grade orchestra) so that the students and the parents can see what is ahead for them in the orchestra program. Concerts of this type are often called All-City String Festivals and the students should be conducted either by the string staff or outside guest conductors. The students should be encouraged to dress-up and look "special" for this first big concert.

Lower Grade Concerts and/or PTA Concerts

After a large, combined concert has been given in the late spring, it is a good idea to have both the beginning class and the advanced class (if the elementary school has one) play a short program during the school day for the lower grades to help with the recruiting of new students in the following years. The teacher should recognize that "students sell students."

The teacher may also want to include the string class as part of a PTA program in the late spring, after the large combined elementary festival, when the classes are fairly advanced and sound good. *Remember:* It is very important that the students sound good in all public performances. A good performance helps recruit future students – a bad one discourages them from joining.

Conclusion

At the end of the first year, the beginning students should:

(1) Have good basic holding and playing positions.

(2) Have a basic knowledge of time signatures of 4/4, 3/4, and 2/4.

(3) Have a basic knowledge of rhythm patterns using quarter notes, quarter rests, half notes, half rests, whole notes, whole rests, dotted half notes, eighth notes and eighth rests, as well as ties.

(4) Understand the first position notes in the keys of D, G and C.

(5) Be able to play pizzicato with a good sound.

(6) Be able to use full bows and play with a resonant sound.

(7) Be able to play with a slower bow stroke, closer to the bridge for an "Intense Tone."

(8) Be able to slur.

(9) Be able to play with a "hooked bowing."

(10) Be able to play some rounds and harmonized orchestra tunes that utilize things learned in the Book I.

The Second-Year String Class 5

INTRODUCTION

The second year is a very crucial year for young string players, as it is a time that they must continue to learn many things before they are ready to play in a secondary-level, performance-oriented (seventh grade) orchestra. Since one year has already been spent learning a multitude of new things (notes, rhythms, bowings, etc.), it has been the authors' experience that unless supplementary materials are used, the students will become bored with such a routine of mainly learning new things in the second year.

Planned Supplementary Materials Are Needed

It is strongly recommended that the teacher use carefully planned and coordinated supplementary materials along with the second year class method book. This will make the students feel that they are making more progress. In planning the curriculum for the second year students, the teacher should take into consideration that the basics of being a mature musician should be introduced – learning to follow a conductor and being aware that it is the player's responsibility to do more with the music than merely playing the notes and rhythm.

"Drill Routine" Needed

During this year there will need to be much use of the "Drill Routine" introduced in the first year, especially when learning the new keys found in most second year books. The authors have written this chapter as if the students are still in a grade school situation. Should the group be in a middle school situation where it meets four or five days a week in 40-45 minute periods, the teacher should understand that *more* should be covered than is mentioned in this chapter. The group should then start the new things listed in Chapter III.

More Musical Activities Needed

It is important in the second year (advanced) string class that the teacher plan for the group to participate in some musical activities that are only for them so that they feel that their second year status is being recognized. Some ideas for possible activities are: (1) play "mini" assembly-type concerts for the lower grades; (2) accompany general music and/or vocal classes or play alone on a program that the general music teacher might present, and (3) combine and play with advanced students from other elementary schools, for PTA concerts, for All-City or All-Area Concerts, etc. It is doubtful in most situations, that a teacher should do all of these things in one year – two or three are probably enough. At concerts where beginning students may also play, it might be fun, and certainly helpful for them to join the younger students on several numbers. However, they must also play alone so that the progress from the first year to the second year is noticeable to both themselves and the audience.

In conclusion, the second year of playing is a very crucial one and the teacher must realize that if this year is not handled correctly, many drop-outs will result.

EXPLANATION OF THE ORDER OF PRESENTATION

The order of presentation of new materials to be learned in this chapter is mainly a categorial listing and is not necessarily in the order that the problems will occur in second year method books.

TEACHING THE CLASS TO TUNE

The students *must* learn to tune themselves during the second year. This is, hopefully, the last year they will be in a small enough class where it will be possible for the teacher to assist individuals with tuning. Once the students progress to a secondary, performance-oriented orchestra, they will have to be able to tune themselves. Constant prodding will be needed by the teacher to see that it can be done correctly and efficiently by the third year.

The teaching of student tuning should start in the first year (second semester) at the end of class each day. The end of class (last 5-10 minutes) is preferable, because if the students try to tune themselves at the beginning of class, it will probably take too long and there will be no time left to play. Wait until they can tune all four strings in five minutes (second year) before having them tune their instruments at the beginning of class rather than at the end. For more detail on teaching the class to tune themselves, see Chapter VII, Part II.

SOME REVIEW OF THE FIRST YEAR NEEDED

Since most students probably will not participate in summer lessons (although they should be encouraged to do so), a review of what was learned in the first year will be necessary. The authors do not basically believe in extensive review because it is discouraging to the students; so the review that will be needed at the beginning of the second year should be handled very carefully. A good second year method book will begin with some review of the first year before going on to present new things. If the book used does not have a "built-in" review section, then the *teacher* will have to review the areas covered during the first year being careful that the students still feel that they are progressing.

The keys and finger positions covered the first year should be reviewed (probably G, C, and D) as well as all the rhythms and time signatures learned. The teacher should make sure that the violinists and violists continue to use their fourth fingers whenever it is appropriate. The bass will need to review the shifting to higher positions that were probably learned in the first year (Key of C – second position, Key of D – third position).

If eighth notes also are to be reviewed, the teacher should have the students again play them using the different parts of the bow (lower half, middle-half, and upper half). Again, a relaxed wrist and finger motion should be taught rather than a rigid forearm motion.

There should be continued use throughout the year of the two basic tones taught in the first year – the "Resonant" and "Intense." During this year, the students should begin to know which tone would be best to use and when, because the teacher has made certain that they understand the differences between them.

LEARNING NEW RHYTHM PATTERNS

DOTTED QUARTER FOLLOWED BY EIGHTH NOTE PATTERN

Several new rhythm patterns will need to be taught to the students during the second year. Probably the most important one is the dotted quarter note followed by an eighth note (♩. ♪) or an eighth note tied to a quarter note and followed by an eighth note (♩♫). This rhythm pattern is not difficult for the students to understand and play if they are taught that the dotted quarter note equals three eighth notes. If they then are taught to play with the tap of the foot as explained in the beginning year, this rhythmic pattern will present no problem.

The authors feel that the teaching of all rhythms should be done by relating the rhythmic figure to the tapping of the foot. This means that they should be taught that a dotted quarter note gets one and one-half beats which equals two taps of the foot. At first this will confuse the students, as it seems to them that two taps of the foot must equal two beats. This confusion can be dispelled, however, by diagramming this pattern on the board as shown in Figure No. 1.

Relationship of Foot to Eighth Notes
Figure No. 1

While the students are tapping their feet, they should then be asked to clap the rhythm pattern over and over until they can do it while keeping the foot beating steadily (the meter). For further detail on the teaching of rhythm patterns by relating them to foot tapping, see Chapter VII of Part II.

Any time a long note value is followed by a shorter note value, there is inherently a problem with young students in handling the bow, unless they are very carefully trained to compensate with the arm. There are several bow techniques that can be used in this situation. The one that the authors advocate is to have the students continue to use a full bow stroke on both the long and short notes (this means the up bow will be faster than the down bow). Thus, on a dotted quarter note followed by an eighth note, the bow would be pulled slowly on the dotted quarter and three times faster on the eighth note. It is obvious then that the up bow, because of its faster speed, will be louder and more accented than the down bow that is travelling slower. The teacher should not, at this point, be concerned about the accent on the up bow. The most important point is that the students first learn how to change speeds from the down bow to the up bow. Unless the teacher expects them to exaggerate the fast up bow, the students will keep the bow speed the same for both the long and short note forcing them eventually to end with their bows at the tip where very little sound can be produced. Do not allow the students to continually play at the tip of the bow because terrible tone problems will result.

After the students have learned to change bow speeds on uneven rhythm patterns and have been doing it for several months, the teacher should then work to eliminate the accent on the fast up bow stroke by asking them to release the weight of the arm by raising the elbow slightly on the up bow stroke.

Quarter Note and Two Eighth Note Rhythm Pattern

Two other rhythm patterns that will no doubt be found in a second year book are: (4/4 ♩ ♫ ♩ ♫ and ♫ ♩ ♫ ♩). These rhythms will be easy for the students to learn if a rigid foot-beat is required as advocated earlier. Be sure that the students tap the meter rather than the rhythmic pattern.

As was learned in the first year – quarter notes (unless the tempo is extremely fast) should use full bows. Eighth notes should use half the bow or less. The part of the bow to use is determined now mainly by the dynamic level and later, by the style of the music. In a rhythmic pattern where a quarter note is followed by two eighth notes or vice-versa, the quarter note will use a full bow (whole-arm) and the eighth notes half the bow or less (forearm stroke) in either the upper half or lower half of the bow. The teacher must watch the students carefully because they will try to use a full bow on the eighth notes also. Do not allow this. *Remember:* Notes that are of shorter value than quarter notes will *never* use a full bow. A good rule to teach the students is: Unslurred eighth notes equal no more than half of the bow, sixteenth notes no more than one fourth of the bow, and thirty-second notes no more than one eighth of the bow.

In patterns using both quarter notes and two consecutive eighth notes, the bow should be distributed as shown in Figure No. 2:

(A) (B)

♩ ♫ ♩ ♫ ‖ ♫ ♩ ♫ ♩ ‖
WB UH WB LH LH WB UH WB

Playing Quarter Note and Two Consecutive Eighth Note Patterns
Figure No. 2

NEW TIME SIGNATURE (6/8)

Sometime during the second year, the students should be introduced to the 6/8 time signature. They must understand that the top number tells how many beats are in a measure and the bottom number tells what kind of note gets one beat. At first, the students will need to count and play this time signature in six. Later on, after they have played 6/8 time for awhile counting six beats in a measure, it will be fairly easy to teach them to count it in two.

The repeated eighth note pattern (six in a measure: ♫♪ ♫♪) is quite easy to play. As before, no more than half the bow should be used on the eighth notes. Eighth notes are easiest to play in the middle of the bow. However, if a dynamic level above mezzo-forte is desired, the lower half of the bow could be used.

Another pattern that will come up in the second year is a quarter note followed by an eighth note (♩ ♪). The bowing for this pattern will be played similarly as for the ♩. ♪ – a slow bow followed by a fast bow. This same rhythm may be found with a slur under it and a dot underneath the second note. This bowing is called either *slurred staccato, detached slur, hooked bowing,* or *linked bowing*. The authors will use the term hooked bowing. This type of bowing will be explained in detail later in this chapter where all the new bowings to be learned in the second year are discussed.

Dotted quarters (♩.) and dotted halves (𝅗𝅥.) will be found in second year books if 6/8 time is presented. These will be easy for the students to understand rhythmically *if* the students are asked to count them out loud and tap their feet. Both will require a full bow – the bow travelling half as fast on the dotted half as the dotted quarter. Playing very near to the bridge and into the string (much weight on to the bow) with the slower bow stroke will be necessary if a forte sound is desired ("Intense Tone").

NEW BOW STYLES AND BOWINGS

There are several bow styles and bowings that will need to be taught to a second year string class. Some of the more important ones are: staccato, accent, hooked bowing, spiccato (off the string bowing), long slurs (three and four in a bow), slurred string crossings, playing two strings at a time and detaché. Work will be continued on the two basic tones introduced in the first year – "Resonant" and "Intense."

Staccato (On the String)

Most composers, when desiring a staccato style, will place a dot either above or below the note ( ), however, often the style of the music itself indicates the need for staccato playing, even though the music is not *marked* staccato. A good example of this might be music that is in a march style.

The *Harvard Dictionary of Music* defines a staccato note as "a reduction of its written duration with a rest substituted"[1] for part of its value. In terms of playing, this means that each note must be shortened so that there is an obvious separation between every note in the pattern. The term commonly used whenever a separation is desired between two notes is "spacing" and it is very important that the students understand the word and what it means to do.

To accomplish the staccato spacing in string playing, the player must pull the bow very fast with a great deal of energy and then stop it suddenly and cleanly *on* the string *before* the duration of the note has ended. In simple terms, staccato bowing is a very fast, detached stroke.

To teach the students to play staccato notes, the teacher should have them use only an open string until they have mastered the correct tone and style. After they can do this, have them play a D-Major scale by playing each tone of the scale four times (see the example in Figure No. 3).

Written **Sounded**

Learning to Play Staccato Style
Figure No. 3

The teacher must explain to the students that when they are playing quarter notes staccato in reality they are playing eighth notes followed by eighth rests (Figure No. 3). Unless the teacher insists strongly upon a definite space (rest) between notes the students will not learn to play staccato notes cleanly.

The staccato stroke is a very tiring stroke for young players and thus they will need to be constantly reminded to put much force and energy into the stroke so a good staccato sound is the result. Once they have developed more strength in their arms it will not be as tiring. The teacher should realize that different sounds are possible from the staccato stroke (just as with a legato bow style). A faster stroke (more bow) will give a more resonant staccato. Likewise, a slower stroke (less bow) will give a more centered, intense sound.

[1]Apel, *Harvard Dictionary of Music,* Harvard University Press, Cambridge, 1958, p. 708.

Accent

Many second year books will present accents. An accent mark (<) found either above or below a note means to give the note extra emphasis by applying additional pressure to the bow. To be able to play a precise accent, the students must be taught to space (or pause) by stopping the bow completely *before* the note that is to be accented. If there are several consecutive accents the player must stop the bow *both* before and after each note. An accent can be considered a form of staccato.

Hooked Bowing

There are many terms used to mean that two notes are to be played in the same bow direction with a space or stop between them. Among the terms that the director and group must know are *hooked, linked, detached slur,* and *slurred staccato*. The term that is probably most widely used is "hooked" bowing.

Hooking two notes together in the same bow direction is frequently used in 6/8 time on a repeated pattern of a quarter note followed by an eighth note (6/8 ♩♪♩♪). Hooked bowing is preferred to each note being played with a different bow direction, because the bow length is divided equally for both the down and up bow. Also, hooked bowing is less tiring than separated bow strokes. This bowing equalizes the bow and makes it possible to use the same amount of bow on the down bow as the up bow without having to compensate by pushing the up bow faster than the down bow. The students will need to be taught to automatically "hook" two notes together on rhythm patterns such as this.

When the students are first learning to hook two notes together in the same bow direction, they should be expected to make a definite space (rest) between the two bows being pulled in the same direction, otherwise a really clean playing cannot result at faster tempos later on. After they have been playing the hooked bows with definite rests between notes for quite a while, the teacher may then want to try barely stopping between the two notes (a brush stroke) especially where this is the musically preferred sound.

Hooking two notes together in a bow is also frequently done so that a phrase can end on a down bow, for instance, on a rhythm pattern of a half note followed by two quarter notes (𝅗𝅥 ♩♩ 𝅗𝅥. 𝄽). If the two quarter notes are not both played up bow, the phrase would come out up bow which is not good musically, because it is easier to diminuendo on a down bow, and, most phrase endings *should* be "tapered" (>).

It is also important to mention that there are several different notations used meaning to use a hooked bowing. The three most common are shown in Figure No. 4.

(1) (2) (3)

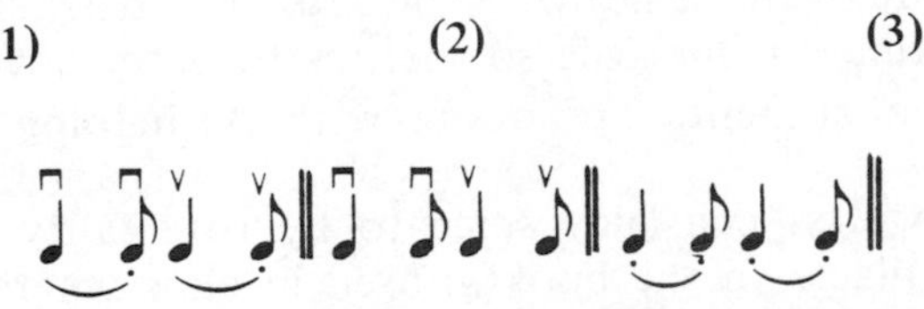

Notations of Hooked Bowing
Figure No. 4

Spiccato (Off the String Bowing)

While the music played in the second year string class probably will not *require* the use of an off the string style of bowing (spiccato), it is fun and makes good sense for the class to go ahead and learn it so that they will know how to do it when they progress to music that requires it or sounds better with it. While Classical style music most often requires some spiccato playing, it can also be very effective in soft passages in other kinds of music when a light, staccato sound is needed or in places where a change of style from a legato type bowing would be effective. The wise director will look for short spots in the assigned music where it is easy for the students to practice some off the string bowing.

The word "spiccato" means to play with the bow *off the string.* Some will use the term, "bounce the bow." The students will need to understand that the bow will be bounced (dropped) from above the string on every stroke and then lifted up again. A small arc-like motion will be made with the forearm, wrist and fingers working together as a unit. The bow hairs make contact with the string at the bottom of the arc. ( ) The students will understand more clearly that the bow must be started to bounce from above the string if it is compared to bouncing a ball – a ball is made to bounce by dropping it from above the floor.

For a controlled spiccato, meaning a spiccato at a slow to moderate tempo, which the students should learn first, it is best to have the students bounce the bow fairly close to the frog end of the bow (no more than one-third to one-fourth of the way out). The teacher can help the students find the ideal place to bounce the bow by having them locate the place on the bow stick where the bow will balance on the hand. When this point on the bow is found, have them move one or two inches *closer* to the frog because young players will have more control of the bow there.

As has always been done in learning new physical skills, the spiccato should first be taught by rote on an open string. The teacher should ask the students to place their bows an inch or so above their D strings (about one-fourth of the way out from the frog) and lightly drop the bow onto the string (using the suggested arc motion). Be sure the students continue to play with a back and forth, down and up motion – they will try to play only down bows unless the director explains that they still will play in a down-up fashion like they have used for *on the string* playing.

The teacher will need to move around the class to be sure that the students are playing light, short, strokes in the correct part of the bow. Also, they will need to be checked to be sure that they don't bounce the bow too high. An inch above the string is high enough, so they will need to be constantly reminded to stay close to the string.

After the class can control some rote spiccato at a fairly slow, steady tempo, they should be ready to try playing a D-Major scale (playing four tones on each tone of the scale) with spiccato. The teacher may also want to use the drill routine on the scale so there is time to move around the class and see how the students are doing with it, helping individuals where necessary.

After the class can play spiccato by rote fairly well, the director should look for places in the book(s) used in class where it would be easy and appropriate to have the students play spiccato. The authors feel that spiccato can and should be introduced much earlier than most teachers introduce it as the students can learn it quite easily and also seem to find it quite enjoyable. It might also be mentioned that spiccato bowing gives the director another opportunity to change the style of the music for more variety and interest with young students.

A Word About Dots Found in Music

There is much confusion and disagreement about how to play music when dots are shown over or under the notes. It is extremely difficult for the authors to give a "black and white" answer as to how the various editors will want the music played when dots are inserted. In general, dots above or below notes merely mean that the notes should be played shortened in rhythmic value with spaces between the notes. If the music is heavy and loud, they probably should be played *staccato* (on the string stroke) particularly if the music is a march or in Baroque style. If the music is lighter in style and not particularly loud, it probably should be played *spiccato* (off the string), especially if the music is in Classical style or it is an accompaniment type of passage. It is always best for the director to try both ways and choose the one that best fits the basic style of the music.

In conclusion, dots above or below notes can mean that the music should be played either staccato (on the string) or spiccato (off the string). In a sense, spiccato playing is a form of staccato, as the notes are still shortened in value and spaced. There may be times when the editor puts no dots in the music but the style of music definitely indicates that the notes should be played shortened in value and spaced.

Other Advanced Bow Techniques

Long Slurs

During the second year, the students should develop the skill of playing long slurs (three and four notes in a bow) without losing tone. To play lone slurs it is necessary for the bow to be pulled at a slower speed which causes a decrease in the amount of sound produced *unless* some other compensation is made in the way the students are handling the bow.

Several things can be done to expand the tone within slurred passages, and the students should know how to do all of them. In reality, they seldom will need to do all of them simultaneously, unless the passage is marked double-forte. To expand tone and play with a clear, solid tone within slurs, the students should do any or all of the following:

(1) Press the left hand fingers more firmly into the strings and fingerboard.

(2) Play firmly with the bow and use additional bow weight (pressure). This is especially necessary using the upper half of the bow where the weight of the arm is less upon the string.

(3) Play closer to the bridge (with slower bow speed).

It may be noticed that if all three of these things are done at once, the technique is the same as that described in the section in Chapter I on producing an "Intense Tone."

Orchestra directors have long thought that it isn't possible for young groups to play with a large sound within slurs. This is true *unless* the students are taught to do the three things above. Many directors, knowing only that keeping the bow moving at a fast speed will give more sound (using full bows) will take out the slurs in passages where more tone is desired rather than teaching the students to learn to play differently within the slurs. Taking the slurs out is of course a way to get more tone but it is certainly an unwise practice to do this automatically, because there is some music where changing the bowing in this way ruins the desired feeling and style. The authors recommend that the students be carefully taught to play with a smooth, solid, forte tone on long slurs.

Remember: The teacher from time to time will need to check the students' bows to be sure they are using rosin. Usually in the second year they are prone to decide that they don't really need rosin anymore. It should be realized also that playing with an "Intense Sound" will not be possible unless the softer, darker rosin is used.

Playing Two Strings At A Time

It may be necessary to introduce some simple double-stop playing (sounding two strings at a time) during the second year. This is really very similar to playing slurred string crossings in that *both* require that the bow hairs be kept very close to the strings. Double-stop playing is really quite easy for the students to learn if they have been taught to play with a firm grip and understand "getting into" the string with the bow. Playing on two strings at once does require equal pressure with the bow on both strings.

It is advisable to have them play the first double-stops on two open strings and sustain the notes for several counts as shown in Figure No. 5.

Learning to Play Open String Double-Stops
Figure No. 5

After the students can handle playing smoothly on two open strings at once, they are ready to try to play some simple double-stops where one finger is used on one string and the open string sounded with it as shown in Figure No. 6.

Learning to Play Fingered Double-Stops
Figure No. 6

After this it would be helpful if the teacher can find some simple supplementary tunes that the class will enjoy that employ some simple double-stop playing. An example of this might be a country-type hoe down where it sounds like some "fiddles" are tuning up for a square-dance.

Slurred String Crossings

When bowing any passage where students must cross strings, the students need to be taught to make a very small motion with their arms while changing from one string to another. The arm will need to be lowered or raised (whichever is appropriate) only a little as the bow is moved from one string to the next. The feeling must be developed of rocking gently from one string to another with a rolling curved motion rather than an angular motion. (◡ rather than ‿). When a small curved motion of the arm is used the result will be a smooth, legato sound, whereas a large, angular motion will produce a rough, staccato type sound. It is difficult to convince the students that it really takes very little motion to change the bow from one string to another, but playing some slurred open string exercises like those in Figure No. 7 will help them to play slurred string crossings with ease.

Rote Exercises for Slurred String Crossings
Figure No. 7

If the students will think of playing two strings at once on slurred string crossings, this will help them to understand that only a very small motion is necessary to change the bow from one string to another.

Detaché

The readers need to be fully aware that there is controversy about what the word "detaché" actually means to do. However, it has been found in recent years that most authorities in the orchestra field now accept the definition that detaché means *only* that each note is to be played with a separate bow. That it is a *legato* stroke rather than a detached, staccato stroke. Ivan Galamian, the most renowned violin teacher in the United States says in his book, *Principals of Violin Playing and Teaching*, that, when playing detache, "a separate bow is taken for each note and the stroke is smooth and even throughout with *no variation* of pressure. There is no break between the notes and each bow stroke has, therefore, to be continued until the next takes over."[2]

[2]Ivan Galamian, *Principles of Violin Playing and Teaching,* Prentice-Hall, Englewood Cliffs, New Jersey, 1962, p. 67.

Mark Lorrin's *Dictionary of Bowing and Tonal Technic for Strings* says, "The definition generally accepted for detaché is that it is a detached or separated bow stroke (with the direction changing for each successive note) including all technics except *slurs and ties.* A minority defines detaché as being synonymous with staccato."[3]

As is obvious from the quotations mentioned, most teachers agree that detaché only means detached in the sense that it means that each bow stroke is to be played in a separate direction – *or not slurred.* In fact, often the word detaché is found after long slurred or staccato passages, and the word is simply telling the musician not to continue to play in the same style as before. The word means to play each note with a separate bow and a legato stroke.

Frequently, composers and editors will simply put lines above or below notes (♩ ♩) to indicate detaché playing. Many directors will then request that the students play staccato. This is incorrect, however, because the tenuto mark (–) indicates that notes are to be held for full value – not separated.

NEW KEYS

Key of F

Learning B-flat on the A-String

The first B-flat that the students should learn is how to play the B-flat on the A-string. As has always been done before, the teacher should tell them how to find the new note, and then have them find it by using some simple rote exercises (made up from the first line of music in their books, if possible).

The violinists, violists and cellists will play their B-flats by sliding their first fingers on the string from B-natural (home position) back a half-step to B-flat. This fingering is often called and marked one-low in music for young groups. *Warning:* Be sure that the students do not slide whe whole hand back but rather, just the first finger.

HALF POSITION (BASSES)

The basses will need to learn to play in a different position for this key. The new position is called *Half Position,* and it is the lowest position the basses will need to play (the hand is farthest back towards the scroll of the instrument). Half Positon is very important to bass players as it *must* be used in the flat keys and the Key of C. The notes for basses in half position on all four strings are shown in Figure No. 8.

[3]Mark Lorrin, *Dictionary of Bowing and Tonal Technics for Strings,* Charles Hansen, Denver, Colorado, 1968, p. 20.

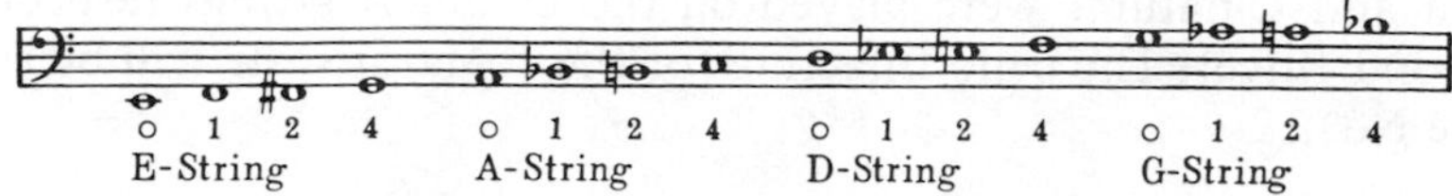

Half Position Notes (String Bass)
Figure No. 8

F-Major Scale

Once the students know how to play the B-flat on the A-string and have played some easy exercises using this note and the other notes in the key on this string, they should next learn a one-octave F-Major scale.

The violins will need to use low second finger for the first note of the scale, low first finger for the B-flat (on the A-string), and low first finger for the high F (last tone of the scale) as shown in Figure No. 9.

Violin Fingering – F-Major Scale
Figure No. 9

The bass will play the entire F-Major scale in Half Positon, and the fingering will be as shown in Figure No. 10.

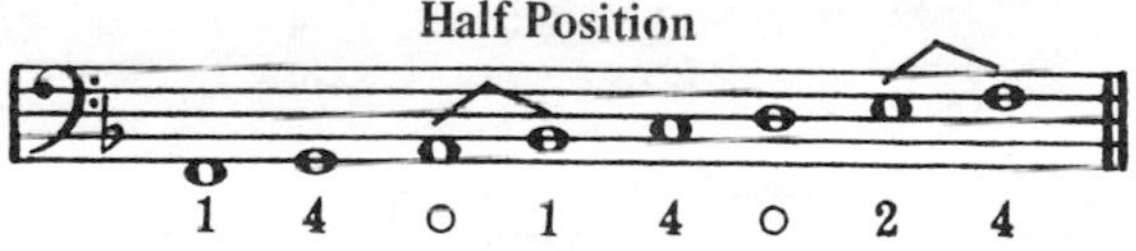

Bass Fingering for F-Major Scale
Figure No. 10

B-Flats on the G-String

To play the F-Major scale, the cellos and violas will need to learn to play the B-flat on the G-string. For the violists, it is simply a low second finger. The F-major scale fingering for violas would be as shown in Figure No. 11.

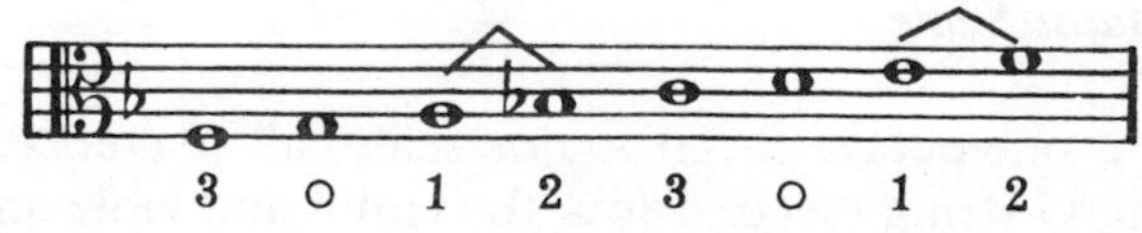

Viola Fingering for F-Major Scale
Figure No. 11

For the cellists, the low B-flat (on the G-string) is played just as F-natural and C-natural were played on the D and A strings respectively – with second finger. The cello fingering for the F-Major scale will be as shown in Figure No. 12.

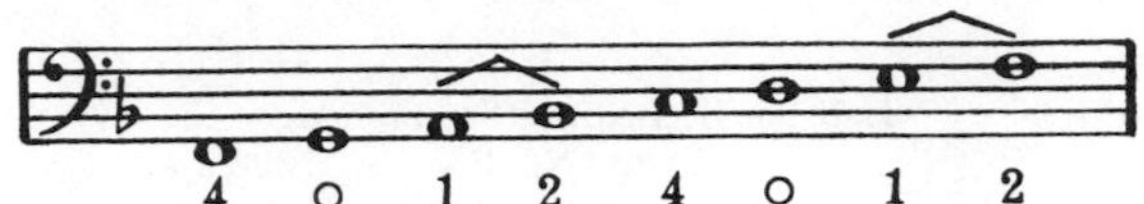

Cello Fingering for F-Major Scale
Figure No. 12

Since both the violas and cellos have learned how to play their B-flats on the G-string so that they could play a one-octave F-Major scale, the teacher might want to go ahead and teach the violins and basses how to play theirs. For the violin, the B-flat on the G-string is simply low second finger (played like F-natural and C-natural were played on the D and A strings, respectively). For the basses, it is played with four fingers on the G-string in half position.

High B-Flat (Violin E-String)

There is just one other B-flat that still needs to be learned in this key, and that is the high B-flat on the violin E-string. The notes on the E-string (in this key) are: F-natural, G, A, and B-flat and they are played as shown in Figure No. 13.

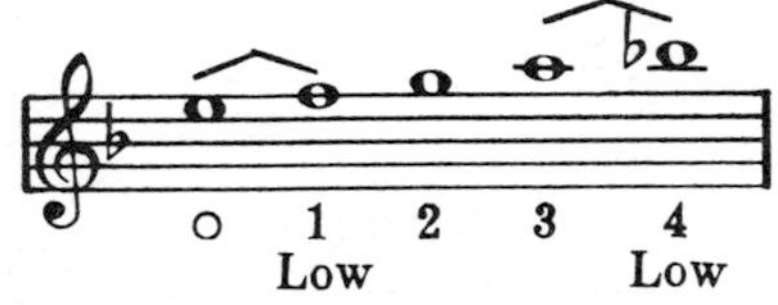

High B-flat (Violin E-string)
Figure No. 13

Key Of B-Flat

In the key of B-flat, the new notes that will need to be learned are the E-flats. For all instruments, the E-flat on the D-string is played first finger low. Only the bass will move the whole hand back and play in half position. Basses must use half position in *all* the flat keys.

B-Flat Major Scale

To play a one-octave B-flat major scale, all players (except the bass) will begin on the G-string (second low for violin and viola and second finger on the cello). The bass will start on the B-flat on the A-string (first finger, half position). Fingerings for the four instruments are as shown below in Figure No. 14.

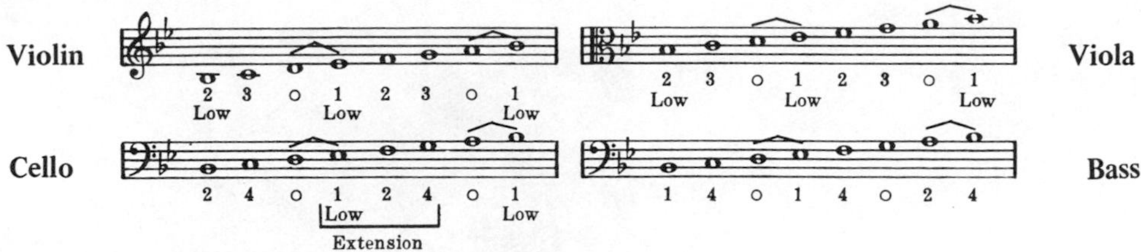

Fingering for B-Flat Major Scale
Figure No. 14

Cello Extension

As will be noticed by looking at the cello fingering for the B-flat major scale, an extension of the hand is required to play it correctly. This is probably one of the most important and most difficult things that the young cellist needs to learn. The teacher must be very insistent and check continually after it has been taught to make sure that the students really use the extension.

The word "extension" literally means "to make larger," so, in the case of string playing, it means to extend the hand and make the interval of the hand span larger than has been previously used in the finger patterns up to this point. At no time when extending back should the player's thumb move or the basic hand position be changed (shifted). Normally, the natural finger position for cellos is a half-step between each finger (four fingers spaced evenly), and there is an interval of a minor third from first to fourth finger as shown in Figure No. 15.

Normal and Extended Finger Spacing on D-String (Cello)
Figure No. 15

With an extension, the cellists can play the interval of a major third between the first and fourth fingers by either lowering the first finger to E-flat or raising the fourth finger to G-sharp (Figure No. 15). The rule that needs to be learned is that: *Whenever there are two consecutive whole-steps to be played between the first and fourth fingers,* an extended finger pattern must be used. In Figure No. 15, the second finger is the one that must be extended from the regular finger pattern. It will now be stretched a half step further and there will be a whole step (instead of a half) between first and second finger (see Figure No. 15).

The notes in Figure No. 16 shown below also require an extended hand position. In this case, however, the second and fourth fingers remain in normal position, and the first finger extends back a half step. (See musical example and photo showing this in Figure No. 16.)

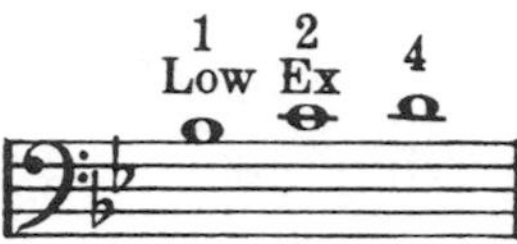

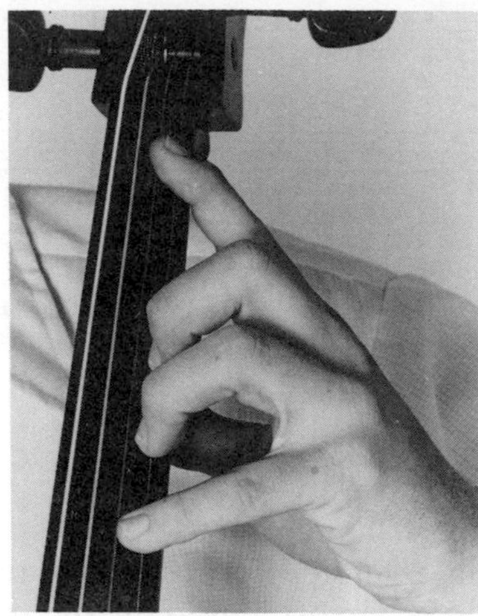

Extension Cello Fingering (A String)
Figure No. 16

When extensions are used, the third finger does not play a note (although the spacing between second, third, and fourth fingers will be the same as in the normal finger pattern). Up until now, there has been a very strict rule of keeping all the fingers down. Now, the students will need to be told it won't be necessary to keep the third finger down on the extension, because it will not actually play a note.

A WORD OF CAUTION

It is imperative that cellists be taught that once the first finger is in position, they must then stretch the whole step to the second finger. As was learned in the beginning, the thumb should stay *under* the second finger, so that when the second finger moves a half-step up, the thumb should move, too. After a while, if both the first and second finger are kept down and the students are *made* to stretch their hands, they will develop the "feel" for the extension, and they will not try to shift or pick up the first finger. They will complain that it hurts at first but the teacher should not be too sympathetic with them – just explain that it will get easier with practice.

ROTE EXERCISE FOR PRACTICING EXTENSIONS

While a two consecutive, whole-step pattern is not generally called an extension on the violin and viola, it really is, and the teacher will find that this stretched fingering pattern is difficult (at first) for young students. Therefore, it is quite helpful for the teacher to have the violins, violists, and cellists make a rote exercise of playing "Mary Had A Little Lamb" using the extended finger position. Be sure that each student keeps his first finger down when going on to play higher notes.

First, the teacher should have the students find E-flats, F's and G's by rote (on the D-string). After they can find these notes then the class is ready to play "Mary Had A Little Lamb" as shown in Figure No. 17.

(Play Also on Viola and Cello)

Practicing the Extended Finger Pattern
(Mary Had A Little Lamb)
Figure No. 17

Unless the cello students keep the first fingers down, an extension has not been played as the extension actually is the whole-step *stretch* from first to second finger.

E-Flat High Register (Violins and Violas)

In the key of B-flat, both the violins and violas will need to learn to play an E-flat on their A-string, and the violins will need to learn to play a high B-flat on the E-string (see Figure No. 18).

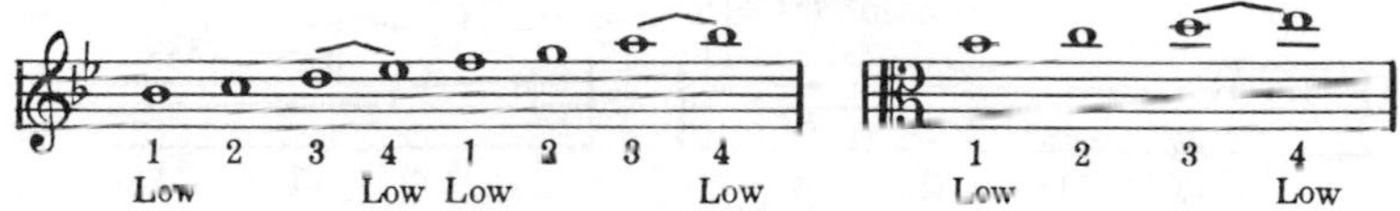

High E-flat and B-flat
(Violin and Viola)
Figure No. 18

For both the violin and viola, these notes are played fourth finger low (the fourth finger close – one-half step from the third finger). *Remember:* The first, second and third fingers are all a whole step apart (extended hand position). After learning these notes, the violins only will be able to play a two-octave B-flat scale.

E-Flat Low Register (Viola and Cello)

In the Key of B-flat, the violas and cellos will need to learn how to play a low E-flat (on the C-string). For the viola this note is played second finger low, and the cello will play it with two fingers. These notes will not be difficult for them to learn. However, they will need to play some on this string alone, because the low register is very difficult to hear when the whole class is playing. Also, they will need to be reminded to use a slower bow stroke (closer to the bridge) for a solid tone on the lowest string.

KEY OF E-FLAT

In the key of E-flat, the new notes that the students will need to learn are A-flats. In this key the violinists and bass players can play only two open strings – their D's and G's due to the fact that the E and A are both flatted.

The first A-flat the violin and viola players will need to learn is shown in Figure No. 19.

A-Flat on the D-String
(Violin and Viola)
Figure No. 19

This A-flat is played by placing the fourth finger a half-step from the third finger (close) on the violin and viola. (The hand position is again extended with whole steps between the first three fingers.)

The cello and bass will need to learn to play an A-flat on their G-strings as shown in Figure No. 20.

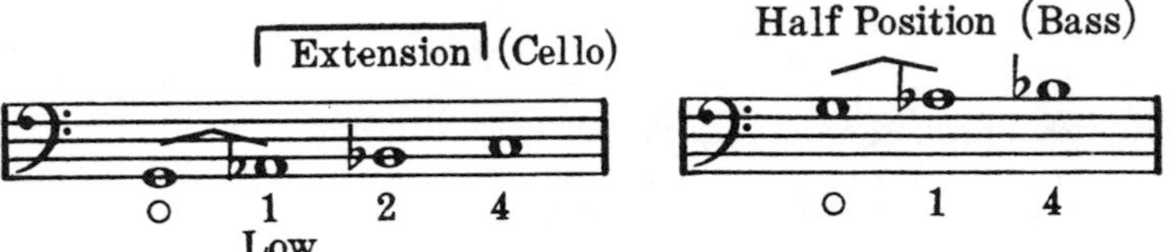

A-Flat on the G-String
(Cello and Bass)
Figure No. 20

On the G-string in this key, the cellists will again need to use their newly-learned extended finger pattern of a whole-step from the first to second finger.

E-Flat Major Scale

Once the students have learned the A-flats they will be able to play a one-octave E-flat Major scale. The fingerings for this scale are shown in Figure No. 21.

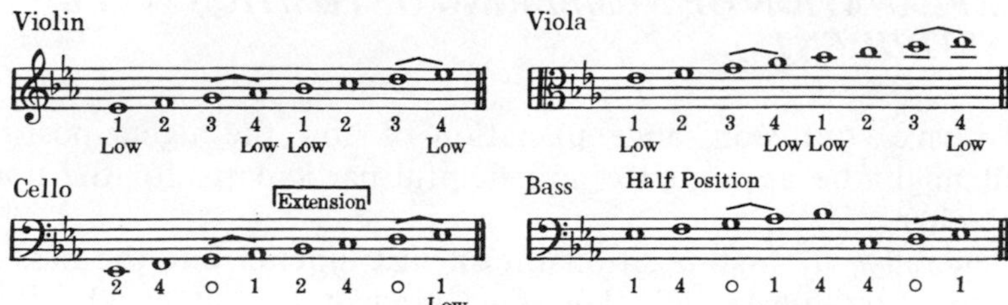

E-Flat Major Scale Fingerings
Figure No. 21

A-Flats (Different Registers)

Each instrument now needs to learn A-flat on a different string before moving on to another key. The violin must learn the high A-flat on the E-string that is played with the third finger close (half-step away from the second finger). The viola must learn the low A-flat on the G-string that is played by lowering (sliding) the first finger from A to F-flat. The bass needs to learn the A-flat (on the E-string) that is played in first position with four fingers (see Figure No. 22 for chart of these A-flats).

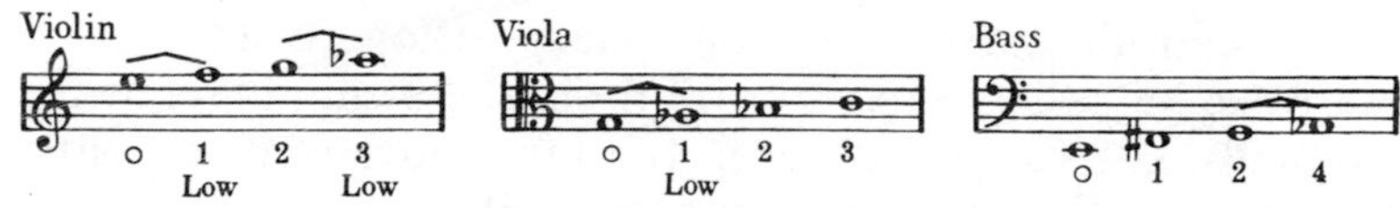

A-Flats in Different Registers
(Violin, Viola, and Bass)
Figure No. 22

Shifting To A Higher Position (Cello)

For the cellists to be able to play the second octave in the Key of E-flat, it will be necessary for them to learn to shift from first position to second position. Learning this position will make it possible for them to play the A-flat on the D-string and the high E-flat on the A-string. The notes in second position on the D and A strings are enclosed in a bracket as shown in Figure No. 23.

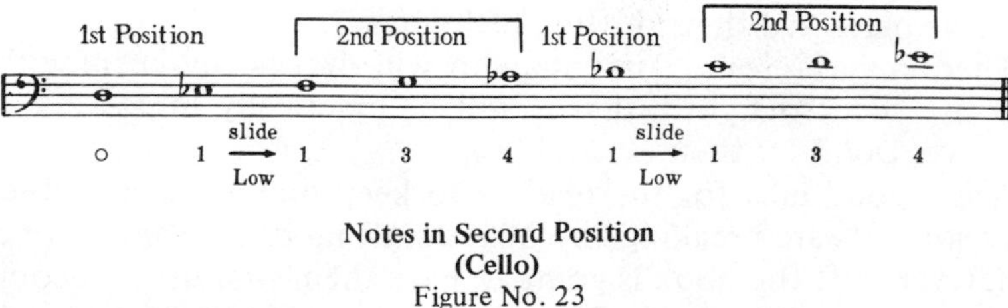

Notes in Second Position
(Cello)
Figure No. 23

EXPLANATION OF NUMBERING OF POSITIONS (ALL INSTRUMENTS)

To save confusion, an explanation of how the higher positions are numbered might be appropriate and helpful particularly for the non-string playing teacher.

Generally, in first position on all instruments but the bass, on the D-string, *the first finger* will play some kind of E – it can be E-natural, E-sharp, or E-flat. When the hand is shifted up to second position (on all instruments), the first finger will be on an F – it can be F-natural, F-sharp, or F-flat. In third position, the first finger would likewise play some kind of G (sharp, natural, or flat). The first finger in fourth position would play some kind of A (sharp, natural, or flat). Positions can be figured in this manner on any string and on any instrument. The basses can follow this rule to find their basic position number, but if the first finger is playing a flat, they must substract a half position. If it is playing a sharp, they will add a half position. This basic rule will make it possible for the director to know almost immediately what position passages are to be played in.

RULES OF SHIFTING

There are two basic rules of shifting that must be followed for accurate and smooth movement from one position to another. Not only *must* these rules be adhered to very strictly in the beginning, but the teacher must continually keep an eye on even the more advanced students to make sure that they are not slipping into careless habits.

The first and most important rule is that, when shifting from one position to another, the *whole hand (and arm) must move as a unit.* The students (especially violinists and violists due to the relatively short distance) will try to move from one position to another by *only* moving the finger that is making the slide and leaving the thumb in the old position. A good exercise to combat this tendency is to ask all class members to freely slide the arm (with first finger pressing lightly) on the string back and forth from the scroll-end to as far as they can reach towards the bridge. The students will quickly see that this would be impossible if just the finger moves and the thumb stays behind.

The second rule of shifting is that the *finger should slide on the string* so as to connect one position to another and make it possible for them to hear where to stop in the new position. To do this, it will be necessary to have the students slide quite slowly at first so the slide will be heard easily. (This obviously audible moving pitch will not be heard later after the students have perfected their shifting technique.)

There may be some students who will over-do by keeping the finger down on the slide so tightly that it will be practically impossible for their arms to move. Don't let them.

It is a good idea for the teacher to keep moving around the class to see if any students are breaking any of the shifting rules. Some rote exercises using whatever shift the book is going to have them first use is recommended before playing from the book. The "Drill Routine" should be used on this rote work. *Remember:* The fingers must be kept on the string – there should never be any "hopping" back and forth from one position to another.

KEY OF A

The last key that most second year books present is the Key of A. All players (except bass) will need to use extended finger patterns on both the G-string (low C-sharp) and the D-string (G-sharp). The violins and violas will play this note with a third finger raised (high). An inexperienced teacher or non-string player might wonder why C-sharp and D-flat (on the violin and viola) aren't played with the same finger. (D-flat is played with fourth finger low and C-sharp third finger high.) The answer is: They can be and are at times later on, but experience has shown that the best basic habit to teach the students is to play all C's with the third finger and all D's with the fourth finger. Later, they may be interchanged for ease of playing where convenient.

The cello players in this key will need to use the extended hand position (a whole-step between first and second finger) on the G and D strings. The bassists will have to use both first and half position for this key. (The half position is necessary on the G-string for the G-sharp.)

A-Major Scale

The fingerings for all instruments for a one-octave A-Major scale are shown in Figure No. 24:

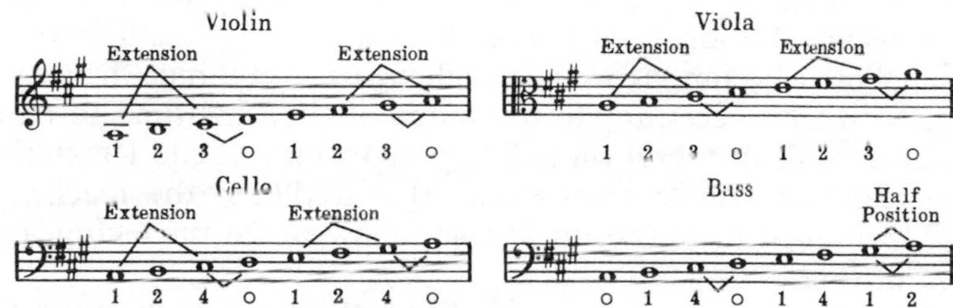

A-Major Scale (All instruments)
Figure No. 24

DEVELOPING FACILITY AND SPEED

By second semester of the second year, the teacher should be starting to develop the students' ability to move around quickly from string to string. This means that the students should play some exercises at faster tempos in order to be ready for full-fledged orchestra playing in the next year. It must be remembered that the teacher should never let students set the overall pace of the class or the tempo of the music. Students need to be constantly pushed to do a little more each day as well as to do what they do a little better than the day before. If they aren't pushed by the teacher, the class will "bog down" and they will never be ready for real orchestra playing.

To be able to pace the class so that the students can gradually learn to play some things at faster tempos (the teacher's tempo – not theirs), the teacher will need to find some lessons in the book that have studies suitable for this purpose. (Possibly something with quite a few eighth notes and possibly some scale-wise passages, *arpeggios*, intervals, and studies.) Studies of this type can also be used with different bowing variations, rhythms, styles, etc. A good book to use for this purpose (written to correlate with Muller-Rusch String Method Book II), is *Muller-Rusch Etudes and Ensembles*. This book has etudes that offer the teacher many possibilities of developing more facility and speed. *Etudes and Ensembles* is written so that the student may play *either* a unison part or a harmony part. Before too long, by working regularly on the development of speed and facility from books such as these, the group will be secure and proficient at faster tempos and be about ready for some real orchestra playing.

USE OF SUPPLEMENTARY MATERIALS

As was mentioned in the beginning of this chapter, it is wise in the second year for the teacher to have the group frequently play some carefully selected supplementary music that correlates and reinforces the skills being learned in the class method book. This supplementary music should be longer, more melodic, and musically more appealing than the exercises and short pieces found in most method books, because the most important reason for using additional music is to help maintain the students' interest. The music should be fun, as well as challenging, but it must be easy enough so that it won't be necessary to use much of the class time to rehearse it.

Students at this level should be able to play Grade I materials quite easily and can also handle most Grade II materials *if* the teacher chooses carefully, has taught them thoroughly, and has covered the technical training advocated thus far.

When choosing music for this level, the teacher should attempt to find music that gives *each* instrument a challenging and interesting part. It should also be of the type that playing with musicianship really makes a difference. The teacher can then start teaching the students the importance of phrasing, playing with dynamics, bringing out the moving parts, etc. The second year should give them a "taste" of the concepts of playing more maturely – being conducted and playing with musicianship. If the "right" music is chosen, upon hearing it, the students will instinctively *know* that the music demands more than the right notes and rhythm.

CONCLUSION

By the end of the year, if the class has met two or three times a week, the students should have covered all the new things in whatever second year method book is being used. The new teacher must realize that this much material must be covered or the students will graduate to a larger secondary school orchestra, and they won't know the keys, rhythms, etc., necessary to play the music they should play comfortably at this level. If the class meets three or more days a week, it will not be difficult to cover this much material. If it meets less than three days a week, the teacher will need to leave out some of the material on every lesson and drill more thoroughly on the lines (or phrases) where new materials are presented. The students can't progress and improve if the material is skipped where new things are introduced. (It is poor teaching to play only the tunes and skip the exercises.)

If the teacher is so lucky that the class meets four or five days a week (often the case if the sixth grade is in a middle-school situation), then it would be wise for the group to go ahead and begin a third year method book that will allow shifting and vibrato to be taught to all. (All students should be taught vibrato no later than the third year.)

In summary, by the end of the second year of playing (if students are started in the fifth grade or later as advocated in this book), they should have learned the following new things:

(1) Be able to tune their instruments.

(2) Rhythm patterns of ♩. ♩; ♩ ♫; ♫ ♩.

(3) Time signature of 6/8.

(4) Bow styles and bowings of staccato, accent, hooked bowing, spiccato, long slurs, slurred string crossings, simple double-stops, and detaché.

(5) Keys of F, B-flat, E-flat, and A.

(6) Cello Extension and Extended Finger Pattern for Violin and Viola).

(7) Shifting (Cellos – Second Position, and Basses – Second Position.

(8) Half Position (String Basses).

(9) To play faster with facility.

There should be continued use of the "Drill Routine" to facilitate the learning of these new things, as well as additional work on the keys and rhythms learned in the first year. Use of the fourth finger for the violinists and violists should now be well-established. The students should be aware of and able to play with some amount of musicianship (phrasing, dynamics, moving parts brought out, etc.) and finesse as well as be fairly adept at following a conductor.

The Third-Year String Class 6

INTRODUCTION

The third year of playing (seventh grade) is very important because it usually marks the end of the time that the string students will be in a string class (string orchestra) rather than a full orchestra. Thus, this is the director's last year to work with them in a smaller group where individual attention can be easily given.

In a traditional school system (6-3-3), the seventh grade year brings together for the first time students from the various elementary schools expanding the group to an orchestra rather than a small string class. Playing in a large group makes it possible to develop for the first time a true feeling of what it is like to play in an orchestra.

String Orchestra or Full Orchestra?

Third year students will either participate in a full orchestra or a string orchestra, and the type of orchestra that they are in effects the kind of curriculum and activities that should be planned for them.

If the students are in a traditional junior high situation (usually 7, 8, or 9), the decision will have to be made as to whether the seventh grade students should participate in the performance oriented orchestra with the more experienced eighth and ninth grade students (who have played four or five years) or placed alone in a seventh grade training string orchestra. The authors feel that the latter is the best way provided that the enrollment of players in the eighth and ninth grade orchestra is large enough to have a string section of from thirty-five to forty students without third-year players. Keeping the third year players separate is best, because it allows the director to be sure that every string player can use vibrato, shift to higher positions, handle seven keys (D, G, C, F, B-flat, E-flat, and A) and understand the basic period styles (Baroque, Classical, Romantic, and Contemporary) before joining the full orchestra where there is participation in more performances, competitive events and performing with the winds.

If it is necessary to use the third year players in the larger, more mature performing orchestra, the director must find some way to teach the skills necessary to play in the full orchestra to the younger students *after* they join the group. Ideas for doing this are: (1) spend a few minutes at each string rehearsal (without the winds) working on the things that the younger players do not know. (A short review of things learned earlier doesn't really hurt the older students and, in fact, probably is a good idea even if the younger students do not play with the group.) A special technique book is recommended for this purpose. *Don't try to do this using the music that will be used in performance;* (2) set aside some time for a special rehearsal once a week (not the regular full rehearsal) to work with the younger students on learning the things that they are deficient in.

It may not be necessary for the teacher to worry about filling in the gaps with the younger students if, during the prior year, they were in a middle-school situation where the class met four or five days a week, and they were able to learn the additional skills necessary for playing in a full orchestra.

It must be realized that in some middle school situations (5, 6, 7) the seventh grade students (third year) will be the performance orchestra if the school is to have one. The authors feel strongly that every secondary level school should have a group that fills the role of the "top" group so the younger students will want to work hard so that they can become members of it in the future. Middle-school orchestras (if composed of string players in seventh and eighth grade) can and should play with winds although it probably should not be quite as often (especially first semester) as one would play with winds in a junior high group due to the time that will be needed to teach the skills needed for full-orchestra playing to the string players.

ACTIVITIES

The teacher needs to understand that at this age it will be necessary for the music program to include more activities of all kinds than it was necessary to have in the first and second year.

Musical

Due to the fact that the third year students are now in a large group, they should be taught all the things that they will need to play successfully in a full-fledged string orchestra (perhaps a full orchestra) which is much more performance-oriented than their string classes in the elementary schools.

The *seventh* grade orchestra should participate in several types of concert activities during a school year. Some ideas are:

(1) Join with the seventh grade band and play a concert once or twice a year.

(2) Play a number or two alone on a concert with the full orchestra (eighth and ninth grade) once or twice a year. (Possibly join with them and play a number together.)

(3) Play recruiting-type concerts at the elementary schools.

(4) Play special concerts at such places as hospitals, nursing homes, etc., at Christmas time or at any other time of year that they can be scheduled.

(5) Participate in the All-City or All-Area Elementary String Festival by performing alone as the Honor group representing the secondary level. This kind of appearance gives the parents and younger students a chance to see what is ahead when these students graduate to seventh grade.

(6) Enter the district contest (festival) if the state activities association allows this age group to participate.

The director of this group should realize that this orchestra *must* be much more active, both musically and socially than the elementary classes were. The teacher must endeavor constantly to schedule activities that will challenge the students as well as build group pride in playing well and participating as a member of the orchestra. The students should look forward to being in this class and be very proud of it.

Supplementary Music

Because this group will present more concerts than the students did while in elementary school, there will be much more need for supplementary string orchestra music that is suitable for performance. At this level, about half the class time should be spent continuing to develop and expand basic playing technique, and the other half of the time on some well-chosen string orchestra music that reinforces the string techniques being learned in drill portions of rehearsals. There are two good ways to split up the time evenly between working on technique building materials and performance type string orchestra music. The first way is to spend the first half of the rehearsal on technical materials and the last half on string orchestra music. The second way is to work Monday, Wednesday and Friday on technique materials and Tuesday and Thursday on performance music one week and then the next week vice-versa. It is felt that the first plan is probably best because it doesn't ask that the students dwell on "drier" materials so long that they get bored.

Technique Books

As well as planning for some correlated string orchestra music, the director will need to decide on the books that will be used to work on raising the technical level of the group. Book III of the Muller-Rusch String Class Method and Etudes and Ensembles in the Muller-Rusch Series are good basic texts to use for this purpose.

Social Events

At this age, the students seem to enjoy occasionally having some kind of "get-together" as a group. This does not need to be anything very fancy and can most easily be done by letting the group plan it for themselves. It is suggested that the group elect officers to work with the director on planning such activities. Some ideas for social events might be: (1) coke and cookie party following a concert; (2) Christmas party or Christmas carolling; (3) poster parties; (4) fund-raising events and (5) end of year picnics, etc. Letting students get together socially helps the group to develop the feeling of "team-spirit" that is essential in developing the morale of a fine performing group.

CLASS ORGANIZATION

There are some additional and unrelated organizational details that will need to be thought about and planned for the seventh grade orchestra. These are: (1) choosing uniforms, (2) promoting full-size, quality instruments, (3) scheduling of sectionals and try-outs for chair seating; and (4) providing for ensemble playing.

Uniforms

A uniform appearance for concerts can contribute much to help build an image of self-confidence and esteem in a performing group. The authors have found that if a group looks nice it seems to have a positive effect on how the group feels about itself and how well it plays.

For young groups like a seventh grade orchestra, the dress for concerts needn't be too fancy or formal. Some ideas that have been used for groups of this age include: (1) vests for both the boys and girls; (2) blazers in school colors for both boys and girls worn with slacks and skirts in coordinating color; (3) dress-up dresses (girls) and coat, tie, and dress slacks (boys), etc.

Full-Sized, Quality Instruments

Beginning with this year, it is very important to encourage the students who are large enough for full-fized instruments to start getting them. If the director doesn't "bug" the students about going to large instruments they will go on playing on the smaller instruments clear through high school. Students playing on instruments that are too small, not only look terrible, but can greatly reduce the amount and quality of tone that the orchestra produces.

The teacher must also realize that student-line instruments, even if full-sized, have a limited amount of tone. So, it is important that whenever students outgrow the small-size instruments that they be encouraged to move up to instruments of higher quality – usually called "step-up" instruments. For the non-string player working with orchestras, it must be pointed out that there will be a much more noticeable difference in tone between student-line stringed instruments and the higher quality stringed instruments than there was between student-line wind instruments and top-line wind instruments. Thus, if the director wants the group to sound mature tone-wise, the better stringed instruments are a necessity.

Sectionals

No matter what year in the students' musical development they begin participating in a group that is more of an orchestra than a string class, both sectionals and try-outs for chair seating will be necessary. The reason for this is that an orchestra-type group should be more of a performance centered group than a technique-building class, and for performance, sectionals and the seating of the orchestra can have a significant effect.

Why Are Sectionals Needed?

In order for regularly scheduled rehearsals with the full group to be spent mainly working on problems that concern all the string players, it is suggested that sectionals be scheduled whenever the director needs to work on problems pertaining to only one of the string sections. Such things as giving out bowings, fingerings, helping the students with difficult note passages and/or having try-outs for chair seating are best handled in sections rather than full-group rehearsals so that many students don't have to sit idle while a few students in a section work on a spot. Avoid all inefficient use of class time.

TRY-OUTS

Try-outs should be used as needed to check students to make sure they are improving, as well as help them to get over the fear of playing alone. The authors feel that either excessive use of, or no try-outs at all can be detrimental to the progress of the students. Not checking and/or grading occasionally can lead to students not practicing at all outside of class because no one ever hears them. However, hearing them too often sometimes causes the students to be too competitive. The authors feel that string students must be seated so that the orchestra sounds best and not necessarily in the order of the students' abilities. Some type of a "buddy" system might be a better solution – a weak and a strong student sitting together. Since string players most generally will play in large sections, they must realize that their chair is not nearly as important as their individual progress. (For more information on chair-seating refer to Chapter VII in Part II – Group Rehearsals.)

When Scheduled? – There are several possibilities for times that sectionals can be scheduled. When they will be scheduled will depend on the individual school system and/or buildings. The ideal, of course, would be to use another class hour than the regularly-scheduled class time, but in most school systems, due to crowded schedules at this level, students don't have the time to schedule another period for orchestra. Most teachers solve the problem by holding sections before or after school, during a lunch period or evenings.

Sectionals probably will not be needed for each string section more than once a month with young groups. Sections are most helpful fairly soon after the students have been given new music so that the teacher can help them to know how to go about learning to play it.

Private Study

To have top-notch performance groups, private lessons are needed to insure that the orchestra will have enough students capable of filling at least the leadership positions. Private lessons are also necessary to help slower students who may be having problems keeping up with the other students.

Unless the teacher encourages private lessons constantly, students just will not get started taking lessons. A good idea is for the teacher to call the parents of both the students showing a greal deal of talent and those that need more help and explain to them the values that can be gained from their children studying privately. Many times, they are just not aware of their child's talent or problems but would be very willing to have him take lessons if it was just suggested to them. It is also a good idea for the teacher to try to make sure that the private teachers that the students study with are those who will reinforce the school teaching. Otherwise, there can be a conflict between the philosophy of the teaching at school and that of the private teachers. This can be very confusing and discouraging to the student and should not be allowed to happen.

Ensembles

If the teacher's schedule allows time for the coaching of string ensembles, these ensembles can be a very valuable teaching tool to help train leaders for the orchestra. Students playing in ensembles at this age (with no previous ensemble experience) must be carefully guided until they are well-grounded in the principles of playing in an ensemble.

To save time and give more students a chance to play in ensembles, it is a good idea to schedule such groups as duets, trios, and quartets with two people on a part. After the students understand how playing in an ensemble works, they can be split into smaller groups (one on a part). (The director must also understand that even though it may take a while before the students will really sound very good when broken down into small ensembles (one on a part), it is still a good experience for the students to play one on a part.)

THE TEACHING

Some review of what the students learned in the second year will probably be necessary, especially if most of the students are not studying privately or playing in orchestra classes held in the summer. (The wise teacher encourages the students to continue playing in the summer.)

As a student progresses, the number of things that they must know constantly increases. Because the human mind tends to forget things previously learned when learning something new, the teacher must constantly keep referring back to all of the old things to prevent the students from forgetting them.

Many third-year books will use the first few lessons as a review of the new materials that were learned in the second year. No matter what type of review the teacher plans to use, it is often possible to find some easy string orchestra tunes that work well as part of the review of the keys and rhythms learned the year before. At all times however the teacher must be sure that the students feel that they are progressing.

This review should include the keys and finger positions (all registers) that were newly learned in the second year – the keys of F, B-flat, E-flat, and A (the students will now know seven keys). Review of these keys will necessitate work on the extensions (cello) and shifting to different positions (cello and bass – the second position, and basses – the half position).

The review should also include the two new rhythm patterns ♩. ♪ ; ♩ ♫) as well as the 6/8 time signature. There should also be continued work on the two basic tones – "Resonant" and "Intense," as well as on the new bowing techniques (staccato, accent, hooked bowing, spiccato). The bow techniques of long slurs, slurred string crossings, simple double stops and detache should also be reviewed.

Class Tuning

By the end of the third year, the students should be able to tune fairly quickly and if handled as advocated in this book (see Part II, Chapter III), the group should be able to begin playing five minutes after the class has started. At this level, it will still be necessary for the group to tune each string separately with the students first listening to the sounded tone, humming the tone and then as quickly and quietly as possible, tuning the appropriate string. The students should be taught to drop out as soon as the string they are all tuning agrees with the hummed pitch. The teacher must continually push the students to try to tune very quickly or the group will dally and take up the whole class period in tuning. Unless a student has a problem with an instrument, the teacher should *never* tune the students' instruments at this level. The students will be very glad to let the teacher tune their instruments forever if the teacher is available to do it.

New Materials

Rhythm Patterns

SIXTEENTHS

Since students must be ready at the end of this year to play in an orchestra with winds where the strings will often need to play fast, technical passages, they need to be introduced to playing 16th notes in various rhythmic patterns.

Just as the students were taught to play unslurred 8th notes with less bow (half or less) than notes of more value, so should they be taught that 16th notes will use even less bow than 8th notes. They should be taught to play unslurred 16th notes with no more than one-fourth of the bow – which part of the bow will depend on the style and dynamic level of the music. Generally it is easiest for string players to play sixteenths more in the middle of the bow where loose finger and wrist action is possible. Students should first be taught to play continuous 16th notes before mixing them up with other note values.

Once the students can play 16ths rhythmically and accurately and with loose, relaxed finger motion, then the director can introduce the rhythm patterns found in most third year method books. Some of these are as shown in Figure No. 1 below.

Rhythmic Patterns
Figure No. 1

In all the rhythmic patterns in Figure No. 1, the player should use no more than one-fourth of the bow on the sixteenths and one-half of the bow on the eighth notes. Strong accents on the beat will help to keep the students together. The patterns shown here would be easiest played by starting about in the middle of the bow where some finger motion can be used.

The next rhythmic pattern that should be taught to the students is the dotted eighth note followed by a sixteenth (♪. ♬). This is perhaps the most important, but most difficult of all those that the director must teach because it is used continually in orchestral music.

The students should be taught to play the dotted eighth followed by a sixteenth pattern first in legato style – slurred (♪. ♬). The students must realize that the pattern is equal to four sixteenth notes (dotted eighth note equals three and the sixteenth one). It can either be counted: "One e and a" or in groups of four – whichever the teacher finds best. The authors have found that a good way to teach this rhythm pattern is to have one-half of the group play the first pattern shown below while the other half plays the second pattern. They can then trade parts. The goal will be for those that are playing Figure "B" to change to the sixteenth note exactly when those playing the Figure "A" play their fourth sixteenth notes. (See Figure No. 2.) At first it may be necessary to use separate bows (take out the slurs) to allow the students to play the rhythm properly.

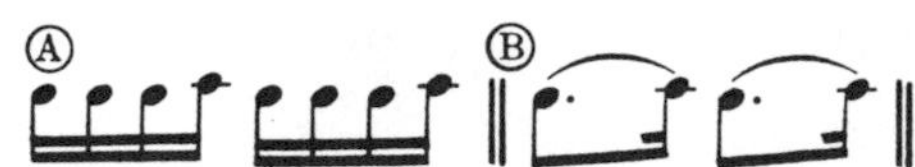

Learning Rhythm Patterns
Figure No. 2

After the students can play the dotted eighth followed by sixteenth note pattern accurately with a legato, slurred style, they should then be taught to play the same pattern with a detached staccato style. The teacher should use the same basic technique to get the students to play the staccato style of this rhythm pattern as was used for the legato style *except* there will now be a rest in place of the third sixteenth as shown in Figure No. 3.

Written Played

Dotted Eighth and Sixteenth Pattern
Figure No. 3

Hooked Bowing – The teacher must be sure that the bow is stopped on the string during the imaginary rest created between the dotted eighth and sixteenth and then pulled again the same direction after the rest. This "hooked" bowing will be used a great deal on this rhythm pattern in orchestral playing. Whether to use legato or detached (hooked) style in playing music is a matter to be decided by the taste of the director *and* the style of the music.

THE TEACHING OF VIBRATO

Introduction

Once the students have mastered the keys that should have been learned in the second year (F, B-flat, E-flat and A), their fingers should be strong enough to begin working a few moments each day on vibrato. If the teacher approaches it correctly and positively (with the attitude that it is easy), the students will enjoy their "graduation" into the more advanced areas of string playing. By now, even if it is not pointed out to them, they will have observed the "polish" and beauty that vibrato adds to the sound of the music from hearing groups play on radio, television or in live performances. The learning of vibrato should be an exciting step for the students, and they will be anxious to learn it if the teacher has correctly prepared them technically and psychologically. The teacher should never say or imply in any way that vibrato will be difficult, as this will cause them to be afraid of learning to do it.

The fingers must be independently strong before vibrato can be started because only one finger at a time is used in vibrato (except in unusual cases). Since only one finger at a time is used, each finger has to be strong enough to hold the string down firmly by itself.

Before vibrato can be introduced, the class must be able to play with fairly consistent and accurate intonation. Their ears need to have been developed to the point that they know when they are out of tune. They also need to have been trained to adjust the pitch as a group. It is essential that they know how to do this, because the learning of vibrato causes the basic intonation of the class to be insecure for a while. It is imperative that the class at least knows that it is out of tune even though they may not be able to do much about correcting the situation during the early stages of learning vibrato.

The teacher should plan on spending about five or ten minutes *daily* teaching the students to vibrate. A good time to do this is when the students are tired or bored with the regular routine of learning technical materials. Vibrato can be taught to the whole class at the same time if the teacher is aware that there are *two* basic vibrato techniques – one for the violinist and violist and another one for the cellist and bassist.

VIOLIN AND VIOLA

Generally speaking, there are three basic vibratos used today by violinists and violists – hand (wrist), arm and finger. Although they will all be used to some extent, no matter which one the player prefers, one will be the dominant one.[1]

HAND VIBRATO

The authors feel that the hand (wrist) vibrato is the one that the students should be taught in a class situation as it is a logical compromise between the very large movement of the arm vibrato and the very small movement of the finger vibrato.

It is absolutely necessary before teaching vibrato that the teacher: (1) make sure that the students have shoulder pads that hold the instrument securely in place; (2) be sure that the students are not holding up instruments with their left hands because it needs to be free to make the "swing" of the vibrato motion; and (3) if the students are still placing the lower joint of the index finger against the neck of the instrument, it must now be taken away so that there is a space between the finger and the neck of the instrument.

PREPARATORY STEPS TO VIBRATO (VIOLIN AND VIOLA)

Sliding in Rhythm – The steps to teaching vibrato to the violin and viola students are:

(1) Have them hold up their left hands and pretend that they are waving good-bye to someone with just their wrists.

(2) Have them next turn the left hands around and wave good-bye to themselves.

(3) Have them place their right hand firmly around the left wrist so that they will not be able to move anything but the hand.

(4) While holding the wrist have them swing or rotate the hand back and forth while their fingers and hand simi-late a normal playing position.

[1]Galamian, Ivan. *Principles of Violin Playing and Teaching,* Prentice-Hall, Englewood Cliffs, N. J. 1962, p. 37.

(5) Keeping the hand in the position as described in steps (3) and (4) "swing" the hand back and forth (pivoting from the wrist) in a steady rhythm while the teacher counts: "1 and 2 and 3 and 4 and." When the students can do this much, the teacher should ask them to observe carefully the swing of their hand going back and forth and then explain to the students that this is the motion that will be used in the actual playing of vibrato on the instrument.

This would probably be enough work on vibrato for the first day with the violinists and violists. The teacher should next move to showing the cellists and bassists the basic motion of their vibratos.

PREPARATORY STEPS TO VIBRATO (CELLO AND BASS)

As with the violin and viola, it is possible on the cello and bass to vibrate either with the hand (wrist) or the arm. However, almost all authorities at the present time agree that the basic vibrato motion for the cello and bass should come from the elbow with the entire lower arm moving as a unit. This type of motion, rather than the predominantly wrist one, gives a wider and freer vibration that most prefer on lower pitched instruments.

It is easy for cellists and bassists to learn to vibrato quickly if they are told that the basic motion is similar to that of sliding from one position to another. First, the teacher can ask the students to make this motion away from the neck of the instruments pointing out for them to observe that the arm, wrist and fingers should be sliding together as a unit. Next, they should be asked to make the same basic sliding motion with the thumb and second finger pressed against something (as if the instrument is being held). A good way to do this is have the students bend their right arm and put it in the middle of their chest (like the fingerboards) then put the left thumb behind and the second finger on the top and lightly slide the left arm up and down an inch or so in each direction. After they can do this, they should be told to try to make the same motion with the arm again but now to lightly press with the thumb and index finger and *not* to slide up and down. At this point, the teacher must carefully check each student to be sure that the arm, wrist, and fingers are still moving as a unit. The cello and bass vibrato must *not* look like the turning of a door knob! It might be helpful to mention that the cello and bass vibrato motion is very similar to the motion that a trumpet player uses when doing a hand vibrato.

STEPS TO VIBRATO WITH INSTRUMENTS (VIOLIN AND VIOLA)

The second time the teacher works on vibrato with the group, it might be well to review the steps that both the violinists and violists and the cellists and bassists learned the first day before going on to add any new steps. After some review, the students should be ready to start learning to do some vibrato on their instruments. The steps are:

(1) Place the instrument into correct position for playing (no bows, however).

(2) Have the students hold up the instruments *without* the aid of the left hands (holding with only the shoulder).

(3) Next, to be sure that the students know exactly where their palms are, have them show the palms of their hands to the teacher.

(4) They should then rest the bottom part of their palms against the shoulders of their instruments. (The teacher should not worry if the students' thumbs are now a little more under the neck of the instruments than is normal for playing.

(5) Have them swing their left hands and fingers back and forth freely (towards the bridge and back). (Make sure that their palms stay against the shoulder of the instruments and that there is no movement of the arms.)

(6) Next, ask them to curve their second fingers and lightly put them down on the lowest string about where the neck joins the body of the instrument.

(7) Next, ask them to lightly slide their curved fingers freely up and down their lowest string. (Be sure that they don't try to press the string clear down to the fingerboard.) It will also be necessary for the teacher to check each student to make sure that the wrist is still swinging back and forth (pivoting) while the second finger slides on the string and, that the bottom of the palm of the hand rests against the instrument and does not move.

(8) After all students can do step (7) correctly, then they should slide their hands back and forth in a *measured rhythm* while counting: "One and two and three and four and" and tapping their feet in the correct down and up fashion.

At this point, after the teacher has made sure that each violinist and violist can slide back and forth on the string while swinging the wrist, he can ask them to continue working on their own in the same way while the teacher introduces vibrato (on the instruments) to the cellists and bassists.

STEPS TO VIBRATO WITH INSTRUMENTS (CELLOS AND BASSES)

After the students are fairly proficient at producing the correct vibrato motion away from the instrument it should be started on the instrument. The teacher should have the students put their arms into fourth position (at the end of the neck where it joins the body of the instrument). Remind them to keep the thumb lightly pressed against the neck. Have them slide an inch or so in each direction as they did on their arms earlier to be sure everything moves together as a unit. Next, have them put their second fingers down lightly on the string (cello C-string and bass E-string) opposite the thumb, and without sliding the hand, try to make the same motion as they were making when sliding. At this point, the students will probably need some individual help from the teacher as some will no doubt begin to make a rolling, semi-circular motion rather than the up and down motion desired. The teacher can keep the students from doing this by taking hold of the students' wrists and moving them in the correct way until they can see and feel how it should be done. Holding on to their wrist keeps them from making a rolling, semi-circular motion with the hand. The students can be taught to hold their left arms like the teacher did. At this point, the cellos and basses can continue working on their own while the teacher works further with the violins and violas.

VIBRATO MOTION (VIOLINS AND VIOLAS)

The teacher should have the students now slide the second finger back and forth just a little bit so that it is almost staying in one place. They will need to be reminded that the palm of the hand should still rest against the instrument and that the wrist should still swing. When the finger stays in one place, the vibrato becomes predominantly a rocking motion *around* the end (tip) of the finger. It is helpful for the teacher to put his hand around each student's finger and help rock the finger for him. This way, the student can both see and feel how it is to be done. The students can be told to do this for themselves as if the teacher was doing it for them.

USING THE BOW WHILE DOING VIBRATO

The students should not be allowed to use the bow while doing vibrato until the basic motion is correct, fairly automatic, and they feel mentally secure about using it. To prepare them to use the bow while doing vibrato, it is best to have them all find the same note with their second finger somewhere on the G-string (in the third or fourth position). Have them hold this tone without vibrato, then next, while counting in a divided beat, have them rotate their hands back and forth to the subdivision of the beat (one and two and, etc.). Once the left hands are vibrating correctly, they can then pick up their bows and play. The sound heard should be an even, *obvious* "pulsing" of the beat in rhythm with the counting. They should be told to not worry about what the bow does – to just change to another bow whenever it is needed. The teacher must be very particular about making the class pulse the vibrato evenly together. They should be told continually to exaggerate the bigness of the physical motion back and forth so that an obvious pitch difference is heard. This helps to overcome their natural tendency to want to go too fast and rotate too narrowly. *Warning:* Allowing a fast, narrow motion to develop in the first few months of using vibrato will keep the students from ever developing a good sounding mature vibrato later on. *Never* allow them to speed up the vibrato in the early months.

LEARNING OTHER FINGERS

Once the students can play vibrato fairly well with the second finger, they are ready to start using the other fingers one at a time with the same preparatory steps used for second finger. The first finger should be taught next as it will be the strongest and easiest for the students to control. It should then be followed by the third and then the fourth finger.

After the students can vibrate slowly and evenly on every finger while still in the higher position, the teacher should next have them play scale-like passages (using the different fingers) in whole notes being sure that an obvious pulse is heard. After the students can play some scale-like passages in whole notes slowly, a little faster tempo can be attempted.

USING VIBRATO IN FIRST POSITION

Once the students are fairly secure playing with vibrato on every finger in higher positions (probably about third position), their fingers should be strong enough to move the vibrato back to first position. In first position there will no longer be support for the left hand against the body of the instrument. The teacher needs to know that it will not be possible to just move the vibrato to first position and stay there – for security it will be necessary to still practice in the higher positions frequently. The same steps can be used in first position that were used in first learning vibrato in the higher position – second finger, then first finger followed by the third and fourth finger. Until the students gain some strength using vibrato in first position, they should only be expected to use it in places where there are half or whole notes and they have time to start the vibrato.

Important Points Concerning Vibrato (All Instruments)

The teacher will need to observe the students closely *every* minute that they are working on vibrato as it is truly amazing how many incorrect ways they can find to do the vibrato. If allowed to practice incorrectly, the students will develop bad habits that are almost impossible to break, and it should be realized that a bad vibrato is much worse than no vibrato at all.

After the students have learned the correct motion for vibrato, it will be necessary to work about five minutes a day practicing it together as a class. This means that they will tap their feet and count aloud: "One and two and three and four and" and vibrate in rhythm with the counting. The teacher must remember that only a *slow*, measured vibrato should be used for several months. Asking them to go faster than it is possible for them to count: "one and two and three and four and" will result in a tense, tight "nanny-goat" style vibrato that is not satisfactory at all. Watch very carefully during the learning of vibrato to make sure that they don't try to do it too fast. They will want to go faster with it *but* they must *not* be allowed to.

Learning to Shift (All Instruments)

In the first year, just the basses were required to do some shifting while in the second year, both the cellos and basses needed to shift (cellos – second position, and basses – half, II and III). However, in the third year, *all* of the students will need to learn to shift to some higher positions. It is very important that a book be chosen that teaches all instruments to shift together at the same time, on the same finger, to the same position, in unison, to keep the teacher from wanting to give up the whole idea of teaching a group to shift. It *is* practically impossible and very disturbing to keep track of a large group of students if they are all trying to do something different.

ROTE SHIFTING

An exercise should be made out of shifting from first position to whatever higher position is going to be learned by the whole group. Most books will present third position first, as it is the one that the violins and violas need to learn to be able to play higher notes (top string) that will occur first in their orchestra music. (For an explanation of how the positions are numbered, the reader should refer to Chapter III, The Second Year String Class.) The group will first learn to play in third position on the D and A strings, as these are the two strings that are common to all instruments. The rote exercise the teacher uses to learn to shift should have the group slide on their first fingers from the lower position (first) to the higher position (third) such as shown in Figure No. 4.

Shifting on First Finger to Third Position
(All Instruments)
Figure No. 4

The basic rules that must be adhered to in learning shifting are:

(1) The whole hand and arm must move as a unit when shifting from one position to another (they should never be allowed to leave the thumb in first position and slide only the playing fingers).

(2) The sliding finger should be pressed lightly into the string during the slide so the two positions can be connected together (they should never be allowed to "hop" from one position to another).

(3) Slide slowly on the shifting finger to make it possible to hear where to stop (later the sound of the slide can be disguised somewhat).

If the teacher is not insistent on seeing to it that *every* student follows the basic rules of shifting at all times, the group will never learn to successfully shift accurately from one position to another.

After the students can move slowly from first to third position fairly comfortably, the teacher can have the students play an exercise where they are required to shift a little faster between the two positions. At this point, it is usually best to write the rote exercise on the board so that the students will start to get used to shifting and reading at the same time. An exercise similar to the one shown in Figure No. 5 is suggested:

Learning to Shift Faster and Reading
Figure No. 5

It has been found that students can best accomplish early shifting if slurs are used to connect the change of position. Once this exercise has been done, the teacher should find some exercises in the method book where students move from first to third position.

Learning the Other Fingers in Third Position

When the students can slide back and forth from first to third position fairly well in the book, they are ready to learn to play the other fingers that will be found in the third position by rote. Third position notes which each finger will play on all of the instruments on their D-strings are shown in Figure No. 6.

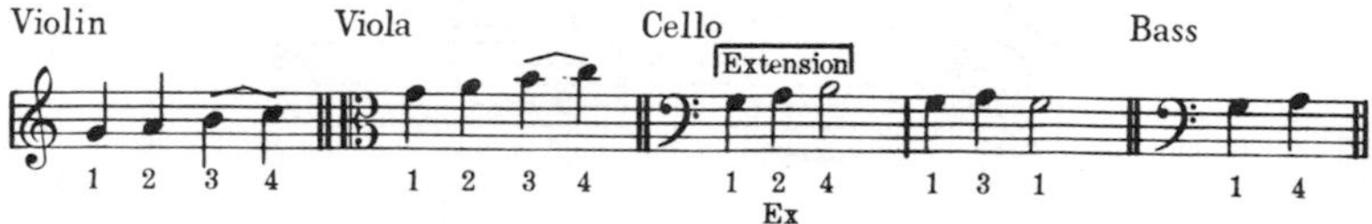

Examples of Some Notes in Third Position
(All Instruments)
Figure No. 6

As will be noticed by looking at Figure No. 6, the students will need to be made aware of where the half and whole steps are in the finger patterns so that they will understand where the extensions occur. (For a detailed explanation of the Extension, see Chapter II.) The reader will notice that there are two different fingerings for A on the cello. Note: When the player is going to play up to a B, the extended second finger must be used to finger A, whereas if the player is not going up to B, the A will be played with third finger.

The students will need to be told that they will be expected to memorize the fingerings in third position just as they have memorized those in the first position. Playing some rote exercises using the notes in third position are suggested before the teacher goes to the book to play these notes.

Third Position Notes – All Strings

Once the students are fairly secure at reading and playing all the notes in third position on the D-string, third position should be introduced on the A-string using the same approach as was used on the D-string. After this, the remaining two strings should be introduced in the same manner. The same techniques should also be used in introducing any other positions that need to be learned.

Rules for Shifting Where a Change of Finger is Involved

A way, accepted by most string authorities, to teach a shift where the slide is started on one finger and ending on a different finger in the new position, is to use the following rule: When leaving a position (either up or down), always begin the slide on the last finger used in the position that is being left and continue sliding on that finger until almost into the new position before changing to the finger needed in the new position. If executed properly, a grace-note like sound will be heard when done slowly.

Further Thoughts About Shifting

Many people fear the teaching of shifting because they feel that it is too difficult for students to learn in a class situation. This is not true – it is much easier to teach than it is to tell about it in this book. If this is done regularly in class (two or three times a week – 15 or 20 minutes) the teacher can expect that after two or three months their students will be able to use this technique in the literature they plan to perform. At first, however, the teacher will have to pick music that only goes into higher positions for relatively short amounts of time.

It must be remembered that to teach this technique efficiently to the whole group, it is far better to use a technique book where all learn to shift at once in unison rather than to try to teach the shifting through the concert music. Also, the teacher must not forget that the students will need much repetition on each new shift learned (use the "Drill Routine").

If the students are thoroughly taught how to shift and play in *one* higher position, they will be able to learn others quite easily, as they will understand the basic principles of how playing in the positions works.

Rudiments of String Playing for the Basic Period Styles

It is very important that the third year students learn to do more with the music than to just play the notes and rhythms. As well as following a conductor and being aware of the dynamics and phrasing in a composition, they should also learn that it is their responsibility to play in the correct style for each period. This means teaching them what the four main periods are and how they affect the way music is performed. Therefore, it will be the director's duty to try throughout the year to select a piece or two from each of the periods so the students can start to learn to play in such styles. Later on, they should recognize and know automatically how to play each style without being reminded by the teacher.

Baroque Period – Students will mainly need to be taught how to play the *faster* movements, because the slower, more lyrical Baroque movements do not require any different techniques of playing than are used in the slower movements in any other style.

Fast movements with non-slurred moving notes will require a very fast and energetic staccato bow stroke in order to duplicate the resonant sound characteristic of the Baroque stringed instruments (the Viols). There should be a space between each note, and this can only be accomplished if the bow is pulled very fast and then stopped. The teacher should realize that this is a fairly difficult bow stroke to teach to young groups. They have a tendency to rush, because they don't want to wait long enough between notes. If the teacher insists on the students using plenty of bow on each note, they will not be as apt to rush.

The director should also teach the students that the "pulse" of the music is especially important in the Baroque period and consequently, it should be very rhythmic. This will mean that they should be trained to play with much accent on the first beat, and that the end of every measure should move into the next measure. Students can easily remember how to play Baroque music if they are told that it is kind of like Rock music that has much emphasis on the driving, accompanying rhythms.

The students will love to play Baroque music, because it is rhythmic, fun, and is often technically not too difficult for them. This music seems to really relate to young orchestras, and will probably be their favorite of all the serious styles.

In order to play Baroque music authentically, the students should be taught that the bow should never be bounced, although there may well be times later on when the teacher might choose to play certain passages off the string for lightness or some other desired musical effect.

Classical Period – For music of the Classical period, the students must be taught that off-the-string playing (spiccato) will be used a great deal. Off-the-string playing is almost always required in non-slurred passages in faster movements. The passages requiring spiccato playing will often be scale-like passages, an accompanying figure, or repeated notes. (Eighth notes almost always will be played off-the-string while quarter notes occasionally will be off-the-string depending on the context of the music.) Sixteenth notes are usually too fast to be played cleanly off-the-string, and it is best to teach students that sixteenths should always be played on the string. If there is to be an exception, teacher will make it.

Explain to the students that Classical music is basically more delicate than the other three period styles and this is why an off-the-string spiccato stroke is generally required. For detailed explanation of how to teach spiccato playing see Spiccato section of Chapter III. In review, the teacher must remember a young group will have more control of the bow on spiccato if they are asked to bounce five or six inches from the frog (lower third rather than more towards the middle of the bow). To begin to bounce the bow, the students must be trained to raise the bow above the string and then lightly drop it on the string while making an arc shape motion with the fingers. The teacher should be sure that the beginning students play spiccato with a soft, light tone, being careful to bounce no more than an inch off of the string. The motion they will make with the fingers will look something like that shown in Figure No. 7.

Arc-Shape Motion Used for Spiccato
Figure No. 7

A Word of Caution: While students will really enjoy learning to play this style of music, and of course, it should be used, the teacher should realize that Classical music is not a particularly good choice for an appearance where the students are to be adjudicated. This is true because, until a group has had a year or two of experience playing some short spiccato passages off the string under pressure, they probably won't have enough maturity and bow control to carry it off without some problems no matter how well they play it in rehearsal. It takes some time and maturity before a group can come off well under pressure with a long section of spiccato playing.

Romantic Period – Understanding the style characteristics of the Romantic period and how the bow is to be used to play in this style is very easy to teach because nothing new must be learned. Most Romantic style music is lush and requires a big full sound. If students have been taught the two basic tones – "Resonant" and "Intense" – they should have the techniques needed for characteristic romantic playing. If a resonant, ringing tone is desired, the conductor should request them to play with full bow strokes. If a more intense, louder tone is desired they should be asked to play with a slower bow stroke, more pressure, and closer to the bridge.

In training a young group to understand the basic period styles, the authors have found that it is probably best for them to think of Romantic style music as being played with a very resonant tone (full bow strokes) so that the music is visually interesting as well as full sounding. However, it must be made very clear to them that this doesn't mean a full bow is to be used on all notes, but only on the notes of longer duration where there is time to use a full bow – quarter, halve, dotted halve, etc. Students should never be told to use full bows on unslurred fast passages of eighths or sixteenths but rather stress that a shorter bow stroke must be used (half or fourth of the bow at most). Also, if the conductor wants a more passionate or intense sound, they should be ready to change to their "Intense Tone" with less bow. Another idea to impart to the students is that romantic music must look like they are really involved and working hard.

Use of vibrato is also very important in Romantic styled music, and students will need to be encouraged to use it whenever there are notes long enough to utilize it (whole, dotted halves, half, and sometimes quarter notes). Daily practice of vibrato for about 5 to 10 minutes will pay off very quickly in the group being able to vibrato. The group must be continually watched to see that the vibrato motion is slow, even, and done with the correct motion, or a nice-sounding vibrato can never result!

Contemporary Period – The director may find that it is difficult to find much good serious contemporary music written for young orchestras, but it is a style the students really do enjoy and certainly need to be taught to play.

Most of the techniques required to play the Contemporary style of music will already have been learned or will be very easy for them to learn. For instance, this style of music often requires them to play with a more harsh or brittle sound than is normally used in the other style periods. So, the director may want to request that pizzicato passages be played with a harsh, brittle pizzicato. The students should be encouraged to experiment with different sounding pizzicatos by plucking the string in different places and different ways. Sometimes this music will want the string plucked so hard it snaps against the fingerboard. "Intense Tone" (playing closer to bridge) may be used more frequently and sometimes *ponticello* will be called for where they should play so close to the bridge that a marsh, ugly sound results.

Sometimes this music will call for *glissandi* (sliding the finger on the string from one note to another) and open-string *harmonics* (lightly pressing the string down an octave above the open string) for unusual sound effects. Harmonics will usually be notated as shown in Figure No. 8.

Open-String Harmonics on G-String
Figure No. 8

The example above shows the harmonic one-octave above the G-string on all four instruments. They are played by lightly pressing down the finger shown on the second note of each example at the mid-point of the open string that is shown on the first note (violin and viola – fourth finger, and cell and bass – third finger). A note one octave above the open string should be heard. All other open-string harmonics will work the same way.

One other string technique that the director may want to use in contemporary music is the spiccato. When using spiccato in Contemporary music, a harsher, louder tone may better fit this style. This can be achieved by asking the students to bounce the bow with a heavier and more vigorous bow stroke that will be more percussive than in the other period styles.

For all the string effects mentioned for use in Contemporary style music, solid, firm pressure of the left hand is also a necessity to give the effects that are being attempted with the right hand.

Developing Facility

The last area of technical training that will need some time periodically throughout the third year is the development of facility in order for the string students to really be ready to successfully handle full orchestra music. The word, facility, to a string player, means being able to move around from string to string and position to position with some degree of accuracy, cleanness and, at least, a moderate tempo. To do this, it is necessary for the students to play some unison etudes that have scale-like passages covering all four strings as well as some that may have arpeggio or interval patterns for all ranges of the instruments. In teaching these etudes that will probably be found in most third books, the director should gradually work from a slow tempo to a tempo fast enough to make it difficult for most of the students to keep up.

The new rhythm patterns that were introduced earlier in this year should be found in some of the etudes included in a good third year book. Reinforcement by further work on these new rhythms is a good idea and will help the students to be secure when playing them. Some of the basic new rhythms to review that would be good to use are shown in Figure No. 9.

Rhythm Patterns to Review
Figure No. 9

Drill on etudes that are planned to develop facility must not be slighted in this last year of string orchestra, or the technique level of the full orchestra in the fourth year will suffer.

By now, it is normal that the string students have tired of the string class situation no matter how large it is and, they will be anxious to join a group that offers more variety both musically and socially. If the third year materials are taught correctly, the students should be ready in every way to join a performance-oriented full orchestra.

The third year students should be at home in seven keys (up to three flats and three sharps), able to play in key signatures of 2/4, 3/4, 4/4, and 6/8, as well as play most of the basic rhythm patterns needed for most junior high orchestra music. They should be able to play with quite a bit of facility and handle short, technically-difficult passages.

They should also have developed the ability to follow a conductor, understand phrasing, dynamics and the four, basic period and style characteristics and how to play them. Vibrato and shifting should also be coming along, although this will need continued attention in the next two or three years.

In conclusion, all of the basic concepts of music, as well as the needed techniques for orchestra playing, should have been fairly well-taught and understood by the end of the third year, so that from now on, the most important goal of orchestra membership will be to enjoy creating music together.

The Junior High Orchestra 7

INTRODUCTION

The fourth and fifth years (the fourth year in the case of a middle school) of the orchestra program will essentially be a consolidation of the fundamentals previously learned. "Resonant" and "Intense" sound, bow placement (between fingerboard and bridge), bowing parallel with the bridge (straight), proper right and left hand position, placement of the fingers on the left hand into the proper patterns for the keys of F, B-flat, E-flat, C, G, D, and A, the use of vibrato and shifting will still have to be stressed constantly during both of these years.

Two new keys, however, need to be introduced and learned during these years. To be able to play the standard orchestra literature before high school, the string students will need to learn the keys of E and A-flat.

TECHNIQUE BOOK IS NEEDED

Even in the best taught and most talented groups, some review will be needed. It is suggested that at the beginning of the year (and until such time that a reasonable proficiency is demonstrated by a majority of the group), a technique book such as *Book 3* of the *Muller-Rusch String Series* be used to review the Keys of F, B-flat, E-flat, and A, as well as the hand positions (both right and left) and shifting to higher positions. The *Intermediate Etudes and Ensembles* of the *Muller-Rusch String Series* is an excellent book to use for the painless reviewing and teaching of such fundamentals as vibrato, "Intense" and "Resonant" tone, less familiar keys and, of course, left and right hand position.

It is felt that technique books rather than orchestral music should be used to review and teach (or reteach) the skills necessary for the students to play with the proficiency required at this level. It is much more efficient to teach all of the strings the same thing at the same time than it is to have some students sit idly while others work. To save time and avoid student boredom, therefore, use technique books to teach skills.

After the fundamental string techniques, scales, and keys being reviewed become usable by a majority of the students, a book such as *Basic Scales and Two-Part Inventions (Muller-Rusch Series)* can be used to further develop technique and teach the keys of A-flat and E. To use a book of this type to best advantage, the teacher should start the scale and arpeggio exercises slowly giving two or even four beats to each note and really concentrating on good straight bowing, correct intonation, slow vibrato, and clean shifting, before speeding up to a tempo where they can be played as sixteenth notes. Have the students play the exercises both on and off the string (after achieving a tempo appropriate for off string playing). These same exercises can be played with both "Intense" and "Resonant" sound as well. Stress the basic good playing habit of keeping all fingers down until they *must* be moved. Do not allow the students to simply play through the music. *Remember:* It is always the teacher's responsibility to see that every student is performing properly (using vibrato, correct right and left hand position, correct bowing (up bow, down bow), and correct part of the bow, shifting properly, keeping all fingers down as long as possible, etc.). The teacher must not only watch the students, but he must also *listen* and make sure that the playing is in tune and the tone is of the quality desired.

EDITING OF MUSIC

At this level, well edited music is an absolute necessity. Bowing, fingering and positions must be plainly marked and observed. Later on, students may be allowed some discretionary choice of the positions and fingering to be used to play some passages. However, at this time, it should be insisted that they all use the same positions and fingerings. Bowing, on the other hand, is always to be done the same by all of the students in any section at all levels.

Because editing music is time consuming, it is a great time saver if the teacher will make the proper editing of the music one of the criteria for choosing music for purchase. It is to the teacher's advantage to examine the publications of various composers and publishers in regard to the editing of the string parts. It will be found that some of them consistently do a fine job of editing, whereas many of the others do it very poorly or not at all.

Teacher May Edit

Occasionally, it will be necessary to buy music that is poorly edited. In this event, the teacher must edit the music, as the students need the consistency of having all music clearly and intelligently edited for bowings, fingerings (in difficult places) and positions to be used if shifting is fairly new.

If the teacher does not feel qualified to edit the music himself, then he should consult with a string player who is aware of the difference between the fingering and bowing that a professional would use and those that are practical for use by young students. For instance, whereas the professional player can get a big sound in all parts of the bow, play long slurs with good control, etc., a young student will have to have the bowing planned so that they are able to play more in the lower half of the bow and do not confront lengthy slurs.

For the biggest sound, young students should be kept in first position whenever possible. This is true because a softer sound is produced in the higher positions. Another reason not to have the students play constantly in the high positions is that students do not have much accuracy in them until after they have used them for a while. When planning bowings, the director should also take into consideration that it is difficult for young string players to slur across two or more strings, especially on fast or difficult passages.

For all of these reasons, it is better to consult a competent string player who also teaches young students and really understands these problems from first-hand experience rather than just any fine performer.

The foregoing discussion was not meant to suggest that the students are not to have the opportunity to learn to play longer slurs, use all parts of the bow or to play in the higher positions. The authors do feel, however, that those things should be taught through carefully selected materials and specially chosen orchestral literature. These skills should not be assumed to be in the young students' realm of competencies, but rather should be carefully and thoroughly taught to them.

THE WINDS IN THE ORCHESTRA

Winds Play One On A Part

It is important to have only one wind person on a part. The rationale for this is that the most important reason given to wind players to encourage them to be in an orchestra is that they need "orchestra" experience. The essence of the "orchestral" experience is that there is one person on a part and a soloistic and very refined style of ensemble playing is required.

To the authors, the argument that this deprives other students of the chance to have orchestral experience is specious, because as soon as *more* than *one* person is put on a part, *no one* is receiving the "orchestral" experience.

Selection of Winds

Should Be The Best

Starting in the fourth year, students should be in a full orchestra (winds and balanced string sections). This will necessitate the recruitment of the best wind players available and the special training in the soloistic style necessary for winds to play in the orchestra's wind section. A group of wind players cannot simply be brought in from the band, seated in the orchestra and told to play.

Since players in an orchestra at all levels should play one on a part and because, many times, orchestral music is not as technically demanding as band music, ensemble problems such as intonation, blend, balance and phrasing become the most important concern for wind players in an orchestra. In a word, the orchestra wind player must play soloistically with the greatest possible concern for his blend, balance and intonation not only in regard to the other wind players, but also in regard to the string sections. This results in orchestral playing being musically more demanding than playing in a band. This is not to say that these considerations do not apply in a fine band, but in a band (due to multiple players on a part), it is not quite so noticeable if every person does not play every little nuance of the music to the best of his ability. In a band, a wind player is a section player just as the string player in an orchestra is. Therefore, the various sections in the band are heard and judged as a group rather than as soloists.

For orchestra playing, especially, the idea that, "It is not *what* you play, but rather *how* you play, is all important. Every attack and every release must be clean and precise. The tone quality and pitch of every note that is played must be a matter of utmost concern lest an out of tune or an uncharacteristic sound be produced. Every phrase, motif, or accompaniment figure must be seen as a musical challenge and an exciting opportunity to play as musically as possible with attention to all of the many musical possibilities that exist.

Instrumentation

If at all possible, the instrumentation of the wind section should be the standard instrumentation for a modern orchestra which is as follows: two flutes and a piccolo, two oboes, two clarinets and a bass clarinet, two bassoons, four horns, three trumpets, three trombones, a tuba and three to five percussionists. If oboes are not available, flutes or clarinets should be substituted. (Clarinet parts would have to be transposed.) Bass clarinet or possibly tenor saxophone could be substituted for bassoon if bassoons are unavailable. Bass clarinet is preferred for reasons of range and tone quality, but the parts will have to be transposed. Saxophones should not be used in the orchestra *unless* a particular piece of music calls for a saxophone (no optional sax parts should be played). The rationale for this is that if the saxophone's are playing optional parts, they are doubling other parts and destroying the concept of one person on a part. Also, the tone quality of a saxophone does not blend well with the woodwind section to create a characteristic woodwind section sound.

STRINGS SHOULD REHEARSE ALONE

It is suggested that the full orchestra rehearse only two or three days a week so that the remaining two or three days a week of rehearsal can be used for strings alone. Because of individual and sectional bowing and fingering problems and the comparative technical difficulty of the string parts, it is felt that it is better *not* to have the winds rehearse every day with the strings. This, of course, makes it doubly necessary that the best available winds be in the orchestra not only because of the musical demands made on them, but because they will have fewer days a week to learn the music.

Key Requirements

The winds and strings will need to know the concert keys of E-flat, B-flat, F, C, G, D, and A to be able to play all of the music that a fourth and fifth year orchestra should be able to play. This means that the B-flat instruments must be able to play in the keys of F, C, G, D, A, *E,* and *B*. The last three keys are rather unfamiliar to most junior high clarinet and trumpet players, so they will need some help when these keys are played. However, even average junior high players can play them if they are expected to do so. The director must not avoid these keys.

The "F" horns must be able to play in the keys of B-flat, F, C, G, D, A, and E. The keys of A and/or E will probably be unfamiliar to most junior high horn players and therefore will need some special attention. Again, these keys should not be avoided, but rather should be used as an opportunity to push the students to master new skills.

Range Demand

At all levels, great care must be taken to make sure that all students, especially brass players, are not asked to play higher (or lower) than where they can control the pitch and tone quality of their instruments. If the players are to be expected to play musically as well as with rhythmic, pitch and note accuracy, they cannot be expected to also be fighting the problem of playing in an extreme range. (See Chapter VII, Part II for some reasonable range expectations for players of junior high level of development.) Brass players, particularly cannot be expected to play higher than they can play with good embouchure and relaxed breath support or they can be handicapped forever.

Style Requirements

By the fourth or fifth year, the concept of playing with a unified style throughout all of the orchestra should be thoroughly mastered. The ability to pay attention to how the music is to be played should be an accomplished skill. There should also be more awareness and understanding of the different styles necessary to play music of the Baroque, Classical, Romantic and Contemporary periods. (See Chapter IV, Part II for detailed explanation of the string techniques needed to perform the music of these four periods satisfactorily.) The teacher should also be sure to select music every year that will allow work toward further development in all of these styles of music.

The students should also be aware that a march, an air, a song, and a hymn, for instance will each be played in a style that will make each of these sound like what they are.

The strings will need to continue developing a good vibrato, improving their shifting techniques and further mastering their control of "Intense" and "Resonant" tone. There will also need to be continuous additional work on mastering the bow techniques needed to play orchestrally. Such things as slurred staccato and staying in the middle, at the tip or at the frog of the bow, can never be assumed to have been learned and will need constant attention.

For good solid orchestral string sound, especially for younger players, much stress will need to be placed on playing as much as possible in the bottom half of the bow (much closer to the frog than the students will find comfortable to play naturally). The skill of "spacing" between notes must also be taught at this time to allow rhythmically accurate and clean playing. String players, especially, find it difficult to stop the sound between notes and phrases for rhythmic and phrase emphasis. Therefore, stopping the bow between notes must be persistently and carefully taught to insure that the students can and will play spaced, rhythmic passages properly.

REHEARSAL PROBLEMS

There will be some problems in rehearsing a full orchestra that will be different than those occurring in an all string or all wind ensemble. Probably the most obvious of these, and perhaps the only one worth mentioning, is balancing the winds with the strings. If the winds are playing one player on a part and the strings are of sufficient number and properly trained in the use of the bow, the problem will be to get the winds (especially the woodwinds) to play out enough to be heard. A forty-member, properly balanced (about 10, 12, 6, 6, 6) and trained string section should be able to produce enough sound that the wind players will have to play with maximum breath support, firm embouchures and noticeably louder than they would have to play in the band. Cornet and trombone players will have to play over their music stands, in order to make themselves heard. Contrary to the conventional wisdom on this subject, if the wind players have to be asked to play softer when playing in the orchestra, *something* is wrong. Either there is an insufficiency of string players or they have not been trained in the proper use of the bow. As a matter of fact, a properly trained twenty-five- to thirty-member string section with top-line instruments can easily balance a wind section (one on a part) *even* when composed of younger players.
composed of younger players.

"STEP-UP" INSTRUMENTS

There is a world of difference between the "student-line" stringed instruments that most students start on and the ones that they should be playing on beginning with the third year (or when they have grown large enough to play a full-sized instrument). "Student-line" stringed instruments are designed to be sturdy, easily playable, mechanically trouble-free, and to have an acceptable tone quality. They do not, however, have the quality or the size of sound that the better quality instruments do.

The better instruments are designed to produce more sound of better quality and they do. Therefore, an orchestra director has a vital interest in the quality of the instruments that are being played in his orchestra. A good way to encourage interest in the students securing better instruments is to have the local dealer bring or loan some of them to the teacher to take to school and let the students take turns playing on them. Another way to convince the parents of the difference is to have a student play for the parents on a "student-line" instrument and then immediately play the same music on a "step-up," better quality instrument. A good place to have this kind of demonstration is at an open house or a special "This is How We Learn" concert.

PRIVATE LESSONS

Another point to remember is that no matter how well the teacher teaches, individual private lessons with a good private teacher, along with the class lessons, are bound to be of benefit to the student desiring to realize his maximum potential. This is especially true for the exceptionally gifted as well as the slower students. Private lessons from a good teacher should be encouraged not only for the musical benefit to the orchestra, but because the serious student will need the guidance of a specialist in the study of solo literature. Some of the very specialized work on individual strengths will probably be overlooked in a class due to the pressure of higher priority concerns. The slower student, who is having trouble keeping up with the class, on the other hand, needs the additional help of private lessons to avoid becoming discouraged and giving up.

Obviously, the top students studying privately as well as in school should be an enormous help as leaders *if* they are being taught by competent teachers who are supporters of the school instrumental music program.

ENSEMBLES

Along with private lessons, ensembles should be encouraged because the students need to feel that they are individually very important, and that they are not just "one of many" as can happen very easily when playing in the larger orchestral sections (strings especially).

SECTIONALS

Sectionals are also very helpful in developing the feeling that every person must learn to play all of their music correctly. This is true, because good teaching procedures will not allow the teacher to take the time of the entire orchestra or even the entire string section to work with individual students which must be done if true excellence is to be achieved. If at all possible, individual string sections (first violins, second violins, violas, cellos, and basses) should be scheduled.

ACTIVITIES

A word needs to be said about activities for this age level. Do not forget that at this age the boys and girls in the orchestra are not as yet dedicated musicians. They are primarily social beings, and if they are to be kept in the program, activities both musical and non-musical must be planned.

When boys are beginning to be aware of girls and vice-versa, and when they have so much energy that they can't sit still, they need additional activities. Suggestions are as follows:

(1) Large group contests.

(2) Solo and Ensemble contests.

(3) Preparation of concerts – socially, physically, and musically (i.e., decorations, refreshments for audience and orchestra, setting up chairs, stands and music, a party or dance afterwards, meeting to plan, etc.).

(4) Exchange concerts with other schools that require all of the activities in (3), plus taking visiting students home for meals and/or staying overnight.

(5) Concerts at nursing homes.

(6) Concerts at children's homes.

(7) Concerts at hospitals.

(8) Skating parties.

(9) Sock Hops.

(10) Carolling parties.

(11) Fund-raising drives (reward for the high salesmen in fund-raising events).

(12) Coke or ice-cream parties.

(13) Picnics.

(14) Elections of officers to run and plan the activities.

If these activities are planned with the students and made to be fun experiences, the teacher will find that the students are much more willing to submit to the discipline required to play the music to the best of their ability. *Remember:* the students must *want* to play well and work hard. They cannot be forced to stay in an elective course and work as hard as an outstanding group must unless they feel that there are rewards other than musical to make it worthwhile. Planning activities such as those suggested here along with the kind of teaching advocated, should result in students not only playing well but feeling involved and happy enough to stay in the orchestra program long enough to achieve the musical excellence that is inherent in them.

UNIFORMS

Another item that can have a good effect on the attitudes and feelings of the students toward their membership in the orchestra is a uniform of some kind to wear at concerts. The orchestra program will benefit from having uniforms that are not the same as the senior high orchestra. The reasons for this thinking are, first: junior high students would look rather strange in an adult, formal type uniform like those that the high school students will probably have; and second: the high school students would be very offended if the junior high orchestra wore the same uniform that they wore.

Many junior high school orchestras use the traditional white shirts and blouses and dark trousers and skirts. Turtle neck "T" shirts with or without an orchestra or school insignia on it would also be a fine alternative to the traditional white skirt or blouse. If the orchestra program has the money, groups sometimes couple this idea with a blazer or vest in the school colors. For non-concert activities, orchestra "T-shirts" or sweat shirts are very much liked by the students and are a real morale booster. Junior high students really need to feel that they "belong" to a group and some type of uniform as mentioned here really helps them to satisfy their needs to identify with it.

The High School Orchestra 8

INTRODUCTION

By the time the string players reach the high school level (sixth year of playing), very little technique-building work should be left to do in class. If the students and their teachers have been following the schedule of development that has been outlined in the previous chapters, the keys with one, two, three and four sharps and flats should have been covered. "Intense" and "Resonant" tone production should be skills already learned. Spiccato, staccato, and legato use of the bow as well as vibrato and use of the upper positions on all instruments should be well in hand.

In short, by the time the students reach the high school level, they should be able to handle much of the standard orchestral literature creditably (if the director chooses carefully). However, due to the summer vacation and new people constantly moving in, it will probably be necessary, for at least the early part of every year, to do some review of vibrato and position work with the group. Some time will also need to be spent reviewing and expanding both the tone production and basic style concepts introduced in the previous year.

TECHNIQUE BOOK NEEDED

A book like *Basic Scales and Two Part Inventions* (from the *Muller-Rusch Series*) is a fine book to use during the first part of the year for review and to further the development of previously learned skills. Again, the value of using a book of this type, rather than actual orchestral literature, is that it is in unison, and thus gives everyone in the string section a chance to be learning any of the necessary skills *simultaneously*. If a teacher attempts to teach basic skills from the music to be performed, it is often difficult to teach all of the sections of the orchestra the desired skills, because the music usually is not written to allow concentrated practice on any particular skill by all at the same time. While skills can be taught from the performance music, it is much more efficient to teach the skills to all sections of the orchestra at one time by using a book designed for this purpose.

As soon as the students have had enough review (three or four weeks) to satisfy the teacher that the basic skills mentioned above are well enough under control to be usable by the majority of the students, the orchestra should begin playing standard literature of several representative styles and periods. There is considerable standard orchestra literature available that can be played by a well-trained high school orchestra. A listing of some of this literature will be found in Chapter VIII of Part II.

MUSICAL ACTIVITIES

At Home Concerts

The high school orchestra should schedule as many educationally worthwhile activities as it can without making unreasonable demands on the students' time. A reasonable yearly schedule of concerts for an orchestra could include a maximum of three or four formal evening concerts and two or three in-school assembly concerts (one for the elementary school(s) and one for the senior high and/or junior high).

Contests, Clinics, and Selected Orchestras

Especially on the high school level, the teacher should make an effort to expose the students to musical ideas and personalities other than his own. Guest conductors should be brought in to work with the group. Individual students should be encouraged to apply for and participate in Regional and All-State select orchestras. The orchestra should participate in any local festivals and/or contests for which they are eligible.

Performances at Music Educator Conventions

To gain recognition and build community and student pride, the director should apply every two or three years (when the orchestra plays well enough) to be invited to perform at a music educators' convention.

A Broadway Musical

Another activity that is very valuable to the orchestra members who are advanced enough to handle the music, is to accompany a Broadway Musical. *Warning:* Much of this music is very difficult for high school musicians.

Combined Choral and Orchestra Works

If the string program progresses as it should, there are quite a few works that can be performed by a high school choir and string orchestra or full orchestra. These are a valuable experience for both the choral and the orchestral students.

Recording

Make a recording of a group every year or so to motivate students to work hard and play to the best of their ability. When good records are produced, they help build pride in the group. Until the group is good enough to have their performances put onto a permanent disc record, the taping of rehearsals and concerts serves as an excellent evaluation of the group's progress and/or current musical achievement.

Summer Music Camps

An activity that can contribute a great deal, especially to a new program, is the participation by the orchestra students in one of the many summer music camps available in all sections of the country. Because these summer camps tend to be attended by the better students and because of the opportunity for concentrated practice, the students will many times return to the home orchestra situation fully "charged up" and revitalized for the coming year. Camps are excellent for developing leads so it is the wise teacher that encourages attendance.

WHY GO TO CONTESTS OR FESTIVALS?

It is important to consider going to contests and festivals (events where groups play for a panel of judges and are rated either in order of excellence or placed into divisions or ratings). Contests, correctly handled by the teacher, are an extremely valuable teaching tool. Properly used, they will motivate students to work on music until it reaches a level of excellence that would be very difficult to achieve in any other way.

Need for Outside Objective Opinions

There is a need to have an outside authority pass an objective musical judgment on what is being done in a music program. This is true for several reasons and some of them follow.

Until a program is really established and the students experience what it feels and sounds like when a piece of music is really practiced to a level of excellence, the motivation to work up to this point has to come from the outside. Therefore, it is useful for a teacher to be able to say: "The judge will never buy that, it needs more work." Conversely when the group reaches a high degree of competency and is able to criticize its own playing, it frequently gets so critical of itself (because it realizes that it is not doing right) that again the objectivity of an outside opinion is needed to convince the students that they are really doing things quite well in spite of the imperfections of which they are aware.

Need to Hear Others

The students also need to hear other groups play. When the group is new and inexperienced, hearing other groups gives them an idea of what can be done. After a group has achieved quality, they can understand after hearing other groups, the reason for the intense, careful practice that prepared them for the contest.

Need to Test Teaching

For the teacher, a contest can be a real test of his own teaching. Especially for teachers now to the field, some objective means of checking the efficiency of their teaching is an absolute necessity if they are to grow professionally. Outside, objective criticism is a necessity for professional improvement. A teacher wanting to do the best possible job should not really trust the opinion of a friend, wife, husband, neighbor, fellow director, etc., as to how the group is playing – no matter how well meaning or objective they may seem!

Builds Pride

Contests can build pride – in the school, in the group, and in the individual. These are all desirable results that can occur as the outcome of contests. *Remember:* Students have a real need to feel that they belong to a group that is accomplishing something.

Social Interaction

Contests give the students a chance to travel with other students, affording an opportunity for social interaction with the teacher and other students. This kind of activity is very helpful in developing a feeling of "belonging" and responsibility in the members of the group.

IMPORTANCE OF UNIFORMS

Because performance should be presented as something special and out-of-the-ordinary, some kind of a special, non-"everyday" type of dress is necessary for any occasion when the orchestra is performing. Many students will state that they would rather not be required to "dress-up" in any special type of clothing or uniform. The authors nevertheless feel that having the students dress in a way that is "special" is positive psychologically. When the students dress in a special way for a performance, in spite of what they say, it makes them feel as if they are doing something out of the ordinary.

This uniform should not be like the band uniform of the school but rather more like the formal concert dress of a symphony orchestra. A long skirt or dress for the girls is almost a necessity, especially for those playing cello or bass, or for those who are sitting in the front row. A tuxedo-type jacket or blazer in either black or the school colors, black trousers, white shirt, and a uniform-color tie looks good and is not too expensive for the boys. For the girls, a long black skirt and a blouse in the school colors (or vice versa), is a practical and inexpensive outfit, particularly if the girls can make their own skirts.

It is important to have a uniform because the ceremony of getting "all-dressed-up" has a good effect on the orchestra members' morale and builds pride in the group. The impression made on the audience is much more likely to be one of organization and of a team that really knows what it is doing. Having students in the orchestra wear uniforms that others recognize (i.e., younger students, other schools, and parents), is also a very effective method of advertising the orchestra program and its activities.

SOCIAL ACTIVITIES

Almost all of the regular musical events scheduled during a school year can bring about opportunities for the orchestra students to interact socially and develop feelings of "belonging" to the group. Sometimes it is also helpful for the director to work with the officers of the orchestra to plan a strictly social event to be held in addition to the musical events that are to occur. A list of activities that have been found helpful in developing these feelings are:

(1) Regular concerts.

(2) Contests and/or festivals.

(3) Exchange concerts with other schools.

(4) Small instrumental groups playing for recruiting concerts at elementary schools, banquets, etc., outside of school.

(5) Helping at parents meetings for recruiting of students.

(6) Fund-raising projects run by the students.

(7) Parties or picnics planned by the students.

(8) Banquets planned by the students (with or without parents).

STRUCTURE OF REHEARSALS

The authors feel strongly that the wind instrument players should not be in orchestra every day for rehearsal. Experience has shown that it is best to have rehearsals at least two days a week with the string players only. Because of the need to work on bowings, fingerings, bow control, and other details of large group ensemble with the strings, it is better not to have the winds in these rehearsals. Full rehearsals should be used to work on ensemble problems affecting the entire orchestra. It is inconsiderate of the teacher to ask wind players to sit quietly during large periods of time when they have nothing to do. Furthermore, it is an open invitation for mischiefmaking to most high school players to ask them to sit quietly for more than four or five un-involved minutes at a time. Also, if the best wind players in the school can be scheduled for orchestra, three days a week of careful rehearsing should be ample time for them to learn their parts as well as the required ensemble with each other and the strings.

Individual sectional rehearsals (first and second violin, viola, cello and bass) will be needed as well as rehearsals of the complete string section, or students will be sitting around at a rehearsal doing nothing while the director works with small groups. An efficient way to plan rehearsals might be as follows.

Full Rehearsals

At full rehearsals, the director should work on such things as wind and percussion (assuming there is no special time for wind and percussion sectional) and full orchestra ensemble problems (intonation, balance, blend, style). If there is time for the wind and percussion section(s) to have sectionals, then the director should work on full orchestra problems only and save the wind and percussion problems for sectional rehearsals.

String Rehearsals

At full string sectional rehearsals, the director should work on such ensemble problems as intonation, balance, blend, and style. Also, such things as whole string section bowings, technical passages involving the whole string orchestra and structure problems (putting string parts together) are appropriate. It is at these rehearsals that general problems such as the teaching of tone production, vibrato, and shifting (if necessary) should be accomplished.

Individual String Sectional Rehearsals
(first violin, second violin, viola, cello and string bass)

It is in the individual string sectional rehearsals that the players can get help with such things as fingerings, bowings, and individual technique problems. It is appropriate to do all checking and drilling of the individuals playing the music (try-outs, challenges, etc.) as well as individual string section problems.

CHOICE OF WIND PLAYERS FOR THE ORCHESTRA

The best wind players in the school will be needed if the orchestra is to perform satisfactorily, because only the best wind players will be able to meet the demands of orchestral playing. They must be able to play in keys of up to four flats and six sharps and be capable of playing independently (one person on a part). Also, due to the nature of much orchestral writing, the wind players must be able to handle exposed, soloistic passages which require control of pitch, tone quality and dynamics in all registers of their instruments. Once the students realize this, being allowed to play in the orchestra becomes an honor rather than a duty (especially for the better players), and the problem becomes one of choosing the best rather than merely trying to get someone to play in the orchestra.

The band director will also want the best students chosen for the orchestra if he is convinced that the orchestra experiences are being offered to his band students. He should know that the skills gained from these experiences will make his students better band musicians. *Warning:* Great pains must be taken by the orchestra director to avoid implying that an orchestra is better than the band or in any way even appearing to compete with the band.

If the wind students are to benefit from playing in the orchestra, the orchestra director must insist that they do all of the things outlined above (play in tune, independently, soloistically, etc.). Do not assume that the wind players will do these things automatically just because they are the best players from the band. The best way to convince the better wind players to play in the orchestra, as well as the band, is to mention to them that orchestral experience is different and that it gives them opportunities to learn many things in addition to those taught in band.

In summary – If the orchestra director wants the enthusiastic support of the band director, he must show the band director that he is helping the band to play better by broadening the experiences of his best winds in the orchestra. Of course, it can only be this way if the orchestra director does his job!

IMPORTANCE OF PRIVATE LESSONS

Individual and small group practice is going to be necessary if the orchestra is going to be of top quality. To develop players able to play soloistically and lead their sections when learning new techniques, private lessons from a good private teacher are almost a necessity. Although class lessons handled as advocated in this book will result in many players of surprisingly high quality, it would be foolish not to encourage private lessons wherever possible. An orchestra trained as advocated in this book will not *need* to have a large number of students studying privately, but at least two or three in each section will save many an hour of group practice.

Private lessons from a good teacher are a necessity for at least a few of the outstanding players in each section to develop the soloistic style of playing and leadership requirements necessary to lead the solid section players developed by these procedures. Also, private lessons are quite important for a few of the very slow students who for one reason or another may have fallen behind the other students over the years. Rather than have these students become discouraged and drop from the program, many times private lessons are just the "shot in the arm" that they need to maintain interest in the orchestra.

It is important to note that a *good* private teacher has been cited. It is the orchestra director's responsibility to know and recommend the qualified, competent teachers in their area that they want their students to study with since there are many poor private teachers available; it behooves the teacher to have his students avoid those who are not teaching effectively. A poor private teacher is worse than no teacher at all.

It qualified teachers are not available in the community, there are at least two alternatives available. It is sometimes possible to persuade talented students to go to a university situation (if within a 30 or 40 mile radius) or many times, a university will have students available to go to a school to teach privately if the local teacher will organize the project.

When attempting to get students interested in studying privately, it is best to talk to both the parents and the student. Everyone involved must be convinced that lessons are desirable before the lessons will actually become a reality.

ENSEMBLE PLAYING

The string students should be encouraged, and helped by coaching, if possible, to participate in string ensembles of all types – duets, trios, quartets and quintets. Playing in ensembles is especially important for the members of the string sections, because without this experience, they will only play with many others on the same part. Playing in ensembles makes students aware of their own part and how it fits into the whole of the music. It makes them realize the necessity for really fine, controlled playing.

In an ensemble, every person is, in effect, a soloist and as such is completely responsible in every way for a part that no one else has. Just as a wind player needs to play in an orchestra to get this experience, a string player needs to play in a small ensemble of some kind to have a complete musical experience.

Rehearsal and Performance Procedures 9

PREPARATION FOR THE REHEARSAL

The first step toward having an efficient well run rehearsal is for the teacher to know what is to be accomplished that day. To plan a rehearsal, the teacher must consider such things as what was done at the previous rehearsal and how well the goals were accomplished. Were the goals completely realized? If they were not, should something new be done; then go back and work on the earlier goals again later? Or, should the teacher start again at the beginning and work on them in a different way? Should the teacher just continue on because the same goals can be achieved either later in the same music or in other compositions planned for rehearsal that day? Another possibility to consider is whether the goals chosen were too advanced for the group and might have to be readjusted either through different music or an acceptance of a lesser quality performance. The first alternative is much to be preferred. The authors feel that: "It is not what you play but how you play it," that is really important.

If the goals planned were completely accomplished, then the next step or area to be covered should be chosen. On the elementary level, especially when playing from a method book, this decision is usually a simple one. Take the next lesson! But, even when working on a lesson in a method book, emphasis can be shifted from rhythm, tone, reading of note names, intonation, bowing or position (or vice-versa) according to what things are most needed by the class at the time. In planning a rehearsal, a judgment must be made as to what is most important, less important, and least important, even at the earliest levels to insure that rehearsals have both direction and purpose. Never just play through a piece without the director and the students knowing exactly what is to be accomplished.

After selecting the music for the rehearsal and deciding what the emphasis and/or purpose of the rehearsal is, the room should be prepared for the rehearsal. To prepare the room for rehearsal, the chairs should be arranged in the proper order – rows for drill (see Chapter II, Part II) or conventional seating for performance. The piece or pieces for the day should be written on the board.

On the grade school level, the teacher should have the instruments tuned and everything needed for the class prepared before the class starts. If possible, arrange to have some of these things done by the custodian, or students (chairs and writing pieces on the board). The tuning will probably have to be done by the teacher until the end of the second year when the students should have learned to completely tune their own instruments. Occasionally, a second year elementary student will be found who can help the teacher tune the instruments for the beginning class.

On the secondary level, chairs and stands should be in place and the titles of the music needed for the day's rehearsal should be written on the board ahead of time. The music to be rehearsed should have all measures numbered, bowings marked and be in the music folders before rehearsal starts. Rehearsal time should not be used for passing out or collecting music, marking bowings, collecting money, passing out tickets, fixing instruments, visiting with students, taking roll, etc. Many of the non-musical activities that must be done can be carried out by students while the group is rehearsing. All of these things are necessary and must be done, but not during rehearsal. Do not allow these things to steal valuable rehearsal time – plan ahead so this does not happen.

There are many things that can be done to help the rehearsal be as productive as possible. Some of them will have a large effect and some of them only a comparatively small effect, but anything that the teacher can do to help the rehearsal advance productively should be done. The areas of discussion that follow are not necessarily in their order of importance, but are intended as a listing of things that affect rehearsals.

SEATING OF THE ORCHESTRA

Strings

Rehearsal

Even such an apparently unimportant thing as seating the students can have quite an effect on the efficiency of the rehearsal. The effect of seating students in different ways will perhaps not be obvious in one or two rehearsals, but can have a decided effect when considered over an entire semester. Several seating arrangements help them learn better and more efficiently.

Use the row seating (described in Chapter II of Part II) rather than the conventional orchestra seating whenever learning a new skill or a passage that requires drill so that there is freedom for the teacher to move around to see and help each student whenever necessary.

The teacher should put the weaker students in front where they can be heard more easily and be more readily helped. Seating in this way also makes it possible for the weaker students to hear the stronger students placed behind them. This will give them more confidence. This type of seating probably should not be used for concerts. While it fosters stronger playing by all of the players, it will cause the weaker players to be heard more than the better players and this will reduce the orchestra's sound quality. For the best sound, the better players should be placed in front.

A "buddy" system should be used as an aid in developing independent and strong players. The "buddy" system means that the stronger players are placed next to weaker players so that the weaker players can learn by watching and listening to the better players. The traditional system of seating players in order of ability is the worst possible way to develop good players throughout the section (unless there is a very small spread of ability levels).

It is wise to put a few good players in the second violin section. It will save literally hours of rehearsal time as they will pull the poorer players along. It is very poor planning to put all of the best players on first violin and all of the poorest players on second violin. This common mistake results either in a very poor second violin section or an inordinate amount of time spent learning the second violin parts.

Figure No. 1 illustrates a recommended rehearsal seating for the string sections of secondary orchestras that will contribute positively and efficiently to the students' collective learning. Number one is considered the best player with the playing quality dropping as the number increases. "A" shows a good rehearsal seating for the cello or viola section. "B" shows a good rehearsal seating for the bass section. A good rehearsal seating for a first and second violin section is shown in "C". "D" is a seating that will "work" if there are more students who can handle the upper positions for first violin. The seating in "D" will give better balanced sections as well as cut down on rehearsal time, but, there must be a player in seat 11 who can handle higher positions and play first violin music.

A		B	C				D			
Cello or Viola		**Basses**	**First Violin**		**Second Violin**		**First Violin**		**Second Violin**	
1	8	1	1	10	3	18	1	11	3	18
2	7	5	2	9	4	17	2	10	4	17
3	6	2	5	8	11	16	6	9	5	16
4	5	4	6	7	12	15	7	8	12	15
		3			13	14			13	14

Recommended Rehearsal Seating by Ability
(Secondary Level)
Figure No. 1

It should also be noticed that there are more players on the second violin part than on first violin part. There are two important reasons why it is best to put more students on the lower part. First, in a school group, additional players are needed on the lower part, because generally, the weaker players are assigned to this part and so it takes more of them to musically balance the parts. Second, the human ear tends to hear the higher part more even if it isn't played any louder. Therefore, the inner parts (in this case the second violin part) need to be played louder to insure their being heard.

Concert

SECONDARY LEVEL

For concerts it may be desirable for the director to change the seating so that the very best people are in front where they will be heard the most (see Figure no. 2).

A	B		C				D			
* Bass	* Viola & Cello		* First Violin		* Second Violin		* First Violin		* Second Violin	
1	1	2	1	2	3	4	1	2	3	4
2	3	8	5	10	11	18	6	11	5	18
5	4	7	6	9	12	17	7	10	12	17
4	5	6	7	8	13	16	8	9	13	16
3					14	15			14	15

***Outside players**

Recommended Concert Seating by Ability
Figure No. 2

To project the best possible sound to the audience, the best players should always be placed to the outside of the stage. Getting the students to accept this type of seating may take a little time if they are accustomed to traditional seating. To help students understand and accept this new idea, it must be explained to them (before auditions) that the purpose of orchestra seating is to make them sound as good as possible. It should also be explained that for the orchestra to sound as good as possible, people need to be placed on the proper parts in the proper proportion, so that all parts are heard and every person has the maximum opportunity to develop their individual capacities. The diagram of the seating should be put on the board, or some seating charts should be duplicated showing how they are to be seated – possibly like the one above.

After the teacher has auditioned all of the students, he should give them the number that they have achieved in their section and let them seat themselves. The people most likely to complain are the top people (3 and 4) that are playing second violin. They can be told that they can get into the first violin section by either improving or getting "beat" in try-outs by some of the people behind them. They usually are not willing to move backwards to get into the first section. To make them sense their importance, the teacher can point out that they are section leaders, and can give them special duties (marking bowings, passing out music, calling and running sectionals, playing solo passages, etc.)

Equally important to the seating of players within the section for the best orchestral sound is the positioning of the sections on the stage. After each section is seated so that it is playing at its maximum potential, it must be positioned so that it can be heard to maximum advantage.

The standard or traditional seating, with the violins to the left of the conductor, and the violas, cellos, and basses to the right of the conductor is probably the poorest possible seating for many school groups. They are often weak numerically in the viola, cello, and/or bass sections. The traditional seating is also poor, because the greatest amount of sound projects from the "F" holes at right angles to the top of the instrument giving the violins (usually the strongest section) the greatest accoustical advantage and the viola, bass, and cello sections an accoustical disadvantage (usually weaker in that order).

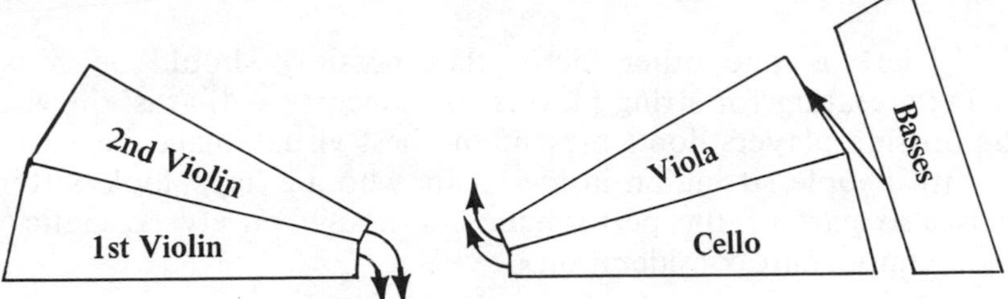

Arrows show the direction of maximum sound.

Direction of Sound in Conventional Concert Seating
Figure No. 3

Two more logical seatings for most school orchestras with weaker second violin, bass, cello, and/or viola sections would be as shown in Figure Nos. 4 and 5.

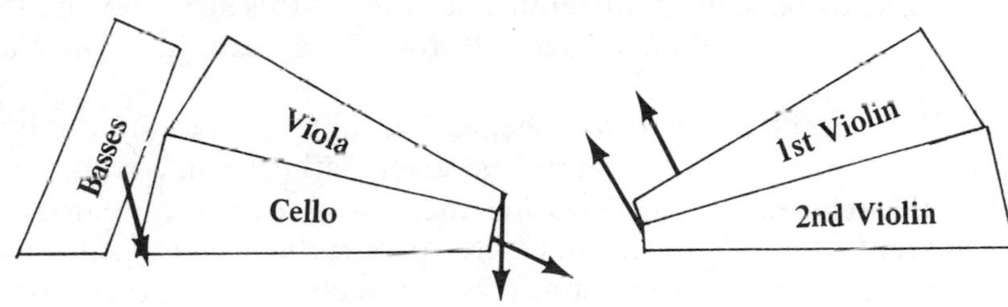

Direction of Sound in Alternate Concert Seating
Figure No. 4

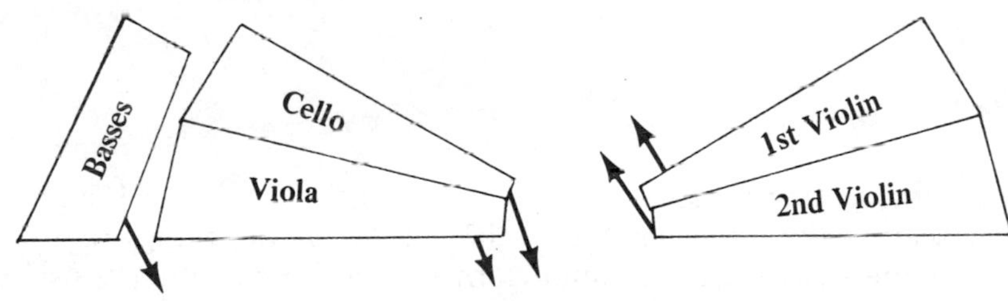

Direction of Sound in Alternate Concept Seatings
Figure No. 5

If the string sections are not in proper balance numerically (approximately one bass, cello and viola for every three violins) or ability wise, it is not wise to use a "traditional" seating. The teacher should experiment with various seatings and find the one that will give the best balance and sound for the orchestra at hand. There is no seating that will give optimum results for all orchestras!

There is one other factor that possibly should be considered in choosing a seating for string players for concerts – that is, the visual effect. If the outside players don't present the best visual image, have them change seats with people sitting on inside chairs who, perhaps, look better. Appearance is also part of the performance; although purely cosmetic, it is definitely an important consideration.

ELEMENTARY LEVEL

If the elementary classes are to give a regular concert where the students are to be conducted, it is best to use a regular concert formation. The students should be seated in a semi-circular arrangement where every student can see the director and follow the baton as the music is directed. (It is suggested that for concerts, even on the elementary level, students be placed according to the general outline as was suggested in the secondary level section so that optimum balance is obtained.) The seating arrangement for this level will need to be slightly different, because at this age, they are used to having their own stand and music necessitating the spreading of the chairs slightly.

It is also suggested that for the earlier appearances in public, a demonstration of "this is how we learn" be given rather than a regular concert, and that the rehearsals "row" seating then be used. Not only does this interest the parents more, but if there are any problems with the music (breakdowns, mistakes, etc.), it is just as it is in the class and no one is upset. Also, during the first semester, the students' repertoire is so limited that a formal concert is impossible. This type of educational concert can also have side advantages. It can help with future recruiting of students and also makes it possible for parents, teachers, and administrators to better understand what the teacher is trying to do with the class.

Winds

The wind seating is essentially the same for both rehearsals and concerts. When seating the winds in the orchestra, all of the things that were considered for the strings are also important for the winds. Other considerations are based on the fact that the winds are all solo instruments and must be placed so that they can all be heard when the full orchestra is playing. This means that the woodwind instruments should be placed as far forward as possible and the brass instruments should be placed behind them. If all the woodwinds are not going to be in one row it is best to put the flutes in front of the clarinets and oboes to help them balance the woodwind section. For ease of hearing on the part of the players, it is a good idea to have the bassoons near the cellos and the basses as they play many parts together. To help a section to hear better in matters of style, intonation, blend, and balance, put the first chair players in the middle seat with the second and third chair players on either side (see Figure No. 6).

The seating shown in Figure No. 6 allows the players in each section to hear their section leaders and also puts the first chair players as close as possible to each other so that they can hear each other. In addition, it puts the high winds and mallet percussionists near the high strings and the low

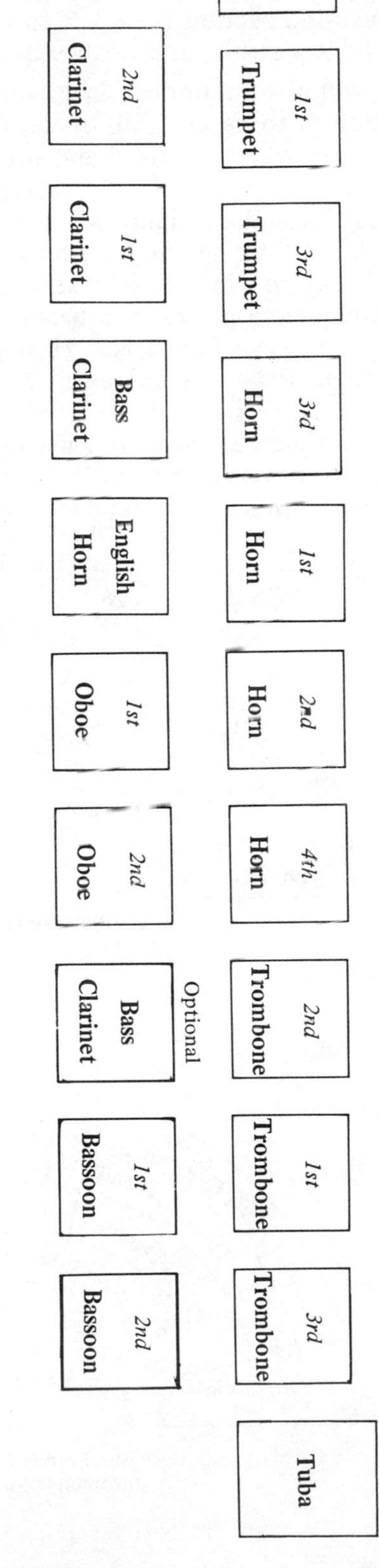

Recommended Wind Section Seating for Balance
Figure No. 6

winds and the other percussionists near the low strings (see Figure Nos. 7A or B for placement relevant to entire orchestra). If for purposes of balance, the string section has been changed from the traditional seating as was suggested earlier in the chapter (Figure No. 4 and 5), then it might be well to reverse the wind section from left to right so that the low wind instruments are with the low strings and vice versa.

It will also be noticed in Figure No. 6 that if a smaller, classical type wind section is to be used, all of the first chair players will be placed even closer together when the third and fourth chair players are eliminated. Two seatings that take all of the above factors into consideration are shown in Figure Nos. 7A and B. Figure No. 7A is a seating that is good to use when there are lots of strings in good balance (maybe even a little heavy on the bass side). Figure No. 7B is a seating that will help an orchestra with a smaller string section with the balance a little skewed towards the violins. The string section in Figure No. 7B is getting small enough wherein balance would be helped by keeping away from Romantic style, and more recent orchestra music requiring large wind sections. Classical and Baroque music are a better choice, because they usually use smaller wind sections. It should be realized, however, that there is some modern music available that requires smaller wind sections, if the time is taken to look for it.

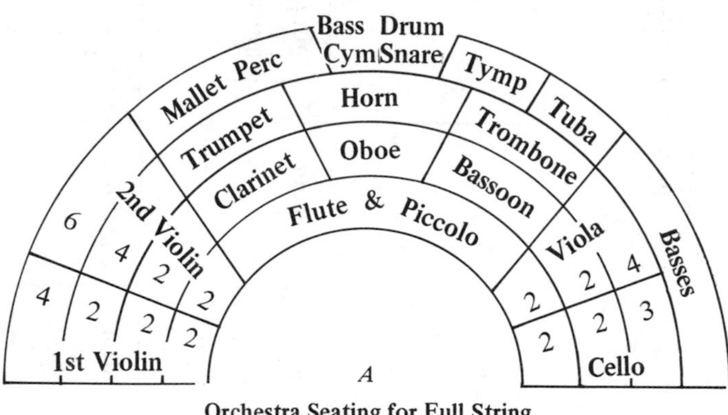

Orchestra Seating for Full String Sections

Snare
Cymbal
Bass Drum
Trombone
Horns
Mallet Perc
Tympani
Tuba
Oboe
Trumpet
Bassoon
Clarinet
Flute & Piccolo
Cello
2nd Violin
Basses
2 2
2 2 3 3
Viola
2 2
1st Violin
2 2 2 2
B

Orchestra Seating for Smaller and/or Incomplete String Sections

Figure No. 7

TUNING THE ORCHESTRA

Strings

On the elementary level, the teacher will have to assume most of the responsibility for the tuning of the stringed instruments. During the first year, the teacher will have to expect to do *all* of the tuning of the instruments. However, about halfway through the year it is a good idea to spend about five minutes at the end of the class period teaching the students how to tune one string. It is best to use the last five minutes of class for tuning rather than the first five minutes, because the students must leave at the designated time making it impossible to take more than the five minutes for tuning. The teacher may wish to make a "race" out of this introduction to tuning and tell the students that they may "pack up" and leave as soon as they get their untuned strings back to correct pitch. A group of students will work very hard to learn to tune quickly so that they can be the first one to be able to put up their instrument!

Recommended steps for teaching the students to tune their instruments are:

(1) Before the beginning of class, the teacher should tune all of the strings on all of the instruments.

(2) About five minutes before the end of class, the teacher should ask each student to hold his instrument up in front of him and place his right hand on the peg that tunes the "A" string (except the string bass players who must use their left hand).

(3) Have them turn the "A" string down one whole turn.

(4) While the teacher plays a repeated A on the piano, or a sustained A on his own instrument, have the students play pizzicato and hum the A while turning the peg until the pitch goes back up to the sounded A. *Warning:* The students must be told to turn the peg slowly and listen carefully, because if they turn it too fast and the string tuned too high, it may break.

(5) The teacher should let them try this for a minute or so being sure to praise highly the ones who can do it and/or who are getting close to pitch.

(6) Announce to them: "That was good; we are getting better. We will do it again at the next lesson."

The above procedure should be continued through the second year, until the students can consistently tune the A string. Then, have them sing down the scale (either using numbers or syllables – whichever they use in their elementary music classes). Have them sing: "Five, four, three, two, one" or "So, Fa, Mi, Re, Do." Ask them to turn their pegs until the "D" string is flat, and follow the procedure as outlined above for the "A" string. When they can do both the D and A strings fairly well, go on and tune the G, C, and E strings in the same manner. Until the students have learned to tune their instruments, do not let them spend more than the last five minutes of the daily class tuning. Then the teacher should retune the instruments (if it is necessary) so the students have instruments that are in-tune to practice on at home. After they have learned to tune, then they should, of course, tune at beginning of rehearsal.

It should be obvious that the authors have omitted tuning by fifths (violin, viola, and cello) or harmonics (cello and bass). This is not an oversight, but was done for a good reason. Unless the strings are all "true" (not false) when tuning is done by harmonics or fifths, the result will be strings that are tuned "out of tune." Strings stay "true" such a short time (especially gut-wound strings) that it is felt it is a mistake to teach this method of tuning, because it is so inaccurate.

By the third year of playing, many of the students should be able to tune their own instruments fairly well, but the teacher will still have to continue to be responsible for the tuning and check carefully from time to time even in high school. If the teacher is not continually picky about the correct tuning of the strings, the students will get careless. (Each one is prone to think he is right and everyone else is wrong.)

After a group is fairly successful and quick at tuning their strings with the whole orchestra by tuning each string together and waiting to go on to another string until all have it, they are probably ready to try to tune with *all* string players tuning their A together. Next, allow them to go ahead and quietly tune the other strings on their own (much like professional orchestras do). The teacher must be sure not to allow loud or fifth (double-stop) tuning, as this makes it so noisy that no one can hear what they are doing. It will probably be necessary after all have tuned to let the cellos and basses check their strings alone, because hearing the pitch is extremely difficult for those playing the lower instruments while everyone else is playing. From time to time, the teacher will need to "spot check" individual strings within the group just to let the students know that someone is paying attention to them.

Winds

The winds should be given their tuning "A" after the strings are tuned and then allowed to tune by themselves. However, it should be understood that this playing of the tuning note by the winds is meaningless and even worse than not playing a tuning note at all, unless everyone understands that playing a tuning note, at best, assures that they are close to the right pitch on only one note: the tuning note. Every note played will still have to be listened to very carefully and adjusted as it is played to assure good intonation. A wind player cannot tune up at the beginning of a rehearsal and then expect to be in tune unless he anticipates that every note he plays for the entire rehearsal might be out of tune. Every note must be carefully placed where it belongs in regard to intonation as well as rhythm.

TEACHING STUDENTS TO FOLLOW A CONDUCTOR

For a teacher to be able to do a good job of conducting, it is not necessary that he be an excellent "stick man." Rather, the first and most important task is to be able to teach the students the meaning of the standard conducting gestures and how to respond to them. Then, and only then, can a group be "conducted." Skill training for following a director can and should be started before the end of the first year of lessons.

There is also a secondary benefit in the procedure outlined below. If followed consistently, it will result in an in-experienced teacher making some basic conducting techniques a real part of his teaching. This happens, because as the teacher teaches these things to the students, he has a chance to practice all of the techniques that were taught to him in his college conducting class. Also, as he teaches the children how everything is supposed to be done, the students in the class become quite knowledgeable about the correct way to do things, and they will be quite willing to tell the conductor if mistakes are made. Too often this is not the case, because the students have unintentionally been taught not to follow the director. This happens when the director constantly reviews a piece exactly (or as closely as possible) the same way every time. In many cases, by the time of a contest or a concert, the director could count: "One, two, ready, play,", leave the room, and the students would play the piece through and never even notice that the director was gone.

Even at the earliest level, the director should purposely vary the tempos, the length of time between phrases, etc. Later on, phrases and dynamics should be changed on the spur of the moment, so that the students never feel that they know what the director is going to do. The students must be convinced that every time they rehearse a piece it is a creative endeavor on the part of the director and that things will vary slightly. There are at least three reasons for this: (1) nobody can possibly do anything twice in a row in exactly the same way, so it is useless to try; (2) the director and the group should constantly be trying new phrasing, dynamics, etc., to see if there is a different and/or better way to play a piece; and (3) the "rules" of playing in a musical group dictate that the director is always right, and if they are not with the director, they are wrong.

As there are many fine books available explaining the mechanics of beat patterns, dynamic indications, etc., no further attempt will be made here to explain what every college music education student learns in conducting class. However, very little has been previously written about how to put these techniques into practice when one is suddenly thrust in front of a school instrumental class, Grades 5 through 12. This is the problem that will be addressed in this section.

There are many things that can be done to teach students, even at the very beginning stages, to be responsive to the director's baton. Our task is to take this area out of the "trusting to luck" and the ""natural good sense" category, and show some procedures that, if followed, will result in groups of all ages that will be able to follow their director. A director should never have to hope helplessly that everything will come out "even" at the end!

In accordance with the basic teaching concept of always breaking material to be presented down into bite-sized "chunks" so that only one new thing is presented at a time, the following step by step procedure is outlined to quickly teach the student the art of following the director. These steps need to be gone through at any and every level if the students are not readily able to follow their conductor.

Step Number One: Finding the First Beat of Every Measure

The teacher will need to explain and demonstrate to the students that the first beat of every measure is a down beat and the last beat of every measure is always an up beat, usually in towards the director's body.

The teacher will also need to explain to them that if they get lost while playing, they can go to the beginning of the next measure and wait until they see the downbeat (the first beat) and begin to play again when the rest of the group gets there.

The following are exercises the teacher may use to help them find the first beat of the measure:

(1) Have them count out loud, "*ONE*-2-3-4, *ONE*-2-3-4" while directing a four-beat pattern with a *huge* upbeat into the first beat of the measure. Be sure they say the ONE very loudly with a pronounced accent.

(2) The teacher should then direct a three-beat pattern with a strong first beat again having them count out loud ONE-2-3, ONE-2-3 with ONE stressed very much.

(3) Likewise, the teacher should direct a two beat pattern with the students counting aloud again stressing the first beat of the measure: "ONE-2, ONE-2."

(4) Next, the teacher should direct the three patterns taught in random order, going directly from one to the other. Have the students count out loud and always stress ONE when it comes.

(5) Finally, the teacher should direct all sorts of mixed meters such as: 5, 7, 9, 10, 13 (any meter) always having the students count out loud with a stress on ONE as a larger than ordinary first beat is given. After a very short time, the students will never miss the first beat again.

Step Number Two: Starting Together

The teacher should demonstrate how the preparatory beat looks and explain what it means. It is a good procedure for the teacher to form the habit of taking a breath as the preparatory beat is given. Doing this seems to have the effect of causing all of the students in the group to take a breath with the director so that they are ready to start when the beat is giver (especially the winds).

The preparatory beat gives everyone a chance to get ready to play. To do this, the strings place their bows on the string at the proper place; the winds take a breath, set their embouchres and put horns to their mouths; and the percussion get their sticks or mallets positioned the proper distance above their instruments.

It is important to explain to the students that the preparatory beat tells the group exactly how fast the piece is going to be played. It is always given at the desired speed of the measures to follow. To teach the students how this works in a real situation, the teacher can give numerous preparatory and first beats only, varying the speeds and having them say: "PLAY-2-3-4," starting on the "ictus" of the downbeat at the speed that has been indicated by the preparatory and first beat. Point out that at the exact time they are to play, the beat will be given a little bounce and this bounce is called the ictus. They should be informed that from now on they must watch for the ictus so that they know exactly when to start playing. (Use the word "ictus" because it is the proper word and because it really pleases younger students and makes them chuckle). When they have mastered saying: "PLAY-2-3-4" at varying speeds, exactly on the ictus of the beat, the group should proceed to play at varying speeds.

The students also need to be taught exactly how they are to produce a tone precisely on the ictus of the first beat. The string students will need to put the bow on the string near the frog, on or before the preparatory beat, grasping the bow securely. Instruct them to start the bow moving quickly when the ictus of the downbeat is given.

To produce a tone precisely on the ictus, the winds will need to take a breath on the preparatory beat with the director, set the embouchure, put the tongue in position to stop air from going through the instruments, start the breath out of the lungs into the mouth (At this point in the procedure, sound will probably be heard from some of the students in the group. It must then be explained that there can be no sound at this point because their tongues should be blocking the air from going through the instruments. Have them repeat steps 1, 2, 3, and 4 and hopefully there will be no sound this time), and quickly pull the tongue back away from the blocking position so the air can cause vibration of the reed, lip, or air column as it should. This release of the air must be sudden and almost percussive as the attempt to breathe air through the horn while the tongue is blocking the air will result in a little extra pressure being built up in the mouth. This will cause a sudden release of air which is necessary for a clean attack on a wind instrument. All tones on wind instruments are produced by air moving and causing vibration (lip, reed, etc.) and never by the tongue as some seem to believe.

The procedure outlined above helps get clean attacks even with high school groups that may be quite advanced. Older students will need to be reminded of these steps from time to time. Many will never have heard this and those who have will need to be reminded.

Step Number 3: Stopping Together

The teacher should explain to the students what a cut-off motion means and show them how it looks on every beat. The teacher can do this by following these steps:

(1) Have them count out loud and tell them to say the word "off" whenever the cut-off sign is given. (The cut-off beat will be the beat after the last beat they are to count.

(2) Have them play music that they already know so that they will be able to think about following the director. Stop at the end of every phrase and then start again with the next phrase. The teacher should make a big cut-off motion on the beat after the last note of every

phrase and give a definite preparatory beat for every new phrase. At this point, it must be stressed that the first beat ends when the second beat begins, the second beat ends when the third beat begins, etc., and that the cut-offs are made accordingly. While playing the music one phrase at a time, the teacher must make the students aware of the fact that they are being started and stopped with the phrases. This is important for them to understand, because it is at phrase endings and at the beginning of new phrases that they must be taught to be especially careful to watch. This is where tempo changes will often be made.

(3) Make a game of seeing if they can be caught by surprise with starting and stopping at all phrase endings and beginnings. Say things like: "I wonder who I'll catch this time," and "Ha, I caught you that time; I wonder who I'll catch next time," or "Will you all be too smart for me this time?", etc.

(4) Stop and start at *every* phrase ending. When the group is stopped, vary the time between the phrases. Give a preparatory beat but don't give the beat of execution, and then laugh with them when people come in before the next beat has been given. Kid them about being "faked-out." By this time they will be watching the director very carefully. *Warning:* They will see everything, especially what it is wished they would not see. Be careful about buttons, socks, runs in hose, shoes, flys, slips, etc. By now, the teacher can do pretty much what he wants to do with phrase endings and beginnings.

(5) Stop and start at places other than phrase endings but only after long notes.

(6) Stop and start at any place in the music.

Step Number Four: Changing Speed Between and Within Phrases

The teacher should explain and demonstrate that tempos can and will change while a piece of music is being played. To accomplish this, have them count out loud as the teacher changes speed from one phrase to the next (one fast, the next one slow, two fast, one slow, etc.), keeping the tempo steady within the phrase. When their attention has been thoroughly focused on big tempo changes between phrases, make smaller and more subtle changes. When they can follow by counting out loud, do the same exercise outlined above with the instruments playing a piece they know. Play a piece that they know and change tempos within the phrases with large changes at first, then gradually smaller and smaller changes.

By following the above procedures, within a fifteen or twenty minute time span, even the very young groups can learn to watch the director and be surprisingly good at following him. The same procedures, used consistently with secondary groups, will result in groups that play very flexibly with clean attacks and releases.

The students need to be taught that volume and volume changes (as well as tempo) can be indicated by the baton. This can be done rather quickly by following a few simple steps:

(1) Demonstrate a very large beat and ask the class how they think they are to play – loudly or softly?. If no one knows immediately, direct with a very small beat and again ask what volume they think they are to play. Usually a student will answer: "Softly." Congratulate the student for being so sharp and immediately beat a very large pattern again and ask, "Are you to play loudly or softly?" At this time, the teacher should get a majority response of: "Loudly." Congratulate the whole class on being so sharp and then say "That's right! A big beat means to play loudly and a small beat means to play softly. From now on that is what we are always going to do!" Then, the teacher must make sure he always does it that way.

(2) Conduct both large and small beats and have them count loudly with the large beats and softly with the small beats.

(3) Have them play their instruments while alternate phrases are directed with large and small beats making certain that they play loudly and softiy at the correct times. Don't accept it if they don't really create a difference in volume, and go back over it until they really exaggerate with a big difference between loud and soft phrases.

(4) Next, try to mix them up on the phrases by doing such things as two loud, one soft, three soft, two loud, etc.

(5) Start a phrase with big beats and gradually make the beats smaller. If they do not respond, stop and ask them: "What do you suppose I wanted you to do"? They will know! Repeat the phrase with gradually smaller and smaller beats and insist that they get softer as the size of the beats is decreased.

(6) As the size of the beat and the volume is increased and decreased and their playing changes, start using the left hand to also indicate the crescendo and decrescendo that the baton is making. As them what the left hand is telling them to do. If they don't know, do it again for them making it obvious that the size of the beat and the direction of the movement of the left hand are directly related to each other. Exaggerate – they will see it!

Step Number 6: Indicating Style With The Beat

Another aspect of playing that can be quickly taught to young players is the concept that a style of playing can be indicated with the baton. To teach them how to recognize the desired style, conduct a four beat pattern with very flowing beats without any clearly defined ictus and ask the students how they think the music should sound. They will say words like "smoothly," and "prettily." The teacher should then agree that that is exactly what he had in mind and that they are to play smoothly and songlike. A song might be defined as a piece of music that is sung – therefore smooth and connected, or *"cantabile."* It is important that words of this type be used as they can learn them from the context of the sentence. Direct the same pattern with a very pronounced ictus, stop between the beats, and ask them how they think the music should be played. They will answer: "jerky," "separated," and "short." The teacher should respond that this is exactly what was wanted – short, separated, very rhythmic, heavily accented music or *"marcato."* Have them count in both the marcato and cantabile styles as they are directed both ways. Any level of student can understand these concepts (fifth grade or above), but the instructor must realize that first and second year students may have considerable difficulty playing the music in these two styles. If they have enough control of their instruments to be able to play the two styles, they should be directed in them to see if they can respond appropriately.

The six steps in teaching students to follow a conductor can be started as early as the middle of the first year and definitely no later than the end of the first year (with the exception of the style indications in step no. 6). They should be used periodically from there on through high school. If this is done faithfully, the group will actually be able to follow anyone that directs them, and will allow the conductor to make music instead of just beating time.

THE REHEARSAL

The objective of every rehearsal should be to do as much as possible qualitatively and quantitatively in as little time as possible. A list of some rehearsal tips to help you to have more efficient rehearsals follow.

Rehearsal Tips (Do's and Don't's)

Stop as seldom as possible and only for a good reason. When stopping is necessary, tell the group why they stopped and what it is that they must do to correct the mistake(s) that caused them to have to stop.

Work for carry-over from piece to piece. Make sure the students understand that they can and are to apply solutions of today's problems to similar problems at other times and in other pieces.

Students must understand the purpose of the drills that they will have to do from time to time. Repetition without a purpose is largely wasted time. To be more effective, the specific purpose of the drill must be known to the students (i.e.: to improve rhythm, intonation, precision, tempo). To be effective, drill of any kind, at any level, must be related to and/or extracted from the music itself.

Work on only one problem at a time. The younger the students are and/or the more difficult the problem is, the more important this rule becomes.

Stop only if the students apparently are not aware of their mistakes or don't know what to do to solve them. Many mistakes will be corrected by the students without the teacher saying anything, so don't waste time commenting about them. Other mistakes will never get better if the teacher does not stop; so point them out, and tell the students how to solve them. To not correct the problems that need to be corrected is to waste time; and to take time to work on problems that will correct themselves is equally a waste of time. If the teacher is aware of this, experience will gradually teach him which are which.

Establish an order of importance for rehearsing problems. A good order might be rhythm, tone quality, notes, intonation, dynamics, and expressive nuance.

Establish the concept that music is not just playing the right notes at the right time but rather how the right notes are played at the right time. After this, the group is ready to start to make music.

Large group rehearsal time should be reserved for problems involving the whole ensemble. Devote it to such areas as balance, phrasing, intonation, rhythm, style, dynamics, tutti passages, etc. Do not use the time of the entire group to work on individual or small group problems. Sectionals or small group rehearsal should be scheduled to work on bowings, seating, fingerings, individual tone production, etc.

Work on music of various levels of difficulty so that students of all ability levels find something challenging as well as something on which they can succeed in each rehearsal.

Locating Problems

When a problem arises, it is very important that both the teacher and the student know first what the problem is and then who has it. When the problem is obvious, there is no difficulty in knowing what needs to be done. Sometimes, there is definitely something wrong but it is not obvious to either the teacher or the students exactly what the problem is. To be able to find out what the problem is, it will often be necessary to literally "tear the music apart." What apparently may be wrong notes can be an intonation problem or a case of either wrong rhythm or lack of precision. *Remember:* Teach the students that the right note at the wrong time is really the wrong note.

To find those problems that are not obvious, it is necessary first to isolate them by having different parts played separately (all of the group playing the same rhythmic figures on the same notes and their octaves). If this doesn't isolate the problem, ask all of the people playing the same rhythmic figures in each octave to play by themselves. If it is still not apparent where the problem is, then have individuals play the problem part, always insisting that a steady beat be maintained, and that the rhythm be played correctly. If the problem still cannot be isolated, surprisingly, it may have corrected itself. To check this possibility, have all parts on the same notes and rhythm play together and see if the problem is gone.

If the problem still exists, obviously someone could be playing right when asked to play by himself but wrong when playing in the group. If this is the case, have all people play the problem part repeatedly and walk around and listen to individuals until the person having trouble can be located. At this point, it must be determined what is causing the problem: rhythm, wrong notes, right notes out of tune, and so on.

If the problem is rhythm, have them mark all beats with a vertical line and tap the meter with their feet. Make sure that all the notes with lines over them are being played when the foot goes down. If there is still a problem, then have the students tap the meter with the foot while clapping the rhythm. They may not be able to do this immediately and it will be necessary to practice it until the students can do it. They will try to tap the rhythm of the passage with their foot. Don't allow this. They must be able to tap a steady beat with their foot no matter what is happening rhythmically. The students must be aware of the relationships of rhythm and rhythmic patterns to the meter (tapping of the foot), or rhythm will always be a guessing game.

If rhythm is not the problem, but notes are, then slow down the tempo and find the problem area. Is it wrong fingering, lip set wrong, right finger, but in the wrong place (strings), etc.? When the problem is found, explain what should be done to correct it. If this does not eliminate the problem then slow the tempo down to the point that it can be played correctly and make a drill out of the problem. Always include at least the note before the problem note(s). Many times, getting to the problem note(s) is the difficulty.

After the problem spot can be played slowly, speed it up gradually. Students will many times say: "I can play it fast, but I can't play it slowly." "Nonsense," the teacher must say, "When you are playing it faster, you don't play it right either. You just don't notice the mistake because of the speed. If you can't play slowly with control, you surely can't play faster with control." If, after three or four minutes of working on playing the passage correctly it is still not correct, it is best to go on to something else after saying, "That's not right yet, but it is getting better." Then come back to it again and again later in the period or on other days until it is learned correctly.

If the problem is "out-of-tune" playing, then each note must be held out while everyone adjusts. The winds should adjust embouchure, try different fingerings (or both), and the strings should change their fingers to the proper spot. When they are all in tune announce: "That's fine! That's the way it should sound." Then, start at the beginning of the phrase, or at least a few notes before, play slowly to the problem spot and again wait until everyone adjusts. Then announce, "That's fine. That's the way it should sound." Repeat the above procedure until the phrase is in tune without waiting. If this does not happen the first day, in a reasonable amount of time (two or three minutes), go on, but come back and do it again the next day, etc. The students will eventually memorize what it sounds like when they are in tune, and be able to adjust intonation quickly or not miss it at all.

There are two facets of music that are the source of most of the problems that are difficult for all directors to solve. These areas are intonation and rhythm. Because they are such a problem, they will be treated at greater lengths in the paragraphs that follow.

Intonation

Intonation is a constant problem for all groups at all levels. Even professionals will play out of tune if they are allowed to. The only way groups can be taught to play in tune is to teach students to listen to themselves and each other. Contrary to what many people think, even the first lesson is not too soon to introduce the concept of playing in tune. This must be started very early before wrong habits are in-grained.

If listening is to produce "in-tune" performance (and nothing else will), there has to be some way to teach students what to listen for. The procedure outlined below will enable the teacher to present specific, concrete methods to help the students learn and gain the confidence needed to continue to strive for better intonation.

Perfect intonation at all times is not possible. Therefore, knowledge of the characteristics of sound and the psychology of human hearing must be used to help choose which intonation problems to attack and solve first. The problems most noticeable to the audience and those most easily solved should be the first ones worked on. Correction of these easily heard and easily solved problems will result in an immediate, obvious improvement.

Intonation problems are more noticeable:

(1) On long notes rather than on short ones (including groups of short notes, fast scale passages, etc.).

(2) On notes before a rest or at the end of a piece or phrase.

(3) On unison passages.

(4) On passages in octaves.

(5) On intervals of fourth or fifths.

(6) On imitative passages at unison or octave.

(7) In thinly scored passages rather than in tutti passages.

(8) In thickly scored tutti passages, *entrances* and *releases* that are *not together* expose intonation that would not be obvious if attacks and releases were clean.

(9) In the extreme registers of the instrument.

(10) When passages are played by *small groups of instruments.* Generally speaking, the larger the group of instruments playing, the less noticeable intonation problems become.

The above list can be used to help improve intonation in several ways. Initially it can act as a guide to help the teacher to select music that will either allow problems to be worked on, or music in which intonation problems will not be easily noticed.

According to this list, music that is mostly tutti, "moves around" or avoids octaves and unison passages, is the easiest to make sound "in tune" to many listeners. This is true, especially if played by a large group. This is why this kind of music is known to experienced school directors as "safe" music for contests.

The order of the items given above is a fairly good guide to the order of their difficulty and, therefore is a good tentative order in which to follow the solution of intonation problems (number 1 is the easiest to correct and number 10 is probably the most difficult).

Playing in tune comes only when performers know when they are in tune – not from a fine instrument, nor from the excellent ear of the leader. The students' instruments and the "ear" of the teacher have relatively little bearing on the ability of a group to perform in tune. The finest instruments in the world will only allow performers to play in tune. They will never cause them to! The ability of the teacher to hear is only helpful in so far as it helps the director to teach the students to hear whether they are in tune or not.

A performer will play in tune (or be miserable) when he recognizes what "in-tune" sounds like, and when, to him, all other sounds are unacceptable. The job of the teacher, therefore, is to make the students aware of what the correct sound is. Once students know what the "in tune" sound is, they will become extremely critical of out of tune performances.

The actual procedures to follow to change pitches up and down has been the subject of numerous articles. Generally, these things do not have to be referred to when working with students. Just demanding the desired "sound" will usually give the desired result. Knowledge of how to produce it however, does make it easier for the student and teacher.

Therefore, a very brief list of things follow that the teacher might have the various wind instrument players try whenever they are out of tune and the pitches need to be changed. Knowledge of alternate fingerings on all the wind instruments can also be of help to the teacher in solving intonation problems, but they are too detailed and exhaustive to be included here. For more information about them, the teacher should study the individual instruments privately, attend clinics and/or read books such as those listed at the end of this chapter.

Brass Instruments

The teacher must remember that once the general pitch level has been established and the main tuning slide has been set, they should not allow the students to change the main tuning slide if a note is out of tune. The student should change pitch with: embouchure (all brass instruments); playing slide (trombone); first and third valve trigger (cornets and trumpets); correct placement of hand in the bell (horn); fourth and fifth valves (some tubas and baritones); and individual valve tuning slides.

The teacher should be very careful about having the students pull valve tuning slides for purposes of intonation, because changing the valve tuning slide to help one harmonic can very well put another harmonic that uses the same valve out of tune. This is true because the length of any tuning slide is set in manufacturing by compromising between the ideal lengths needed for the various pitches that use any valve alone or in combination. Therefore, if one note is helped, there is a strong chance that other notes are being hurt.

Remember: The embouchure is used constantly on all brass instruments for fine tuning of all notes. If adjusting the embouchure, plus using the other suggestions, can't put a brass instrument in tune, the instrument is not usable and should be discarded. The chances of finding an instrument that just cannot be played in tune are very slight. Today's standard brand brass instruments are generally very satisfactory in this respect.

CLARINET

A clarinet has considerable flexibility of pitch downward but practically none upward. This is because clarinetists have been taught that to get a good sound they must play with a very firm embouchure. This means that a clarinetist that plays with a good sound plays very close to the top of his pitch at all times. Therefore, a clarinetist must set his barrel (in) so that he is a little sharp so that the pitch can be favored down with the embouchure because there is little or no room to go up.

A really good clarinetist will almost never play flat. If the clarinetist is using the correct embouchure (very firm) and he is still flat, either the barrel is too long, or the orchestra is playing at too high a pitch level. If the orchestra is playing at too high a pitch level, and the conductor prefers not to lower the pitch level to 440 CPS, the clarinetist will have to get a shorter barrel which probably will cause many pitch problems throughout the entire range of the instrument. It is much better to make sure that the group is playing at the proper pitch level rather than expect the wind players (particularly the clarinetists) to make radical pitch adjustments.

SAXOPHONE

Unlike the clarinet, the saxophone has a very large range of pitch control both up and down, and the pitch can and should be controlled by the embouchure. Many high school saxophone players use much too tight an embouchure, and as a result, play very sharp, especially in the higher registers. *Do not allow this.* Have them put their mouth on the mouthpiece until they can relax the embouchure and get the lower register in tune. Then, if the embouchure is kept loose and it is a good instrument, the saxophone should be fairly well in tune in the upper register as well. From this type of relaxed embouchure setting, a slight adjustment either way should allow the students to play in tune.

OBOE AND BASSOON

There are many reasons why an oboe or bassoon will play flat or sharp. The causes and their remedies are listed below:

The Instrument is Flat:

Cause	*Remedy*
Not enough reed in mouth	Put more reed in mouth
Embouchure too relaxed	Firm up embouchure around the reed
Reed too open	Squeeze reed by the wire so that the reed blades close a little
Lack of breath support and too relaxed an embouchure	More breath support and a firmer embouchure
Cracked reed	New reed

The Instrument is Sharp:

Cause	*Remedy*
Too much reed in mouth	Pull reed out of mouth
Embouchure too tight	Relax embouchure
Lack of breath support coupled with pinched embouchure (especially in high register)	Relax embouchure and add more breath support

When using any of the above remedies for pitch problems on the oboe and bassoon, the teacher must be aware of tone as well as pitch. Tightening and loosening the embouchure and moving the reed in and out of the mouth both cause both pitch and tone to change. If the wrong choice is made, it will affect tone quality adversely as well as change the pitch.

FLUTE

If there are pitch problems with a flute, the teacher should first check the head joint adjustment. Slide the cleaning rod gently into the head joint (solid end first) until it stops. The line around the end of the cleaning rod should be exactly in the middle of the embouchure hole. If it is not, adjust the head joint cork so that it is. When this is right, and the flute is generally in tune with itself (most standard American brands are), pitch adjustment will still need to be made on individual notes that will be slightly high or low.

Basically, there is one way to adjust the pitch of the flute while playing – the more the air stream is aimed down into the embouchure hole (i.e., the less the lower lip covers the hole), the lower the pitch will be. The more the air stream is aimed out towards the edge of the hole (the more the lower lips cover the hole), the higher the pitch will be.

There are three common ways to vary the direction of the air stream and/or the amount of lip covering the hole. They are rolling the flute in (lowers pitch) or out (raises pitch), ducking the head (lowers pitch) or raising the head (raises pitch), and moving the jaw in (lowers pitch) or out (raises pitch).

The teacher should be warned that flute teachers and players can be very vehement and combative about which are the correct ways and which are the wrong ways to change pitches. The safest way to approach this problem is to ask the students what their teacher has told them to do, and then have them do it that way. If there is no private teacher involved, the orchestra director will have to suggest one of the methods described here to the student. Generally, the rolling of the flute is the least popular method at this time. The moving of the jaw for pitch adjustment is the most recent method; however many fine teachers and players still move the head up and down with great success.

Ensemble

Some basic procedures to develop awareness of pitch and the ability to discriminate between pitches in the students will be detailed in the following paragraphs. Obviously, the whole procedure will not be followed all of the time on any grade level and only a very small part of it (the unisons) will be used in working with beginning students.

VERTICAL INTONATION

Tuning Unisons – The procedure, which must be a constant one, is as follows. First, the teacher should pick a tone from a piece (any tone will do). Have the students sustain this tone while the teacher says such things as: "Listen to that! It is terribly out of tune. How many people can tell?" Hopefully some students will raise their hands. If they do not, ask them to repeat the tone and the question. At this time, hopefully many students will raise their hands and say that it is wrong. Then, if it is a triad, the teacher should sing the chord to them: "1-3-5-3-1" or "Do-Mi-So-Mi-Do." If the note is a unison, as it would be in a beginning class situation, the teacher should skip to the procedure given to tune up unisons.

Second, the teacher should say: "Everyone is supposed to be playing one of the tones I just sang. Can you pick your tone out? NO? Then play the chord again and listen to yourself. Pick which tone is yours." The teacher then sings: "1-3-5-3-1" again and directs everyone who has "1" to play while everyone else listens. Some wrong tones will be played the first few times because some of the students will not yet know which pitch they are playing (one, three or five). Next the teacher should comment that some are playing wrong tones. He should sing 1-3-5-3-1 again and ask the class how many can hear that everyone is not playing or singing the tone asked for. When they can identify the pitches wanted by sound, then the comment should be made that the tones do not sound the same – that is, they are out of tune. Ask the students how many can now tell. If most or many still cannot tell, then ask for only a specific octave or even one section of instruments to play a unison. Again, the teacher should comment that it is still out of tune (it will be) and ask how many can hear that it is.

If the class still does not hear that it is out of tune after doing all of the above, have one student play the tone and another one pull out his tuning slide or move his finger until it is obviously flat and then tell him to slowly come up to pitch. (The trombone or cello is excellent for this.) Instruct the class to raise their hands when they hear the two pitches matching perfectly. Someone will probably comment, "That's fine, I can tell when they do it, but I cannot tell whether *I* am sharp or flat." The teacher's answer to them should be: "You do not need to know whether you are sharp or flat, you just need to know that it is *not right*."

The next step is to teach the students how to change. Logic dictates that if a tone is not in tune, it must be either sharp or flat; so if the pitch is changed, it has to either get better or worse. If it gets better, obviously the student is going the right way – if it gets worse, the student should then go the opposite way. After a while, making such necessary adjustments will be automatic and quite easy for the students. It becomes a matter of reflex – not an intellectual problem.

After all of this has been done, ask for a section to play the tone again. Point out that the tone sounds "rough" when it is out of tune and smooth and "clear" when it is in tune. Every time they play again the teacher should become harder and harder to please (it does not take long to get one tone perfectly in tune).

The tuning of unison procedure just described is the most basic and the key step to the whole process of hearing pitches. This particular part of the procedure can and should be used from the very earliest stages of teaching (even in the first year). *Caution:* Don't be discouraged if children of all ages apparently don't learn to do this immediately and also don't remember to do it every time. Learning to tune a unison is a long time, repetitive process.

Tuning Octaves – The next step would be to add the other octaves of the same tone (one octave at a time), and have the students listen for the "roughness" between the tones (beats).[1] If octaves are not in tune with groups of instruments, then the teacher should take two individuals at a time. Have one play one note and the other try to match it at the octave. Have one student move the pitch up and down so the class can hear the difference when it is in tune and out of tune. Have them raise their hands when they think that it is in tune. The teacher must give them immediate positive reinforcement by telling them when they have made the proper judgement.

Tuning Fifths and Thirds – The next step is to follow the same procedure used for octaves with the fifth of the chord. The teacher should sing "1-3-5-3-1." Ask for the "1" of the chord to be played in tune as above and then add the fifth. The teacher should teach them the sound of the perfect fifth in the same manner that the sound of the unison and octave were taught earlier. The next step is to teach them the sound of major and minor thirds in the same manner.

Tuning Sevenths – Last, the teacher can teach the students the seventh of the chord. Sing "1-3-5-7-5-3-1" and follow the same procedure as used before – root, fifth, third and seventh.

Perfect Intervals Are Not Flexible – Perfect intervals *must* always be tuned *first*, as they are the most obvious to hear and also, because there is the least room for differences of opinion. An octave or unison is *unquestionably* in or out of tune. A perfect fifth or fourth must also be played perfectly in tune.

Major and Minor Intervals Are Arbitrary – A major or minor interval can be played in several different places and still be acceptable to most ears because of the fact that opinion as to sound is a factor in these intervals (high third, low seventh in a seventh chord, leading tone, etc.). *Note*: Even though major and minor intervals can be played in different places and still be acceptable depending on who is listening, it is absolutely necessary that every teacher teach his students where he (the teacher) wants these intervals played. As has been indicated, this will be an arbitrary, personal decision, but it is one that must be made and then carefully taught to the students. This can be done by the application of the same principle that was used to teach the perfect intervals. Have the note played where it has been decided that it is to go and have them do it often enough that they memorize the sound of it.

[1]The "roughness" is a result of the sonic beats which occur when two pitches are rather close but not exactly the same. The lower the beats become the closer the pitches are to being the same. When the pitches are exactly the same, the beats will disappear and the tone will sound "smooth." The phenomenon of beats is much more noticeable when the wind instruments are playing than it is when the stringed instruments play.

HORIZONTAL INTONATION

By regularly following the procedure just discussed, good vertical intonation (simultaneous tones) can be taught successfully to junior high as well as high school performing groups. There still is horizontal intonation (consecutive tones) to conquer, but it is much less noticeable to any but the most discriminating audiences, so it can be approached after vertical intonation has been brought under control. That is not to say, however, that horizontal intonation is not important nor that it need not be a concern before groups reach this level. Actually, horizontal intervals should have been taught all along and the vertical intervals that are being learned now will serve as a "check" to make sure they are accurate.

Most problems of horizontal intonation can be simplified (using the above procedure) by extending the idea of learning the sound of chordal intervals to all major scale intervals. This is accomplished by having one person or section hold the first tone of a major scale while following the above procedure of listening and having students raise their hands whenever the sound is correct. Have one student play each note of a scale and compare it with the sustained tonic tone. This not only makes it easy to hear if the scale is in tune because of the constant reference to the sustained tonic, but it also develops a really definite idea of exactly where the notes have to be "put" to make a scale in tune.

The suggestions given in this intonation section by no means exhaust the things that can be done to improve intonation but, if they are followed consistently, will result in any group playing with fine intonation.

Rhythm

Because rhythm is primarily a physical reaction, it is felt by many music educators that rhythm should be taught as a physical reaction. This is done by teaching it through the physical act of tapping the foot. The "purists" will immediately react with alarm and say: "But we don't want the students to tap their feet when they are playing." The answer to this objection is twofold: (1) Use of the foot to help learn rhythm does not mean that tapping the foot is to become part of the performance. All agree that obvious tapping of the foot while playing a performance is distracting to the audience and should not happen. (2) Even among the professionals in the world's finest orchestras, feet (or toes) can often be seen tapping so it certainly cannot be said that tapping the foot keeps one from learning to play well. Why not, then, let the students use this as an aid to learn to play if the "pros" still use it at their level occasionally?

From the very first lesson, the child should be taught that in every time signature some kind of note gets one beat. Further, a "beat" is every time the foot comes down when it is tapping the tempo of the meter for that particular piece. They should never be permitted to practice anything without tapping the foot evenly at whatever speed the meter of the piece is going. From the first lesson on, *never* allow the students to tap the rhythm of the piece, only the meter. Thus, if they are playing quarter notes on the beat in 4/4 time, they must start each quarter note when the foot goes down (see Figure No. 8).

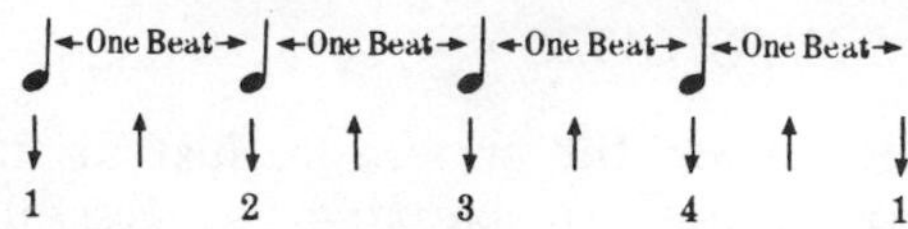

Relationship of Quarter Notes To Foot Movement
Figure No. 8

At this point the teacher should not mention that the foot also goes up, because it will only confuse the students. If they are playing half notes, then the note is held for two beats which last until the *third* tap of the foot (see Figure No. 9).

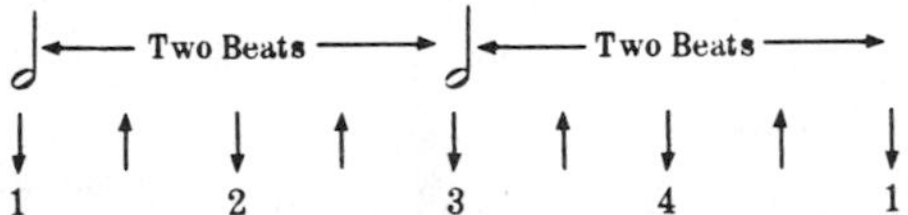

Relationship of Half Notes to Foot Movement
Figure No. 9

A dotted half note ges three beats which last until the fourth count and a whole note gets four beats which ends on beat one of the next measure (see Figure No. 10).

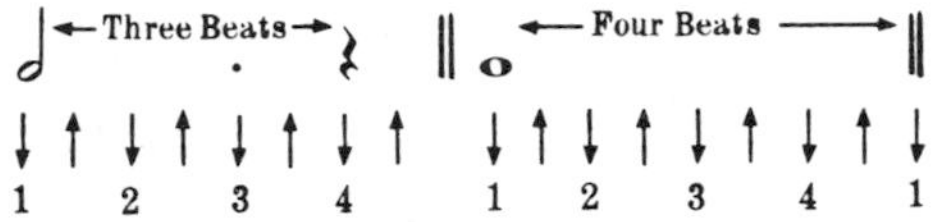

Three Beats   Four Beats

1 2 3 4   1 2 3 4 1

Relationship of Dotted Half and Whole Notes To Foot Movement
Figure No. 10

At the same time as they are learning these note values, the students should be taught that a quarter rest, half rest, and a whole rest get the same number of beats as their corresponding notes. By teaching this thoroughly, the teacher can reasonably expect children to know and be able to read these notes and rests (see Figure No. 11).

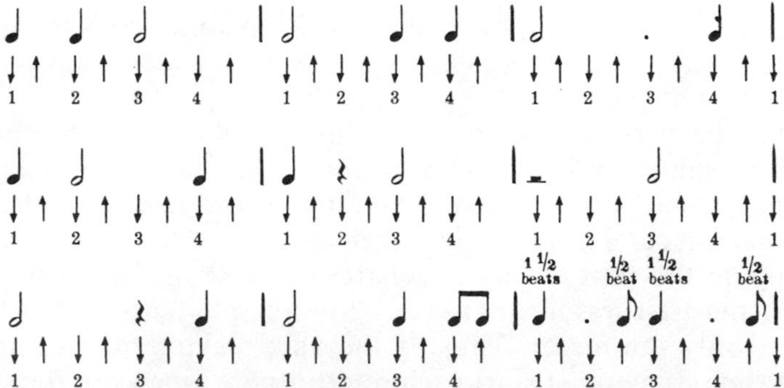

Rhythms Combining Several Note Values
Figure No. 11

Stringed Instruments

THE INSTRUMENT AND ITS ACCESSORIES

A very important area of concern that has a great effect on the tone quality of the string section is the quality, condition, and/or the adjustment of the instrument and its related accessories (bow, strings, rosin, height and shape of bridge, etc.)

Not only does the quality of the instrument, the type of strings, etc., affect the tone, but even such frequently overlooked details as the type of rosin, its use or lack of use, the tension and amount of bow hair and the placement of the bridge on the instrument can have considerable effect on the overall quality and quantity of sound produced.

Bows - Generally, students use the bow with too much tension and not enough rosin. For maximum sound, the bow should be as loose as possible and still allow the player to do spiccato and fortissimo playing without having the bow hair hit the bow stick. Many students, and some teachers, think that for maximum sound, a tight bow is needed. This is not so.

Rosin – As soon as the students have gained some bow control (when lots of rosin begins to come off on the top of the instrument), they should be asked to replace the light, ambered colored rosin (beginners rosin) with darker rosin. Require them to use it every day (most young string players do not use nearly enough rosin to get a good full tone from their instruments). Rosin on the tops of the instruments is a sign that the students are starting to add more bow weight into the string and thus need a softer rosin (dark rosin) that will grip the string more. The light, beginners rosin is sometimes marked violin, viola and cello. In reality, however, it is all the same as is the dark rosin that should be used from the second year on. Basses are the exception, and they must use rosin marked "Bass" and numbered 1, 2, 3, 4, or 5 (the higher the number, the harder the rosin; the lower the number, the softer the rosin). All bass rosin is softer and stickier than even the dark violin, viola, and cello rosin. This is a necessity so that the bass bow can grip the string firmly enough to be able to completely set its thicker strings in motion.

The teacher should have the bass beginners use the harder, less sticky rosin. As the beginning bass player progresses, he will eventually need to change to a stickier, softer rosin, but only its number will change – not its color. Another even more basic reason for the five hardnesses (stickiness) of bass rosin is to allow for variation in room temperatures and climate. The warmer the climate or temperature, the harder or less sticky the rosin and vice versa. Most players will have a harder "summer" rosin and a softer, winter rosin. However, with climate control that exists today (thermostatically controlled air conditioning and heating units), it may be unnecessary to have more than one kind of rosin. *Warning*: Do not allow bass players to use violin, viola, or cello rosin – it won't do the job.

IMPORTANCE OF CORRECT USE OF HANDS

Tone quality and tone production must be a constant concern. In the beginning stages (the first two or three years), this concern will consist mainly of the teacher being insistent that the students use both hands correctly. How the hands are used greatly affects how much or how little tone the group will have. Areas that the teacher *must* be concerned with are:

(1) The right thumb is curved (away from the hand).

(2) The bow is moving in a straight line.

(3) Ability to use the whole bow (the designated amount for each student) for quarter and longer notes on all legato (detaché) passages.

(4) No more than half of the bow is used for eighth notes.

(5) Ability to execute a smooth change of bow direction.

(6) Each up bow is pushed clear back to the frog (provided the down bow was started at the frog).

(7) All bows within each string section are going in the same direction.

(8) All students exert solid pressure into the string (fingerboard) with the fingers of the left hand.

The above areas are studied in greater detail in Part II, Chapter II.

ADVANCED BOW SKILLS

While the above areas must be constantly and forever stressed to the students, the instructor should realize that as the students develop the ability to use the bow correctly and consistently, they will need to be taught other more advanced bow skills, as well as left hand skills. Eventually, the student should be able to play with a slow moving bow placed closer to the bridge and pushed into the string to give a louder, more intense sound. This is especially necessary for a solid tone on slurs and longer notes. The ability to play off the string (spiccato) and, in particular, be able to change back and forth from on the string to off the string playing should also be developed.

ADVANCED LEFT HAND SKILLS

At about the same time that the students are learning more advanced bow skills, there are some advanced left hand skills that the teacher will need to make sure the students are learning: (1) Use of the fourth finger on the violin and viola to eliminate the harsh sound of the open string, (2) Shifting to higher positions on all instruments so as to be able to play with a softer tone and quality than the same notes would have in first position, and (3) Vibrato.

Wind Instruments

Tone quality must be a constant concern for winds as well as strings. Since it is almost a lifetime project to learn all there is to know about proper tone production on any *one* instrument, it would be presumptuous to pretend to tell all there is to know about all of the wind instruments in this book. However, there are some general principles, which if known and followed, will enable a teacher to help solve at least some of the more common problems faced in a public school instrumental music situation. The most fundamental factors involved in achieving good sound from the winds are breath support and/or control, embouchure, mouthpiece, reed, and adjustment and condition of instruments.

BREATH SUPPORT

For all wind instruments, improper breath support is probably the most important single cause of tone problems. For the brass players, this means keeping the throat open and a good flow of air from the diaphragm going clear through the instrument. The concept should be that the breathing be as effortless and relaxed as possible. Any resistance to the movement of the air stream should come from the mouthpiece and/or the instrument – never from the performer (throat, embouchure, etc.).

For the woodwinds, the breath should also come from the diaphragm in a steady, intense flow of air through the instrument. The difference in the woodwinds is that the air stream is not as large nor as fast moving as with brasses, but rather, more of an intense, steady push against resistance. (The reed in the case of the clarinets, saxophone, oboe, English Horn, and bassoon, but the embouchure in the case of the flute.)

The order of the next three items is an arbitrary one because the embouchure, mouthpiece and reed are so interdependent that it is hard to know which one really is the most basic. If the mouthpiece is not matched with the proper reed (clarinets and saxes), then even a proper embouchure will not allow a sound to be produced. Likewise, a good reed is an absolute necessity for a double-reed instrument or a good embouchure will produce out of tune playing and/or a bad tone.

EMBOUCHURE

The embouchure is the second factor to check if a bad sound is coming from the instrument of a wind player. Occasionally, a player will produce a good sound with an apparently terrible embouchure. But, this is not the person we are concerned with, unless the teacher is an expert on that particular instrument. Even then, it is best to be extremely careful about "fooling" with an embouchure in orchestra rehearsal. If a person is getting a bad sound and they are apparently breathing correctly, then the teacher should next check the embouchure. If the embouchure is not a "standard," legitimate type embouchure, then this is the logical place to start. Pictures of good embouchures on clarinet, saxophone, flute, oboe, bassoon, trumpet (cornet), trombone, French horn and tuba follow with a brief discussion of what to look for when a student is suspected of having trouble in this area (see Figures No. 12-19).

With brass instruments the embouchure problems generally fall into just a very few categories. Perhaps the most common error to watch for is the "collapsed" embouchure with air pockets under the cheeks and/or the lips. The entire area from the nose to the chin and from corner to corner of the lips must be firm and flat to prevent this. Another cause of bad sound and upper range problem is when the lips are allowed to roll out so that the inner part of one or both of the lips is being pushed into a buzzing position instead of having both lips slightly rolled in. The teacher should check also to see that the lips are not pulled back in a smile but rather pushed forward (see the pictures in Figure Nos. 12-15).

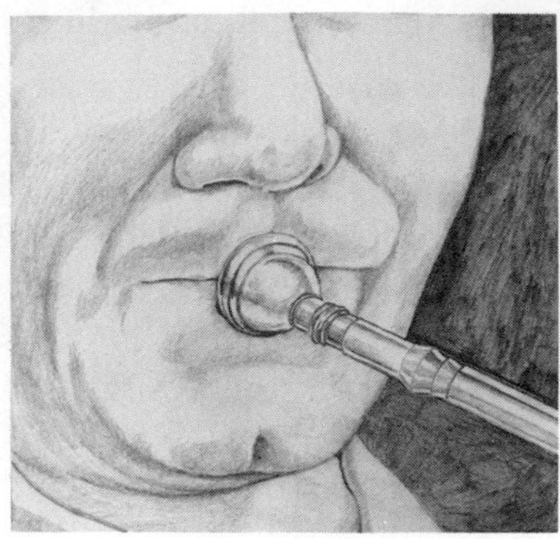

Trumpet Embouchure
Figure No. 12

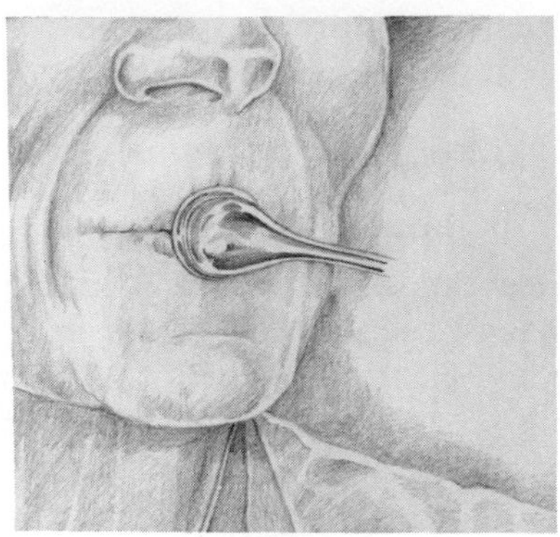

French Horn Embouchure
Figure No. 13

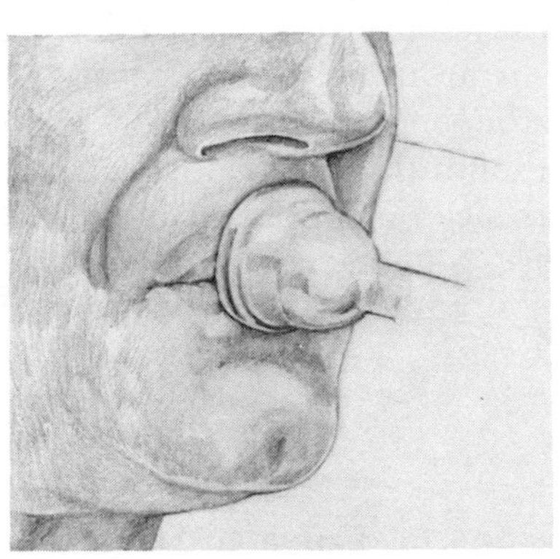

Trombone Embouchure
Figure No. 14

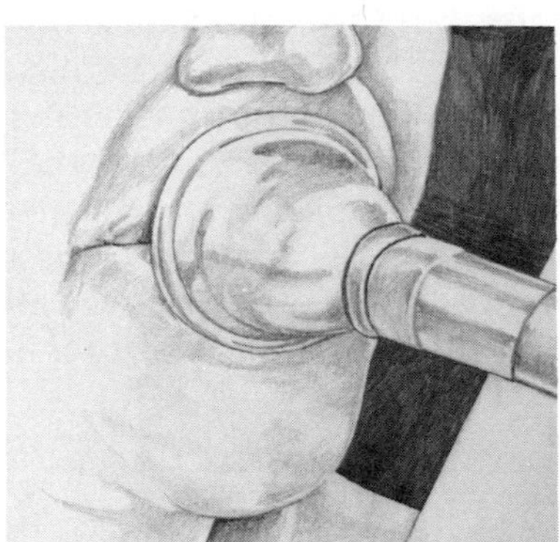

Tuba Embouchure
Figure No. 15

The clarinet embouchure problems usually will be of just a few types. The most common one is the collapsed embouchure. Here the chin bunches up and, the corners of the mouth are not firm and there is too much lip in the mouth. To correct this, the teacher must insist that the student's chin be pulled down until it is pointed. The corners must be firm and there must be just enough lip pulled into the mouth to cover the teeth with as small a part of the edge of the lip as is possible. The lips, upper and lower, should be shaped into the form of an oval. No pressure is to be put on the reed by the teeth, as only the corners of the lips should be controlling the tension on the reed (see pictures in Figure No. 16).

The most common embouchure problem for the saxophonist is an embouchure that is too tight. A saxophone player must have an almost completely relaxed embouchure (both against the reed and around the mouthpiece) or the instrument will play out of tune in all registers and be very sharp in the upper register. A good clarinet embouchure will not work for a saxophone (see pictures in Figure No. 17).

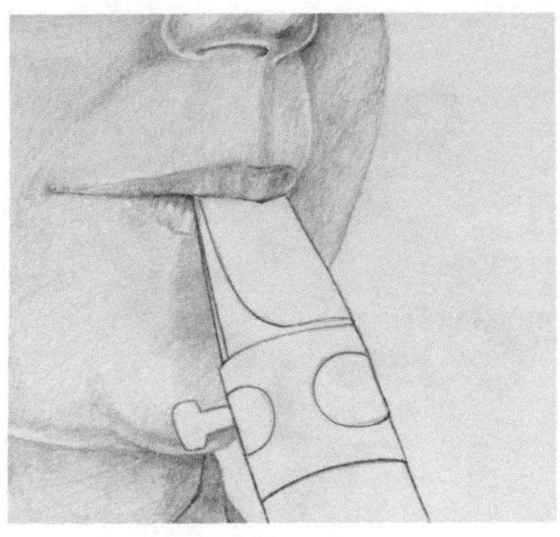

Clarinet Embouchure
Figure No. 16

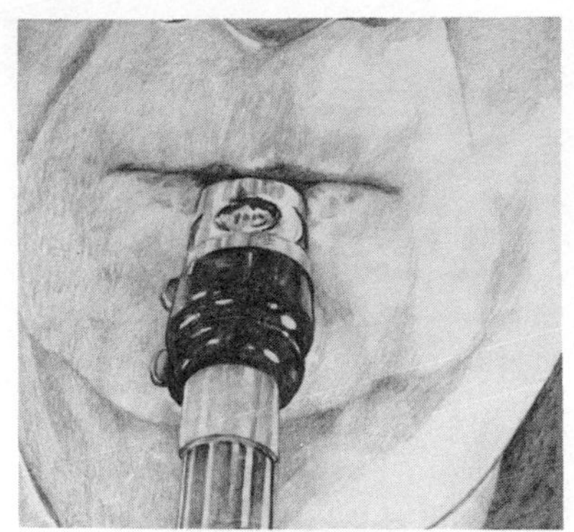

Saxophone Embouchure
Figure No. 17

The most common embouchure problem for the oboe and the bassoon is too much tension – squeezing the blades of the reed together with the lips. The embouchure should be formed around the reed and not squeezed against it (see Figure No. 18). *Note*: The "proper"' embouchure as just described can only be used if the reed is adjusted correctly (see the section on pitch).

(A)

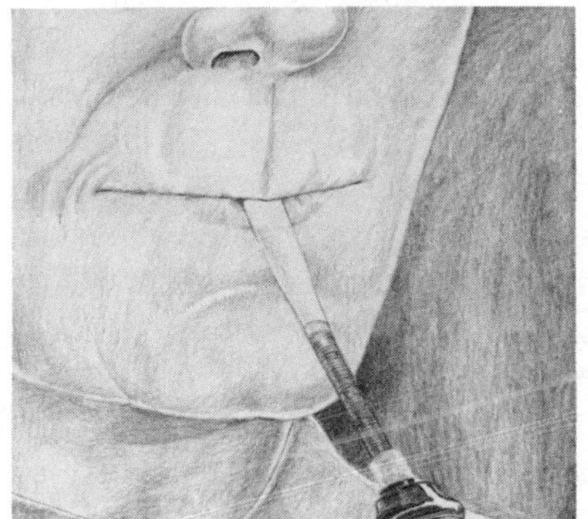

Oboe

(B)

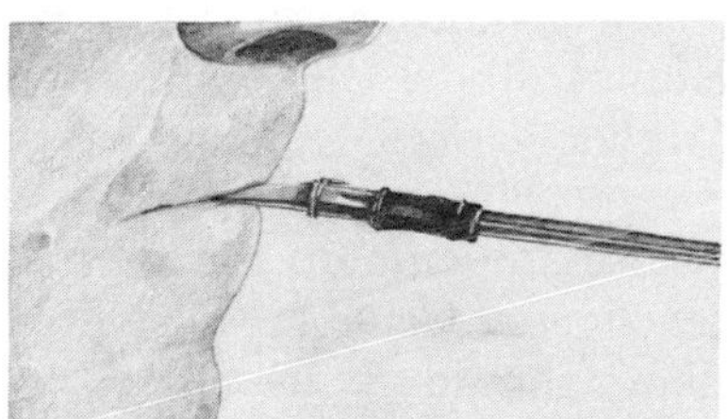

Bassoon

Oboe and Bassoon Embouchures
Figure No. 18

The most common problem with flute embouchures is the lack of centering the flute on the lips or not having the air stream centered as it comes through the lips. The lips must be centered vertically over the embouchure hole of the flute. The flute must be centered horizontally on the lips so that the amount of upper and lower lip showing are equal. Further, the air stream causing the sound should be centered as it leaves the lips (see Figure No. 19).

Flute Embouchure
Figure No. 19

MOUTHPIECE

Brass Instruments – Mouthpieces are extremely important in determining the type of sound that an instrument will get. Generally, for high school brass instruments, a good medium mouthpiece is best. Do not allow students to use extremely shallow mouthpieces to "help" their high register. They do not really help and in any event, they will not give a good legitimate, resonant sound. A list of recommended medium mouthpieces that will give good sound if played properly are: Cornet and Trumpet (Bach 7C or 5C); French Horn (Giardinelli C8 or Conn 5BW); Tenor Trombone (Bach 6½ AL); large bore Tenor Trombone with F attachment (Bach 5G); American Tuba (Bach 18), European Tuba (Helleberg C3); Clarinet (Selmer Golden Tone #3, Noblet Model 2B, or Portnoy BP02 – advanced players); Alto Saxophone (Meyer 4 or 5M), and Tenor Saxophone (Meyer 4M, Brillhart Eboline #4).

The preceding list is meant only as a guide for the use of teachers whose students do not have access to fine private teachers. If a good private teacher is available, take his or her advice as to what mouthpieces the students should be using. It should be mentioned, however, that the trend in brass mouthpieces is towards deeper, larger mouthpieces because they give a bigger, more resonant sound. Don't be tempted to recommend larger mouthpieces, because they may require more breath control and maturity of playing than most players can achieve without lessons with a specialist on the instrument.

Clarinet – The choice of mouthpieces has even more effect on the tone quality of a clarinet than it has on a brass instrument. A good mouthpiece and reed on a poor clarinet will give an acceptable sound. A poor mouthpiece and/or reed will make even the finest clarinet sound terrible. The correct mouthpiece with the wrong reed can also prevent the tone quality from being characteristic. The most important quality in matching the reed to the mouthpiece is the hardness of the reed. The reed should never be less than a 2½ on the Portnoy BP02 and even beginners should use at least a 2½ reed on a good beginning mouthpiece such as a Golden Tone No. 3 (Selmer) or Noblet 2B. If the 2½ reed won't work, either the embouchure is too loose, the mouthpiece is not far enough in the mouth, the angle is wrong or the mouthpiece is not suitable. (There are cheaper beginning mouthpieces on the market that are designed for a softer reed and a more relaxed embouchure. These should not be used because they prevent the young student from developing an embouchure that allows a good sound).

The other qualities of the reed that affects tone are the cut of the reed and the quality and the type of cane used in the manufacture of the reed. The choice of the proper cut, brand of reed, etc. is a very personal one and rather controversial. It would be easy to get an argument going in any group of clarinetists about the relative merits of various brands, cuts of reeds, etc. Nevertheless, some workable combinations of reed and mouthpieces are: For the beginners, the Noblet 2B or the Selmer golden tone works well with the #2½ Rico or LaVoz reed. For more advanced players, a Portnoy BP02 mouthpiece works well with a #3½ Van Doren or LaVoz reed.

Saxophone – The matching of the reed and the mouthpieces are as important for the saxophone as they are for the clarinet. Again, it is necessary that the student have a good medium mouthpiece and reed so that he can use a relaxed embouchure which will give the best results. Some workable combinations for the alto saxophone are Meyer 4M or 5M or the Selmer Selmer C Star mouthpiece with a La Voz medium or Rico 2½ reed. For the tenor saxophone, the Meyer 4M or Brillhart Eboline #4 mouthpiece works well with the Rico 2½ or La Voz medium or medium soft reed.

Double-reeds – For the double reed instruments – the oboe, English horn and bassoon, the reed is the mouthpiece and reed all at once. The sound and pitch of these instruments is almost completely dependent on the reed. Ideally, they should be custom made for the person and the instrument. Many times, a local college will have a double reed person who will do this for students even though they do not study with them. If this service is not available, then the next best thing to do is to have the student get a reed from a dealer, by mail or the teacher can have some reeds on hand for resale. There are reeds commercially available that can be depended upon to be at least somewhat uniform from one purchase to the next, and of the proper design, hardness, etc. to allow the student to get a good sound without distorting the embouchure.

A reed available nationally that seems to be generally acknowledged by oboe and bassoon teachers as satisfactory (if a custom made one is not available) is the medium Meason reed. If it is necessary to use commercial reeds, the teacher and/or students should learn how to "doctor" the reeds as soon as possible (shave a little wood away in certain spots) by going to a college reed-making and adjusting clinic. All double reed players agree that if their reed is good they can play – if it isn't good, catastrophe! One last word on oboe and bassoon sound – an oboe should not sound like a duck! A good oboe or bassoon sound is a smooth resonant sound – not a raspy cutting sound. If there are no good teacher-performers available in the local area, the teacher should make records available for listening by the students as the first step in being able to create a good sound is to know what a good sound is.

Flute – The flute should have a resonant sound in all registers and a rather "reedy" sound in the lower register. As with all the other wind instruments, the breath needs to be supported from the diaphragm. The air stream needs to be "centered" across the embouchure hole for the best sound. Usually when the sound is not what it should be – lack of "centering" the air stream or improper direction of the air stream is the cause.

CONCLUSION

For further, more detailed, information about the intricacies of reed-making and adjustment, as well as the fundamentals of tone production on wind instruments, the teacher should refer to the list of materials at the end of this chapter.

Style and Musicianship

Hopefully, as soon as the orchestra is able to play the right notes at the right time with good tone and intonation (a considerable undertaking), a desire to make music out of all of these things will arise. Doing all of the above things right (notes, rhythm, good tone and intonation) is not the end goal of music making but rather how the notes are played. Music is an art rather than a science. One of the tests of the validity of a scientific experiment is that if it is done properly by many different people, the results will always predictably be the same. If the results are not the same, either a mistake was made or the project was improperly designed. Because music is an art, rather than a science, each performance of a piece of music should be unique to the performer and probably even to that particular performance. This is true because it is probably impossible for anyone to play a piece of music twice in exactly the same way.

The reason that music can be played "right" by many different people and still be different is that the expressive elements of music are all incapable of being indicated precisely on the printed page. These expressive elements are volume and changes of volume, tempo and changes of tempo and the amount of space (time) between notes. By varying these things within a piece of music there are virtually limitless ways of performing a piece. This is not to imply that all of the ways that these factors can be varied would be musically acceptable to most people. Fortunately however, the options for a logically acceptable musical performance grow out of certain rather well-defined musical considerations. Many musicians make these decisions on a purely intuitive basis. This is very good except that at certain times, intuition may fail to function, so it is a good idea to have an intellectual foundation from which to start in order to get the "creative juices" flowing. Years of observations have shown that intuitive musical decisions are based on underlying reasons that can be abstracted, generalized and categorized for use in other situations having similar musical considerations.

Probably the most basic concept of all in interpretation is that all notes of a phrase are not equally important. To play musically, one must choose some notes to emphasize while others are played with less emphasis. Subtle changes in dynamic levels and length of beats and notes within a phrase can serve to distinguish the more important from the less important notes. Further, there are underlying general principles, which, if applied, limit the number of choices that can be made in order to produce a "musical" performance. This is not to suggest that musical playing can be reduced to a formula that will result in a performance that will please everyone, but that there are limits within which most musicians will accept what is done interpretively even if they may not agree with it.

The application of general principles to come up with an interpretation need not result in a stereotyped performance, as it will be noticed that some of the principles are contradictory and thus allow several choices. A very effective device, for example, is to do the unexpected and consciously ignore the principles, or apply them in reverse. A good thought to keep in mind is that any attempt to play "musically" is better than no attempt at all.

There are several ways to examine the music for clues as to what to do. Consider melodic line; rhythmic and metric structure – beats (basic accent pattern) and length of notes; harmonic structure; style of piece – type and period; and relative importance of parts, particularly in music of a polyphonic nature.

Many of the suggestions given here are known to most musicians; but they are many times not applied consciously and consistently, and they are generally not taught to young groups.

Melodic Line

Possibly the first and most important step in deciding how to play a melody is to decide where the phrases begin and end, because a phrase must be played as an entity, not as unrelated parts. It is true that any mature musician knows intuitively where phrases begin and end, but there are times when phrases are ambiguous. In such cases, an arbitrary decision must be made. The director should realize that any decision that establishes phrase definition is better than no decision at all.

Fortunately, most music does have a recognizable phrase structure. In addition, most conventional music (marches, overtures, symphonies) will use phrases that are two, four or eight measures in length, with the majority of them having four measure phrases. As a rule, phrases within a piece will all start on the same beat. They will usually also all end on the same beat.

Once a phrase has been isolated, the next step is to know how to play the phrase. An important principle is that a phrase must start from a point of rest, build tension (usually with a crescendo and/or a slight stringendo) and then return again to a point of relative rest (usually with a decrescendo and/or a slight rallentando). Another obvious idea is to play ascending melodies with a crescendo and descending melodies with a decrescendo. A variation of this idea can be used with melodies involving sequential or repetitive figures. Here, a general dynamic change should be made between the figures as well as between the notes within the figures. Generally, *a figure repeated at a higher pitch level can effectively be played at a louder dynamic level; a repeated figure played at a lower pitch level can effectively be played at a softer dynamic level.* These differences cannot be too subtle, or they will not be observed by the audience.

Rhythmic and Metric Considerations

The major considerations here are order of importance of beats and leading-tendencies. The most important beat in any measure is the first. The last beat in a measure has a tendency to lead to the first beat of the next measure. The other beats in a measure, depending on their position, have similar (but less strong) functions. In a 4/4 measure for example, the first beat is the strongest, and the fourth beat (unless it ends the phrase) leads directly to the first beat of the next measure. The relationship of beat two leading to beat three is similar to beat four leading to one, only not quite as strongly.

An understanding of the function and order of importance of beats is especially important in the playing of pick-up notes. In three-note pick-ups, such as this: (4/4 ) the first note should not be accented, since it falls on the relatively weak second beat, but rather, the second note should be stressed as it falls on the strongest beat that is left to be played (the third beat). By extension of the same logic, in groups of three eighth or sixteenth notes following rests, the second note is again the note to be accented *(Notes on the beat are more important than notes off of the beat). Example:* 2/4  .

The other rhythmic consideration is the relative length of notes found in the melodic line. Generally, the longer the duration of a note, the more important it is and the louder it should be played. Conversely, the shorter the duration of a note, the softer it should be. This is important as many unmusical effects are produced by musicians trying to play sixteenth note figures as loud as the surrounding longer notes.

Harmonic Considerations

In conventional tonal music, dissonances used to increase tensions are followed by non-dissonant chords of rest or resolution. The feeling of tension on the dissonance may be heightened by a slight increase in volume and the feeling of relaxation on the resolution by a diminuendo. (The "ooh-ah" effect). Some very fine performers also increase the rate and size of their vibrato on dissonances and decrease or remove it completely on the resolution in order to heighten this effect.

Stylistic Considerations

Stylistic considerations also effect the way in which a piece of music is performed. A dance, such as a minuet or waltz, may be associated with a specific tempo or manner of playing. Be sure to read the name of the piece as obviously a piece named "Gypsy Dance" should not be played like a piece called "Lullaby."

The name of the composer also can be a valuable clue as to how a piece of music should be played, because many times, the composer's name will enable you to place the piece in the proper period (Baroque, Classical, etc.). This is important because each period has idiosyncracies that, if known, affect how the music is to be played. For example, in the Baroque period, it is customary to use block dynamic contrast on repeated motifs. Classical music is very light and delicate and a great deal of use is made of the spiccato articulation for the strings. Music of the Romantic period is likely to give more opportunity for rubato treatment of certain passages.

Relative Importance of Parts

Some very obvious rules to be followed are:

(1) The accompaniment is to be softer than the melody

(except on many phrase endings where the accompaniment sometimes becomes a counter melody).

(2) Moving parts are almost always to be stressed more than stationary parts.

(3) In imitative music, entrances are to be heard at the expense of the continuing part.

(4) When two or more things of apparently equal importance are happening to the music, choosing an order of importance (arbitrarily if necessary) will help the audience to comprehend the structure of the music. If a section is repeated, stress a different part the second time.

Obviously all of the things mentioned as possibilities for making music more expressive and giving the opportunity for creativity on the part of the performer(s) cannot be used on the elementary and junior high level. However, the general principles of musical playing can and should be taught from the first year on. As soon as the students begin to play they should be made aware that a piece of music, or even a line of music, divides into parts called phrases and that one phrase is distinct from another. Even the youngest students should be taught that a repeated phrase is played at a different dynamic level the second time to avoid boredom.

By the second year, the students should also be aware that the first beat of a measure should be stressed and that it is a good idea to crescendo as the melody ascends and decrescendo as the melody descends. If part music is being played (it should be) then the students should be aware that at different times some parts are more important than others and why.

During the third year, within the limits of their capabilities, pretty much everything outlined in this section on Musicianship should be a part of their rehearsal and musical experience. Don't ever underestimate the ability of the students to learn to try to "do something" with the music. They can be concerned about musicianship at any level and they have a great interest in doing so. This may be the very thing that really "turns on" the brighter students in the class.

The biggest obstacle to musical playing for most people is the fear that they will do something wrong. Actually the only thing that is truly "wrong" musically is to do nothing at all. Nothing that is done for a musical effect can be "wrong" although some people may not like it, or may question the taste of the conductor. This is a gamble that the director must take if music is to be an expression of individuality and creativity. This is where the excitement and thrill of teaching and directing school groups must be. Something (anything!) is better than doing nothing at all musically. The conductor must be the one to do this – if it is to be done, as there is no way that a composer and/or an arranger can possibly indicate everything that needs to be done in the score. Wolfgang Mozart said: "Play – with plenty of expression, taste, and fire."

The students' attitudes towards the teacher, the music and what is supposed to be happening at the rehearsals is probably the most important single factor that influences what is or isn't going to happen with a musical group.

If the students want to do what the teacher wants them to do, then anything the teacher is able to teach is possible for the students. On the other hand, if the students do not want to do what the teacher wants them to do, nothing can be accomplished. Therefore, if the teacher is to have goals and accomplish them, a primary task is to somehow make the students feel that they want to work and learn to play music beautifully no matter how hard it may seem. In order to teach this sort of an attitude to the students, there are some things that, if done consistently, will result in students that will not only work hard and long but will also enjoy it!

Success is the greatest motivator of all, therefore, if the teaching situation can be structured in such a way that the students leave class every day feeling that they have been successful in even some small way, they will keep coming back to class and trying to succeed again. Success can not just be the teacher saying "That's fine." It must also be apparent to the students that progress has been made and that they are playing better than when they came into class. To do this, it is necessary that the problem to be solved be broken down into parts that can be accomplished in a period or less. Also, the task to be accomplished should be defined to the students in such a way that they know exactly what they are to do and will know when they have done it. For instance, the teacher might say: "Today we are going to play this passage perfectly at metrenome marking equals 116 instead of at 112 where we played it yesterday." Or: "Today we are going to learn both high second finger and low second finger on the violin and viola A string."

The teacher must set the goals in such a way, and then teach so efficiently towards these goals, that the child *has* to succeed. As soon as possible, the idea should be implanted in the students' minds that the teacher is there to help them achieve their goals. The students should not feel as if the teacher is making them do things.

Some rules that will help the teacher to develop positive attitudes in the students and help them to avoid frustration, if followed consistently are:

(1) The group should never be stopped without being told what was wrong and what to do about it.

(2) Full rehearsals should not be used to work on individual or small group problems.

(3) The group should be stopped *only* if the students are not aware of a problem or don't know how to correct it. Many mistakes will correct themselves – some will not. It is frustrating to a student to be stopped for a mistake that he already is aware of and is possibly already a little embarrassed about anyway. It is also frustrating to a student when a teacher asks him to keep playing a part over and over that he can't handle and the director doesn't give help on it.

(4) Although the students must practice for perfection, and they cannot stop trying to improve until this goal is reached, they must realize that they are not failures if they do not achieve perfection.

(5) The teacher must give constant encouragement, but never let the students feel that they have achieved perfection. Goals should be set that are just a little bit out of their reach, but never so far removed that they seem unobtainable. The director should say things like: "That was really much better but now we need to do this."

(6) The students should have pride in their playing and always play to the best of their ability. The teacher should insist on high standards and give the group the tools to achieve the goals that have been set for them.

(7) The teacher must make sure that the students think about what they are doing and why they are doing it so that they can eventually function without the teacher and make independent musical decisions.

(8) The students must be made to realize that a criticism of their playing is *not* a criticism of them personally.

(9) The teacher *must* realize that deserved praise for improvement and accomplishment is far more effective than censure in motivating the students to excel.

(10) If much of the rehearsal has been spent on intense work on a small portion of a composition, it is a good idea for the director to put the problem passage back into the context of the piece before finishing the rehearsal so that the students can see that progress has been made.

(11) Each student must feel that it is his responsibility to play every note of every piece as though it were a solo performance. If the student *cannot* do this, the music is too difficult, improperly rehearsed, or the right attitudes have not been developed by the teacher.

(12) The director should end each rehearsal on a positive note. If possible, it should be ended with music that will show the improvement made that day and/or something that the students like to play.

The Importance of Competition for Seating

Introduction

Competition is a fact of life and it can and should be used by a teacher as long as it helps the group to play better. It should not be allowed to become cut throat nor an end to itself. Students should want to play better so that they can assume more responsibility and help the group to play better, not so they can "beat" someone else. It is also good psychologically to have the students feel that they have some control over where they are placed in the section.

Tryouts for positions in the section should be routinely held at least twice a year and, at any other time when it seems that people are either playing much better or worse than they should be for their positions in the section. Also, if someone is really unhappy, they should be able to request another tryout (or to challenge) the person or persons that are ahead of them. The tryouts or challenges should *never* take time from a full rehearsal. They should be done during sectionals that are held at some other time.

Challenges

A challenge differs from a tryout in that, in a tryout everybody plays and is evaluated. A challenge, however, involves only two or three students playing for an evaluation and possible reseating (more of an individual contest). Challenges should not be done even in sectionals more than once or twice. After that, the students should be required to come in on their own time to decide these matters. In matters of seating, once the seating plan has been decided on, the students should no longer be allowed to influence the seating plan but only the seating order (see Figure No. 1). The students must be made to feel that the seating order is important only in so far as it affects the sound of their section and/or the orchestra.

SECTIONALS

Sectionals should be scheduled regularly as needed before or after school, during study halls, etc. Individual and small group problems should be saved for sectionals with each of the string sections, the woodwinds, brass, percussion or possibly all of the winds, as it is inefficient to have large groups of people sit and do nothing while a few people rehearse.

Sectionals are necessary on every level to insure that every person has a chance to be checked and helped on all of the myriad of details that many times may involve only a few people. When preparing for a contest or any other performance where the highest standards of excellence are desired, it is necessary to go these extra lengths to see that things are being done properly on *every level!* Most students cannot be depended on to work to the utmost of their ability *unless* they are individually helped and checked periodically.

HOME PRACTICE

The authors feel that individual home practice is desirable and a good thing to encourage. It is felt, however, that the emphasis should be on the students being able to play the music properly rather than trying to check up on the students to see whether they have practiced a specific amount each week. The important thing is not how much they have practiced that counts but rather whether they can do what is asked of them. Some will need to practice a lot and others won't need to do much. It is far better to be concerned about how well they play the music rather than demand a specific amount of practice time.

The importance of the percussion section must not be overlooked as its potential to help or hurt a fine group can not be overstated. Fortunately, while a fine percussionist is a rare treasure, and the knowledge, training and musical ability required for excellence in the field cannot and must not be unappreciated, the director must know comparatively little to have a good functional percussion section.

Probably the greatest contribution the director can make is to help instill a sense of pride in the percussion section by making them feel that they are so important that he is aware of everything that they do. They must be made to feel that good tone production by the percussion section is just as important to the director as good tone production by any other section. Tone production in a percussion section is affected mostly by how the instrument is struck, where it is struck and with what it is struck. The relative importance of these factors varies with the instruments being considered and in this short section on percussion instruments, only the *most* important points will be mentioned.

Another way to build pride in the section is to have every percussionist have a case for snare drum sticks and mallets which should be individually owned. This way every percussionist can come to orchestra with a case full of equipment just as the other players do.

Cymbals

CHOOSING THE INSTRUMENT

The cymbals are probably unknowingly misplayed more often than any other percussion instrument. First of all, the cymbals must be chosen for the sound desired. Cymbals vary in size (diameter), thickness, and quality. When buying cymbals, several sets of cymbals of various sizes, thicknesses, and brands should be tried before deciding on the set desired. If the sound produced from the cymbals is not the desired sound, perhaps making different sets by mixing thicknesses will give the wanted sound.

PLAYING

Cymbals should not "clang." They should not "thunk" or sound like two garbage can lids being hit together. They should have a nice bright "ring" or "zing" to the sound. To achieve this effect, the player must know several things about how to strike the cymbals together (see Figure No. 20). First, the cymbals must not ever hit together so that the circumferences of the two cymbals are flat together (Figure D). Rather, one of the cymbals is held at about a 60 degree angle to the floor (Figure A) and the other should be brought up against it in such a way that the edge of the bottom cymbal strikes below the edge of the higher (descending) cymbal (Figure B). This will cause the bottom of the rising cymbal to swing in and hit above the bottom edge of the descending (upper) cymbal (Figure C). At no time must the cymbals be allowed to assume the position shown in Figure D.

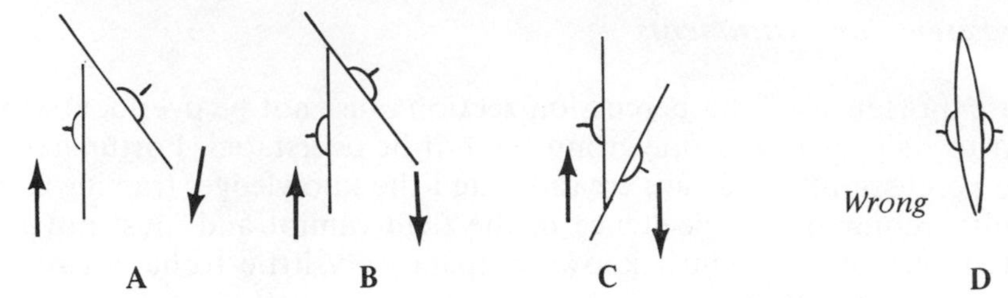

Proper and Improper Striking of Cymbals
Figure No. 20

If the cymbals are very large, percussionists sometimes bump them on their knee to get them vibrating before a big "crash" for better sound.

Snare Drum

STICKS

Do not allow snare drummers to use the "clubs" (big heavy sticks) that they use for marching band. To get a nice "buzzing" sound and good clean articulation, the orchestra drummer should use light sticks and tighten the heads and the snares.

WHERE TO PLAY

The snare drum has different sounds when played in different places. (Distance from the center and/or the edge of the head) and if not tuned evenly, it will even have different sounds when played in different places around the head.

The teacher should take the time to have the percussionists play in different spots around the head and more from the edge of the head to center and back to find the spots where the sound is what the director wants, then insist on that particular sound.

Bass Drum

There are two important things that the director must watch for to make sure that the bass drum is producing the best possible sound. The drum must be hit with a glancing blow – (Right) ↗ (Wrong) ↓. Also, as with any other drum, where the head is struck definitely affects the type of sound. Generally, about half-way between the center and edge will produce the best sound. This can and will vary, however depending on how the bass drum is tuned. Again, the best procedure is to experiment and have the drummer move around on the drum head until the spot is found that gives the sound that is desired. After this spot is located, the teacher must listen for and insist on that sound or the percussionists may get lazy and hit the drum improperly and/or in the wrong spot.

Tympani

There are two major problems to deal with in regard to the tympanist. One, is that the head must be tuned properly so that the tone quality will be clear and in tune. To get a clear in-tune sound, the tympani head must be in tune with itself. To accomplish this, the pitch must sound the same when the head is struck all around the edge by each tuning knob. If the pitch varies, the knob nearest the spot that is being struck should be changed until the whole head sounds the same. *Warning:* The process can take two or three times around the head if the head is badly out of tune to begin with. After the head is in tune with itself all the way around, then the tympanist must also make sure that the tympani is tuned to the right pitch for playing. As with the snare and bass drum, have the tympanist experiment to find the right spot to strike for the best sound.

The other concern is the hardness of the tympani mallet. For rhythmic figures a hard mallet is required. For rolls of a "rumbling" sustained quality, a soft mallet is required. For in-between playing, a medium type mallet is needed.

Orchestra Bells

Orchestra bells should never be struck with anything but a beater designed for use on them. Usually a nylon type plastic will be the material used, however for really loud playing there are special metal mallets available.

Xylophone-Marimba

This instrument should also never be struck with any beater not specifically designed for use on the wooden bars of a xylophone. The wooden bars of a xylophone split rather easily so caution must be used in demanding too much volume.

Chimes

Chimes should be struck with rawhide mallets for best sound, and to avoid damaging them, the player should never use anything harder than this kind of mallet to strike them.

The chimes should never be struck on the side – only on the side of the "cap" on top:

BIBLIOGRAPHY OF USEFUL BOOKS ON WIND PLAYING FUNDAMENTALS

Clarinet

Bonade, Daniel. *Clarinetists Compendium.* Kenosha, Wisconsin: Le Blac Publishers, 1962.

Bonade, Daniel. *Manual of Reed Fixing.* New York: Bonade-Falvo, Pupa Corp., 1947.

Opperman, Kalmen. *Manual for Making and Adjusting Single Reeds for All Clarinets and Saxophones.* Chappell and Company, 1956.

Stein, Keith. *The Art of Clarinet Playing.* Summy-Birchard, 1958.

Oboe and Bassoon

Spencer, William. *Art of Bassoon Playing.* Revised Frederick A. Mueller. Summy-Birchard, 1969.

Spratt, Jack. *Double Reed Players Handbook.* Jack Spratt Publishers, 1969.

Sprinkle, Robert, and David Ledet. *The Art of Oboe Playing.* Summy-Birchard, 1961.

Flute

Kincaid, William. *The Art and Practice of Modern Flute Technique.* Belwin Publishers, 1967.

Putnik, Edwin. *The Art of Flute Playing.* Summy-Birchard, 1970-1973.

Saxophone

Teil, Larry. *The Art of Saxophone.* Summy-Birchard, 1963.

Brass

Farkas, Phillip. *The Art of Brass Playing.* Rochester, New York: Wind Music, 1962.

Farkas, Phillip. *The Art of French Horn Playing.* Summy-Birchard, 1956.

Selection of Music and Recommended Materials 10

SELECTING MUSIC FOR A GIVEN GROUP

When examining music to determine its suitability for any given group, there are many things that need to be checked carefully by the director. Some of the most important factors are range, key, relative size, and ability levels of the various sections of the orchestra.

Range

Range demands are extremely important for the teacher to check because with *both* the strings and the winds, the higher they play, the more intonation and tone quality are going to become extremely difficult if not impossible for the students to control. This is especially true of junior and senior high school wind players (brass, oboe, bassoon and clarinet). Even with good junior and senior high school players, it is best for the director to use music that does not make *continual* range demands that are beyond the point of being produced in tune with good tone most of the time.

Senior High School Orchestra

The practical range limits for senior high school players are as follows:

Strings – First violins (F# one octave above the staff), second violins (D one octave above the staff); violas (A harmonic one octave above the staff); cellos (A harmonic one octave above the staff); and basses (G harmonic one octave above the staff).

Winds – Trumpet-cornet (B-flat above the staff and A below the staff); horn (F top line of staff and G below the staff); trombone (B-flat above the staff and E below the staff without trigger and B-flat below the staff with the trigger); tuba (fourth line F and G below the staff); oboe (G above the staff and D below the staff); bassoon (G above the staff and C below the staff); clarinet (E above the staff and E below the staff); flute (A, an octave above the staff and D below the staff); and piccolo (A, an octave above the staff and E bottom line of the staff).

With young instrumentalists, it should be understood that occasional notes above or below the limits listed here can be handled, but compositions have parts that are continually higher or lower than these limits should not be attempted unless the calibre of a particular section is just so outstanding that there is no doubt about the ability of the students to handle them. *Warning:* For brass players especially, the above limits of practical ranges are for students who *can* play a fourth or fifth higher than the given upper limits.

Junior High School Orchestra

With junior high students, the teacher must be even more careful not to make extreme range demands, especially on young brass players. Great harm can be done to a developing brass player by asking him to play higher than his embouchure development and breath support will allow him to play properly. It is much better to under estimate their upper range potential than to demand too much. Some reasonable junior high range limits follow:

Strings – First violins (harmonic E above the staff), second violins (B above the staff); violas (E above the staff); cellos (harmonic A above the staff); and bass (D above the staff).

Winds – Trumpet and cornet (Top-line F and B-flat below the staff; horn (E top of the staff and B-flat below the staff); trombone (F above the staff and F bottom of the staff); tuba (third line D and B-flat below the staff); oboe (G top of the staff and F bottom of the staff); bassoon (E above the staff and C below the staff); clarinet (C above the staff and E below the staff); flute (G one octave above the staff and E bottom of the staff); and piccolo (F one octave above the staff and first space F).

Key

The key definitely must be considered when judging the difficulty of a piece of music. Although it is reasonable to expect a really top notch high school orchestra to be able to play in the concert keys of up to four sharps and four flats, until the orchestra matures, it is probably better to only play in keys of up to three flats and three sharps as the four sharp and four flat keys cause many problems for the strings (especially the cellos and basses because they can use only one or two open strings as a reference point).

For junior high groups, a reasonable key limit would be the keys of F, B-flat, C, G, D and possibly E-flat. The thing that must be kept in mind by the teacher is that the keys chosen must be easy enough to allow the students to concentrate on playing in tune, musically and with good sound. When the music gets so involved, in any respect, that the students' entire efforts must be bent toward playing the notes, the music is too hard!

Size of Various Sections

The size of the various sections also has to be considered when choosing music for an orchestra. If an orchestra has a complete wind section, music from the Classical Period would be a poor choice as a regular diet because the clarinets, piccolo, trombones, one of the trumpets, two of the horns and the percussion section (except for the tympani) would have nothing to do. Conversely, if the orchestra is short of horns, trombones, and/or percussion, music of the Contemporary and Romantic period would be a poor choice because this music cannot be played without them. In the event that the orchestra has a full wind section, it still should play some Classical and Baroque music, which will mean that some arrangements must be made with the school adminstration to send the students not needed for this music somewhere else.

The size of the string section also needs to be considered. A small group of strings demands that music be played that does not call for a full wind section (especially if block-scored) *or* the orchestra will sound like a band with a few strings added. If the string sections are not balanced well numerically, this can also influence the choice of music. The teacher should realize that with student orchestras, Baroque music generally requires a large, strong cello and bass section due to a usually dominant continuo bass line and that Classical music needs a larger violin section due to the extreme technical demands this music makes on the first violinists. (This, of course, would not be true with professional players.)

Ability Level of Sections

The ability levels of the various sections of the orchestra also need to be considered when choosing music for a group. The winds especially, must be absolutely first quality to play much of the Classical repertoire, as their parts are so exposed that there is no room for any lack of finessse. Much of the Romantic literature is not playable by student orchestras *unless* the strings have mastered the upper positions and have much left-hand facility. Baroque music, because of the moving bass line, requires better than average cello and bass players and they especially need to be very accurate intonation-wise.

Summary

Whenever choosing music for a student orchestra, it is not enough to generally know the grade level of the music, but rather, to examine the music carefully to ascertain where the difficulties are. Observe whether the harder parts are written for the stronger sections in the group and the easier parts for the weaker ones. For instance, it would be impossible to play Bizet's "Carmen Suite" no matter how well the orchestra plays as a whole if there is not a fine solo oboist, flutist, and trumpet player for the solos in the various movements.

PURCHASING MUSIC

Constructing A Budget

In many school systems, the teacher will have the responsibility of making a recommendation for the buying of music. There are several areas the teacher must be concerned with. One of these is projecting a reasonable and defensible budget figure.

To construct a reasonable budget figure, a good procedure for the teacher to follow would be to multiply the number of concerts to be given during the year by the average number of pieces required to fill the amount of time needed per program (thirty to forty-five minutes total for junior high groups and sixty to seventy-five minutes total for senior groups). For a thirty minute program, the director will need to plan on twenty to twenty-five minutes of music. For a seventy-five minute program, from fifty-five to sixty-five minutes of music should be planned for depending on whether several shorter pieces or a few longer pieces are to be played (the more pieces to be played, the more time will be used between numbers). The teacher should take the number arrived at (concerts times the average number of pieces) and multiply it by the average cost of orchestrations for the grade level involved. Next, the teacher should add the cost of any books that may be needed for technique building (if the school is going to provide them). Then, in order to allow for pieces that may be bought and found to be unusable for some reason, about a 10% margin should be added plus about another 10% for shipping and/or mailing if the music cannot be picked up conveniently from a local supplier.

Music should be selected in such a way that after about three years it can be pulled from the files and used again. By selecting music that is enjoyable, well written, well-edited and that contains opportunities to teach the techniques needed on any given level, a library can be amassed that only needs occasional additions of outstanding new works and/or some (not too much) "pop" music. It must be kept in mind that pop music is "one-time" music and is comparatively more expensive than other music and therefore cannot be used to *build* a library that is long-lasting.

Importance of Selecting Well-Edited Music

When choosing the music to be used for groups on any level, but particularly on the junior high level, a very important consideration should be the quality of the editing of the music. The younger groups need to have their bowings done especially for them. Professional bowings usually will not work for younger groups. Younger groups need to play music that is edited so that they play fewer notes on a bow, fewer notes within a slur and music where they normally pay attention to starting measures and ending phrases with a down bow.

Well-edited music for younger groups will also indicate (at least the first few times) the fingerings in the higher positions and the position changes. For the cellos, the extensions should be marked. The use of the fourth finger to avoid open strings on the violin and the viola, when appropriate, should also be indicated through Grade III music. Grade I and II violin and viola parts should also have low and high second fingers indicated (the first few times) for the Keys of F, C, G, and D. First finger low and normal position should be indicated for the Keys of F and B-flat.

If music to be played does not come edited as mentioned above, then the teacher must accept the responsibility for doing it himself or seeing that it is done by someone else that is competent in this area so that the students can develop good bowings and control of finger placement. Selecting music that is already edited will save much of the teacher's time and is well worth searching for.

Learning to Edit Music

In the event that a competent person that understands each level is not available to mark the bowings for a non-string person, Elizabeth Green's fine book *Orchestral Bowings,* explains thoroughly all of the basic rules of bowing in terms that are easily understood.

Knowing the best fingerings for students to use is much more involved and will take years of observation of young students and private lessons on the various stringed instruments to understand completely. Attending clinic sessions given by people familiar with the problems of young students is probably the best and least difficult way to learn this very involved skill

Locating Sources For New Music

The best way to select music for any group, of course, is to personally examine the scores to the music with all of the things in mind mentioned in this chapter. If this is not possible, or if some pre-selection of materials is desired, there are lists of graded materials available.

Many states have either a permanent publication or a yearly list of contest and/or festival materials. The Music Educators' National Conference, American String Teachers' Association and National School Orchestra Association all publish lists of graded materials that are available to their members at nominal cost. The ASTA and NSOA publications constantly review new music in their periodical publications. *The Instrumentalist* and *School Musician* also review new music in each issue that they publish. Also, the program for the annual Mid-West National Band and Orchestra Clinic held each December in Chicago lists almost all of the new music published for orchestras and bands each year.

Other good ways for the teacher to become aware of new and good materials to use with student groups are to attend conventions of music teachers and visit the publisher exhibits and talk to colleagues about materials they have used or are using successfully. Publishers are also very willing to send teachers announcements and sample scores of their newly-published pieces. A teacher can have his or her name put on a list of this type by registering at a publisher's exhibit or by writing directly to the publisher and requesting it.

Some other ways to secure information on new music are:

(1) Write to the music publishers to request catalogues that list their compositions that are currently in print.

(2) Attend conventions and workshops that have reading sessions where the attending teachers play the newly published music.

(3) Purchase books that have lists of orchestral literature in it. There is at least one book available that lists all (as nearly as can be done) of the standard orchestral literature as well as the instrumentation needed for each composition: *Orchestral Music* by David Darnell, published by The Scarecrow Press, Inc., Metuchen, New Jersey, 1972.

(4) Check books about the teaching of orchestras as they sometimes have lists of selected and graded materials as this one does.

There is a wealth of good materials available for both string and full orchestra on almost all levels. New compositions are constantly being added to this body of materials and consequently, no list of materials can be complete. Nevertheless, the following list of materials that has been used with success by the authors and/or other successful teachers, will be helpful to others looking for music to use with student groups of varying abilities. The lists contain an ample selection of good materials to use until the teacher himself becomes familiar with materials to use. "Pop" music of temporary interest has been excluded because of its short term appeal. However, there is much of this type of music available that is of good quality and useful for teaching various string and ensemble problems so necessary for orchestral players to learn.

FULL ORCHESTRA MATERIALS
Grades Two through Six

GRADE TWO

These materials are mainly block-scored and require no soloistic wind playing. They are in easier concert keys of F, C, and G. There will be no position work required of the strings. This literature will be *easy-to-medium* in difficulty for most junior high orchestras.

Title	Composer/Arranger	Publisher	Comments
Air from "Indian Queen"	Purcell/Ployhar	Wynn	
Bach Triptych	Bach/Leroy Walter	Lydian Orchestrations	2½–3

Title	Composer/Arranger	Publisher	Comments
Cappricietto	Telemann/Wayne Livingston	Lydian Orchestrations	
Carillon from "L'Arlesienne" Suite No. 1	Bizet/Stone	Boosey Hawkes	2–3
Cowboy Rhapsody	Ralph Matesky		
English Suite, An	Purcell/Scarmolin	Ludwig	2–2½
Four Centuries for Orchestra (Collection)	Phillip Gordon	Carl Fischer	2–3
From Sea to Shining Sea	Ward and Bates/ Whitney	Warner Bros.	2–3 Also Chorus
He Shall Feed His Flock (from "The Messiah")	Handel/Rizzo	Kendor	2–3
Highlights from "The Sound of Music"	arr. J. Frederick Muller	Williamson	2–3
Hymn of Joy	Beethoven/Benoy	Oxford	
Hymn to Diana	Gluck/Reibold	Sam Fox	2–3
Intrada and Elegy	Arthur Frackenpohl	Kendor	2–3
It's A Small World	Sherman/Chase	Hansen	
Junior Philharmonic for Young Orchestras (Collection)	Forsblad and Livingston	Shawnee Press	2–3
Little Baroque Suite	Phillip Gordon	Carl Fischer	
Little Suite for Orchestra	Corelli/Phillip Gordon	Carl Fischer	2–3
March in G	Purcell/Edward Jurey	Belwin-Mills	2½
Matchmaker from "Fiddler on the Roof"	Harnick/Chase	Plymouth	
Matilda (Calypso)	Ployhar	Wynn	2–2½
Merry Widow, The	Lehar	Pro Art	
Minuet from Symphony No. 17	Haydn/Hanson	Ludwig	
Musical Sleigh Ride	Mozart/Isaac	Highland	2–3
Oh, What A Beautiful Morning	Rodgers/Ralph Matesky	Williamson	2
Prelude	Bach/Edmund Siennicki	Forest Etling	
Russian Folksongs (Set 2)	Liadov/David Stone	Boosey Hawkes	2–2½
Scherzo	Edmund Siennicki	Neil Kjos	2½
Silver Bells	Livingston/Chase	Paramount	
Silver Bells	Livingston/Gordon	Hansen	2–3
Slovakian Folk Songs	Cechvala	Hal Leonard	
Springtide (Miniature Overture)	Charles Woodhouse	Boosey Hawkes	2½
Star Spangled Banner	arr. Ralph Matesky	Neil Kjos	
Sunrise, Sunset from "Fiddler on the Roof"	Harnick/Chase	Hansen	2½
Symphony Number 40 (Themes)	Mozart/Carlin	Carlin	
Three Songs by Brahms	Brahms/Woodhouse	Boosey Hawkes	2–3
Tick Tock Clock and Flow Gently Sweet Afton	Bruce/Spilman	Shawnee Press	
Three Trees of Christmas (Cherry Tree Carol, Holly & Ivy, O Tannenbaum)	Traditional/Heinen	Kendor	2–3
Trumpet, The (Suite in D)	Telemann/Christenson	Carlin	2–3

Title	Composer/Arranger	Publisher	Comments
Two Pieces for Young Orchestra	Weber and Handel/ Klauss	Kendor	2½
Village Dance	Rameau/Phillip Gordon	Kendor	2½–3
Western Strings	Martin and Pizzuto	Kendor	2–3
When Johnny Comes Marching Home	arr. Ralph Matesky	Neil Kjos	2½–3
Youth Symphony for Young Orchestras (Collection)	Herfurth and Stuart	Shawnee Press	2½–3
Yuletide Festival, A	Phillip Gordon	Warner Bros.	2½–3 Also band, string orchestra, and choir

GRADE THREE

These materials are in concert keys of F, C, G, D, and B-flat. There will be larger range demands made upon both the winds and strings. The strings will need to be able to play some simple positions. There are some brief exposed solositic wind passages. The music is more involved and typical of traditional orchestra scoring. These materials should be playable by average to fine junior high orchestras.

Title	Composer/Arranger	Publisher	Comments
Adagio and Allegro	Corelli/Jerry Lehmeir	Forest Etling	3½–4
Adagio and Allegro	Corelli/J. Frederick Muller	Ludwig	3½–4
Aegean Modes (Aeolin, Dorian)	Vaclav Nelhybel	E. C. Kerby	3–3½
Air from "Peasant Cantanta"	Bach/Phillip Gordon	Kendor	3–3½
Airs from "The Beggar's Opera"	Gay/Phillip Gordon	Alfred	
Allegro	Stamitz/Edmund Siennicki	Forest Etling	3½–4
Allegro in C	Mozart/Stone	Boosey Hawkes	
Alleluia	Mozart/Isaac	Forest Etling	3–3½
A Love For All Seasons	Bill Holcombe	Musicians Publications	3–4
America the Beautiful Fantasy	Traditional/J. Frederick Muller	Ludwig	3–3½
Andante from the Symphony in G Major (The Surprise)	Haydn/Merle Isaac	Carl Fischer	
Arirange	Korean Folk Song/ Bauernschmidt	Lydian Publications	
Ballet Parisien	Offenbach/Isaac	Carl Fischer	
Berceuse and Finale from "The Firebird"	Stravinsky/Isaac	Belwin-Mills	3–4
Brahms First Symphony (Fourth Movement)	Brahms/Vernon Leidig	Highland	3½
Bratislava	Holesovsky	Elkan-Vogel	3–4
Bunker Hill Fantasy	Jack Johnson	Elkan-Vogel	3–4

Title	Composer/Arranger	Publisher	Comments
Can Can	Porter/Cacavas	Chappell	
Capriccio Italian	Tschaikovsky/Isaac	Forest Etling	3½–4
Carmen Prelude	Bizet/Kriechbaum	Forest Etling	3–3½
Catskill Legend	Paul Whear	Elkan-Vogel	
Cherish (Pop)	Kirkman	Studio PR	3–3½
Chilean Folk Song	Harold Rusch	Tempo	3½
Chorale Fantasy	William Presser	Forest Etling	3½–4
Christmas Music for Orchestra	Cacavas	Bourne	
Christmas Orchestra Folio	Merle Isaac	Belwin-Mills	
Concertino in G	Sammartini/Muller	Ludwig	3–3½
Concerto No. 2 (Third Movement)	Seitz/Isaac	Forest Etling	Solo violin(s) & orchestra
Coronation Festival	Handel/Kirk	Neil Kjos	Also band & brass ens.
Courante	Bach/Muller	Neil Kjos	Soli cello section
Dance of the Tumblers from "The Snow Maiden"	Rimsky-Korsakov/Stone	Boosey Hawkes	3–3½
Dancing Seargeant, The (from "Five Images")	Norman Dello Joio	Belwin-Mills	3½–4
Danse Infernal from "Firebird Suite"	Stravinsky/Isaac	Belwin-Mills	3–4
Danse Macabre	Saint-Saens/Isaac	Carl Fischer	
Die Meistersinger	Wagner/Siennicki	Ludwig	3–4
Divertimento in G Major	Haydn/Leroy Walter	Lydian Orchestrations	3–3½
Ensenada		Carl Fischer	
Festique	M. L. Daniels	Ludwig	3½–4
Festival Overture	Diemer	Elkan-Vogel	3–4
Fiddler's Day	Ralph Matesky	Wynn Music	
Fifth Symphony, Finale	Beethoven/Woodhouse	Boosey Hawkes	
Fifth Symphony, (First Movment)	Beethoven/Herfurth	Carl Fischer	
Fitzwilliam Suite	Phillip Gordon	Marks	
Good Daughter Overture, The	Piccini/Scarmolin	Ludwig	3–3½
Grand March from "Aida"	Verdi/Isaac	Belwin-Mills	
Great Gate of Kiev, The	Moussorgsky/Stone	Oxford	
Hemis Dance	Kirk	Carl Fischer	
Hungarian Dance No. 6	Brahms/Isaac	Forest Etling	
Jesu, Joy of Man's Desiring	Bach/Walter	Berkeley	3–4
King and I, Highlights	Rodgers/Herfurth	Chappell	3–4
March from "Athalia"	Mendelssohn/Isaac	Belwin-Mills	
March from "Scipio"	Handel/Woodhouse	Boosey Hawkes	
March of the Boyars	Halvorsen/Isaac	Forest Etling	3½–4
March of the Meistersinger	Wagner/Herfurth	Carl Fischer	
March Slav	Tschaikovsky/Herfurth	Carl Fischer	
Maria Theresa Symphony Themes	Haydn/Carlin	Carlin	
Matador	Cacavas	Bourne	
Menuetto from Fifth Symphony	Schubert/Weaver	Belwin-Mills	
Minuet and Polonaise	Telemann/Livingston	Wynn	

Title	Composer/Arranger	Publisher	Comments
Modo Espagnol	Ployhar	Hal Leonard	
Music Man, The	arr. Merle Isaac	Frank	
My Fair Lady, Highlights from	Loewe/Herfurth	Chappell	3–4
Northern Saga	Phillip Gordon	Colombo	
Now Thank We All Our God	Cruger/Spire	Pro Art	
Orchestral Transcriptions (Collection)	Richard Weaver	Belwin-Mills	3–4
Overture in G dur	Telemann/ Bauernschmidt	Lydian Orchestrations	3½–4
Overture on Jewish Themes	Gearhart	Shawnee Press	
Overture, Prayer and Dance	Robert Clark	Forest Etling	
Overture Russe	Merle Isaac	Carl Fischer	
Passacaglia	Vaclav Nelhybel	Colombo	With solo piano
Perpetual Emotion	Bauernschmidt	Tempo	3½–4
Petite Caprice	Rossini/Isaac	Forest Etling	
Prelude (from Cantata 156)	Bach/Siennicki	Forest Etling	
Prelude for Christmas	A. Benoy	Oxford	3–4
Preludio and Danzetta	Corelli/Livingston	Lydian Orchestrations	3½
Presto (from Concerto in C)	Giordani/Muller	Colombo	
Proloque, Hymn and Dance	Holesovsky	Elkan-Vogel (Presser)	3–3½
Quantum Suite	Paul Whear	Ludwig	3½–4
Queen Anne Suite	Eccles/Gordon	Alfred	3–4
Rigaudoon	Bohn/Matesky	Wynn	3–4
Rosamunde Overture	Schubert/Weaver	Belwin-Mills	
Russian Chorale and Overture	Tschaikovsky/Isaac	Carl Fischer	
Salute to Bach, A	Bach/Gordon	Marks	
Salute to Handel, A	Handel/Gordon	Pro Art	
Scherzo for Christmas	A. Benoy	Oxford	3–4
Selections from "Fiddler on the Roof"	Harnick	Sunbeam	
Sibelius Second Symphony (Fourth Movement)	Sibelius/Leidig	Highland	3–4
Siboney	Merle Isaac	Big Three	
Slavonic Dance No. 3	Dvorak/Isaac	Forest Etling	3½–4
Slavonic Dance No. 8	Dvorak/Isaac	Forest Etling	3½–4
Sound of Music, Highlights	Rodgers/Muller	Chappell	
Star Spangled Banner, The	Smith/Damrosch	G. Schirmer	
Star Spangled Spectacular	Cohan/Gordon	Marks	
Stonehenge	Matthews	Forest Etling	3½
Symphony in D Major	Sammartini/Scarmolin	Ludwig	3½–4
Symphony No. 3 (First Movement)	Hadyn/Isaac	Forest Etling	3½
Symphony No. 5 (Finale)	Beethoven/Woodhouse	Boosey Hawkes	
Syncopated Clock, The	Anderson/Applebaum	Belwin-Mills	
This Land Is Your Land	Guthrie/Ployhar	Hal Leonard	3–4
Three Pieces for Orchestra	Robert Jager	Elkan Vogel	
Three Rustic Dances	von Weber/Gordon	Kendor	
Trepak from "Nutcracker"	Tschaikovsky	Oliver Ditson	

Title	Composer/Arranger	Publisher	Comments
Two Orchestra Minuets	Beethoven/Denny	Oxford	
Typewriter, The	Leroy Anderson	Belwin-Mills	
Valse Triste	Sibelius	Kalmus	3½–4
Variations on a Theme by Beethoven	Beethoven/Matesky	Alfred	
Vocalise, Opus 34	Rachmaninoff/Gearhart	Shawnee Press	3½
Waltz of the Flowers	Tschaikovsky	Carl Fischer	
Water is Wide, The	arr. Ployhar	Wynn	
Winter Frolic	M. Lombardo	Belwin-Mills	

GRADE FOUR

There is much more emphasis on solo wind passages. The music is more fragmentary and rhythmically difficult and endurance will be required of the group. Both winds and strings need wide ranges. The strings must know some basic positions. Concert keys of F, C, G, D, B-flat, E-flat, and A will be found. These materials could be played by an exceptional junior high group and by most average to fine high school orchestras.

Title	Composer/Arranger	Publisher	Comments
Allegro con Brio (from Symphony No. 1)	Beethoven/J. Frederick Muller	Neil Kjos	
America the Beautiful Fantasy	Traditional/J. Frederick Muller	Ludwig	Optional choir
American Celebration	Bill Holcombe	Musicians Publications	4–4½
American Fantasie, An	Grossman	Ludwig	
American Salute	Morton Gould	Belwin-Mills	4–5
Bach Double Violin Concerto (First Movement)	Bach	Neil Kjos	Solo violins
Battle Hymn of Republic	Wilhousky	Carl Fischer	
Capriccio Espagnol, Opus 34	Korsakov/Woodhouse	Boosey Hawkes	4–5
Carousel, Highlights from	Rodgers/Bourdon	Chappell	
Carmen Suite, No. 1	Bizet	Kalmus	Needs fine solo winds
Carnival Selections	arr. Holesovsky	Big Three	
Carousel Selections	Rodgers/Bourdon	Harms	
Cassation	M. L. Daniels	Forest Etling	
Choreo Primo	Ralph Matesky	Neil Kjos	
Christmas Festival, A	Leroy Anderson	Belwin-Mills	
Concerto in D minor for Two Violins and Strings	Bach	Breitkopf	4–5 Solo violins
Concerto in G Major No. 3 (for Violin)	Mozart	Associated	4–5
Crown Imperial March	Walton/Stone	Oxford	4–5
Decade Overture	Paul Whear	Ludwig	4–4½
Declarative Essay	Coker	William Presser	4–5
Dream of Scipione	Mozart/Thor Johnson	Neil Kjos	4–5
Excursion for Orchestra	Robert Washburn	Oxford	
Faithful Shepherd, The	Handel/Beecham	Boosey-Hawkes	
Fanfare and Celebration	Claude T. Smith	Wingert-Jones	4–4½
Fantasia on Alleluia Hymn	Gordon Jacob	Galaxy	4–4½

Title	Composer/Arranger	Publisher	Comments
Fantasia on "Greensleeves"	Vaughan-Williams/Stone	Oxford	
Farandole	Bizet/Stone	Boosey-Hawkes	
Festival of Alfred Burt Carols, A	Alfred Burt	Shawnee Press	
Fiddler on the Roof	Harnick	Sunbeam	
Finale (from Ninth Symphony)	Beethoven/Leidig	Wynn	
Finlandia	Sibelius	Fischer or Kalmus	4–5
Great Gate of Kiev, The	Moussorgsky/Reibold	FitzSimons	
Gypsy Selections	arr. Bennett	Chappell	4–5
Hatikvah	Ovanin	Ludwig	
Heart Wounds/Last Spring	Grieg/Wilson	Carl Fischer	4–4½
Highlights from "West Side Story"	Bernstein/J. Frederick Muller	G. Schirmer	
Hispania	Q. Hull	Wynn	
Hymn of Hope (Variant of Battle Hymn of Republic)	Vaclav Nelhybel	E. C. Kerby	Also chorus and band
I Am an American	Carmen Dragon	Carl Fischer	Chorus and narrator
I'll Be Home for Christmas	Ployhar	Hal Leonard	
Iphegenia En Aulis	Gluck	Carl Fischer or Kalmus	4–5
Jesus Christ Superstar	Mancini	Leeds	4–4½
Jubilee	Ron Nelson	Boosey Hawkes	4–5
La Bamba de Veracruz	Tucci	Sam Fox (J. W. Pepper)	4–5
Lancaster Overture	Paul Whear	Ludwig	
Lullaby and Scherzo	Otto Frohlich	Shawnee	Piano or celeste needed
Manfred Overture	Schumann/Muller	Neil Kjos	4½–5
Man of La Mancha	Lang	Sam Fox (J. W. Pepper)	4–4½
March to the Scaffold	Berlioz/Carter	Oxford	4–4½
The "Messiah"	Handel	Peters	4–5
Mighty Fortress, A	Vaclav Nelhybel	Joseph Boonin	4–4½
Monterey Blues	Francis Feese	Young World	4½–5, with jazz ens.
Movement for Orchestra	Vaclav Nelhybel	Colombo	
Music for Orchestra	Vaclav Nelhybel	Colombo	
Music from "The Royal Fireworks"	Handel/Johnson	Neil Kjos	4½–5
Musicianship and Repertoire for High School Orchestra, Volume I	Elizabeth Green	Theodore Presser	Etudes, Scales Symphonic excerpts
Night in Mexico	Paul Creston	Shawnee Press	4–5
Ode to Freedom	Robert Washburn	Oxford	4–4½
Oklahoma, Highlights	Rodgers/Bourdon	Chappell	
Old Devil Moon (Studio Orchestra Styling)	Lane/Joe Reisman	Kendor	

Title	Composer/Arranger	Publisher	Comments
Old Hundredth Psalm Tune, The	Vaughan-Williams/ Stone	Oxford	Also band & chorus
Oliver, Selections	Bart/Reed	Plymouth	
Overture and Allegro from "La Sultane Suite"	Couperin/Milhaud	Elkan-Vogel	4–5
Overture 1812	Tschaikovsky/Jerry Lehmeir	Forest Etling	
Overture in Italian Style (In C)	Schubert	Kalmus	4½–5
Overture in D Major	Schubert/Johnson	Neil Kjos	
Overture to "Samson"	Handel/Muller	Ludwig	
Pavane	Faure/Gearhart	Shawnee Press	
Petrouchka	Stravinsky/Isaac	Belwin-Mills	4–4½
Polka from the "Golden Age Ballet"	Shostakovitch	Carl Fischer	4–4½
Prelude	Shostakovitch/Isaac	Forest Etling	
Procession of the Nobles	Rimsky-Korsakov/Isaac	Forest Etling	4–4½
Romeo and Juliet	Tschaikovsky/Muller	Neil Kjos	4–4½
Russian Sailors' Dance	Gliere/Isaac	Carl Fischer	
Saint Lawrence Overture	Robert Washburn	Boosey Hawkes	
Second Symphony (Fourth Movement)	Sibelius/Leidig	Highland	4–4½
"Showboat" Overture for Orchestra	Kern/Gordon	Harms	
Sinfonia Piccola	Suolahti	Boosey Hawkes	
Sleepers Wake	Bach/Brown	Pro Art	4–4½
Soft Winds	Bill Holcombe	Musicians Publications	4½
Sounds of Simon and Garfunkel (Vol. I and II)	arr. Robert Lowden	Keynote	
South Pacific, Highlights (Pop)	Rodgers/Bourdon	Chappell	
Suite No. 1 and No. 2, Water Music	Handel/David Stone	Oxford	
Sunfest	Daniels	Ludwig	
Symphony in D (Third Movement)	Franck/J. Frederick Muller	Neil Kjos	4–4½
Symphony No. 1 (First Movement)	Beethoven	Kalmus	4½–5
Symphony No. 2 (First Movement)	Borodin/Isaac	Forest Etling	
Symphony No. 5 (Fourth Movement)	Mendelssohn/Leidig	Highland	
Tournament of Temperaments	Dittersdorf/Khan	G. Schirmer	4½
Toy Symphony	Haydn	Kalmus	String orch. and toys
Triptych	Tommy J. Fry	Carl Fischer	
Variations on a Shaker Melody	Copland	Boosey Hawkes	4½–5
Where or When (Studio Orchestra Style)	Richard Rodgers/Joe Reisman	Kendor	
William Byrd Suite	Gordon Jacob	Boosey Hawkes	4–5

GRADE FIVE

Among these materials will be found much standard orchestral literature. non-simplified. Sometimes only one movement of a symphony will be feasible with high school students. The keys found will include up to four flats and four sharps. Transposition may be necessary for winds and cellos and trombones will need to be able to read tenor clef. Violins will need to know up to fifth position, violas treble clef, and cellos some thumb position.

This category is playable only by exceptional high school orchestras. Most usually used with youth orchestras or college/university level groups.

Title	Composer/Arranger	Publisher	Comments
Abduction from the Seraglio	Mozart/Isaac	Belwin	
Academic Festival Overture	Brahms	Kalmus	5–6
Allegro Appassionata, Opus 70	Saint-Saens	Durand	Cello solo
An Outdoor Overture	Copland	Boosey Hawkes	
Buckaroo Holiday from "Rodeo"	Copland	Boosey Hawkes	
Capriccio Espagnol (Opus 34)	Rimsky-Korsakov	Boosey Hawkes or Kalmus	5–6
Choral Prelude (Sleepers Wake)	Bach/Ormandy	Boosey Hawkes	
Dance Rhythms	Wallingford Riegger	Associated	
Danse Macabre, Opus 40	Saint-Saens	Kalmus	
Egmont Overture	Beethoven/Sopkin	Carl Fischer	
Elegy	Faure	Kalmus	5–6 cello solo
Elsa's Procession from "Lohengrin"	Wagner/Campbell	Kalmus	5–6
English Folk Songs	Vaughan-Williams/ Gordon Jacob	Warner Bros.	
Festival Prelude, A	Reed	Marks	
Festival Overture	Robert Washburn	Oxford	5–6
Finale to the "New World" (Symphony No. 5)	Dvorak/Roberts	Carl Fischer	5–6
Fourth of July, The	Charles Ives	Associated	5–6
Francesca Da Rimini	Tschaikovsky/Muller	Neil Kjos	
Fugue in G minor ("The Little")	Bach/Cailliet	Carl Fischer	
Hansel and Gretel, Prelude	Humperdinck	Kalmus	5–6
Hoe Down ("Rodeo")	Copland	Boosey Hawkes	
Intermezzo from "Harry Janos"	Kodaly	Boosey Hawkes	5–6
Kol Nidrei	Bruch	Kalmus	Solo cello
Komm Susser Tod	Bach/Stokowsky	Broude	5–6
L'Arlessiene, Suite No. 2	Bizet	Kalmus or Peters	
Lincoln Portrait	Copland	Boosey Hawkes	5–6 Narrator
London Symphony No. 2 (#104) in D	Haydn	Kalmus	
Music from "The Sting"	Joplin/Cacavas	Belwin-Mills	
Night on Bald Mountain, A	Moussorgsky/Sopkin	Kalmus	5–6
Noyse of Minstrells	Gordon Jacob	Oxford	

Title	Composer/Arranger	Publisher	Comments
Our Town	Copland	Boosey Hawkes	
Outdoor Overture	Copland	Boosey Hawkes	
Overture to Prometheus	Beethoven	Kalmus	
Overture to "The Impresario"	Mozart	Carl Fischer	
Peer Gynt, Suite No. 1 (Fourth Movement)	Grieg	Kalmus, Peters or Fischer	
Polonaise from "Christmas Night"	Rinsky-Korsakov	Kalmus	
Pomp and Circumstance, No. 1 D Major	Elgar	Boosey Hawkes	
Porgy and Bess	Gershwin/Bennett	Chappell	
Prairie Night and Celebration from "Rodeo"	Copland	Boosey Hawkes	
Rhosymedre	Vaughan-Williams/ Foster	Galaxy	
Ride of the Valkyries, The	Wagner/Roberts	Fischer	
Rosamunde Overture	Schubert	Kalmus or Peters	5–6
Sheep May Safely Graze	Bach/Cailliet	Boosey Hawkes	
Short Symphony for Orchestra	Jean Berger	Boonin	
Symphony in D minor	Franck	Boosey Hawkes	
Symphony in E minor, No. 5	Dvorak/Roberts	Fischer/Kalmus	
Symphony No. 1	Beethoven	Kalmus	
Symphony No. 1, C Major	Bizet	Universal	
Symphony No. 2, B minor (First Movement)	Borodin	Kalmus, MCA	5–6
Symphony No. 2 (Romantic") (First Movement Excerpt)	Hanson/Van Hoesen	Carl Fischer	5–6
Symphony No. 3, D Major	Sibelius	Associated	5–6
Symphony No. 5, G Minor	Beethoven	Kalmus	5–6
Symphony No. 6	Haydn	Kalmus or Carl Fischer	5–6
Symphony No. 12	Haydn	Kalmus or Carl Fischer	
Symphony No. 32	Mozart	Kalmus	Uses 4 horns
Symphony No. 94, G Major ("The Surprise")	Haydn	Kalmus	
Toccata	Frescobaldi/Kindler	Belwin-Mills	
Tragic Overture	Brahms	Associated	5–6
Unfinished Symphony, The (Symphony No. 8)	Schubert/Dasch	Fischer, Kalmus or Peters	
Waltz ("Billy the Kid")	Copland	Boosey Hawkes	
Water Music Suite	Handel/Harty	Chappell	
West Side Story, Overture	Bernstein	G. Schirmer	5–6

GRADE SIX

This category is only for extremely advanced orchestras that are able to play in all keys, have much technical facility and unusually mature musicianship. There are many other selections from the standard literature that orchestras at this level could handle in addition to those listed.

Title	Composer/Arranger	Publisher	Comments
Bacchanale from "Samson and Delilah"	Saint-Saens/Reibold	Sam Fox	
Carnival Overture	Dvorak	Boosey Hawkes or Kalmus	
Die Fledermaus, Overture to	Strauss	Kalmus or Peters	
Fingal's Cave ("The Hebrides")	Mendelssohn	Fischer or Kalmus	
Les Preludes	Liszt	Kalmus	
Nutcracker, The (Suite)	Tschaikovsky	Kalmus or MCA	
Oberon, Overture to	Weber	Kalmus	
Overture to "Candide"	Leonard Bernstein	Schirmer	
Roman Carnival Overture	Berlioz	Associated or Kalmus	
Russian Easter, Overture	Rimsky-Korsakov/ Sopkin	Fischer, Kalmus Boosey Hawkes	
Russlan and Ludmilla	Glinka/Sopkin	Fischer	
Symphony No. 1, C Minor	Brahms	Kalmus	
Symphony No. 2, D Major	Sibelius	Kalmus	
Symphony No. 4, A Major ("The Italian")	Mendelssohn	Kalmus	
Symphony No. 6, F Major ("The Pastorale")	Beethoven	Kalmus	
Symphony No. 40, G Minor	Mozart	Kalmus or Peters	
Toccata and Fugue in D Minor	Bach/Cailliet	Fischer	

STRING ORCHESTRA MATERIALS
Grades One through Six

GRADE ONE

These materials could be used near the end of the first year of string playing and completion of most Book One string methods. They are all in keys of D, G, or C and use easy rhythms with 4/4, 3/4, or 2/4 time signatures. The piano is usually necessary on performance to give a full sound and add rhythmic interest.

Title	Composer/Arranger	Publisher	Comments
First Orchestra Program Album (Collection)	Edward Jurey	Belwin-Mills	Also full orchestra
Gavotte	Haydn/Abbott	Kendor	
Kathleen Album, The ("Polychordia String Series")	James Brown	Galaxy	1–2

Title	Composer/Arranger	Publisher	Comments
Late Baroque Music	Bach/Cechvala	Kendor	
Loch Lomond	Noah Klauss	Kendor	
March of the Metro Gnome	Fred Hubbell	Kendor	
Melody Book for Strings (Collection)	Merle Isaac	Carl Fischer	Unison (except bass) 1–2
Orchestra Performance I (Collection)	J. Frederick Muller	Neil Kjos	1–2 (Also full orch.)
Sight Reader for Young Strings (Book I)	Norman Ward	Shawnee Press	Augments beginning methods
Sound of Strings (An Animal Survival Suite)	H. Alshin	Boston Music	Narration and Piano
Southwestern Suite	Clifton Williams	Southern	1–2
Steptoe	Metcalfe	Kendor	
Stringing Along (Collection)	Stoutamire-Henderson	Pro Art	1–2
Symphony for Young People	Clifton Williams	Witmark	1–2
Two Tone Pictures	Phillip Gordon	Skidmore Music	1½ 2
Twenty Easy Pieces for the Young Orchestra (Collection)	Norman Ward	Kendor	

GRADE TWO

These materials can be used during the second year of playing and completion of most Book Two string methods. They use keys of G, D, C, F, and possibly B-flat. The rhythms and bowings are more difficult than Grade 1. There will be no position work. Use of piano is recommended in most cases for performance of these materials.

Title	Composer/Arranger	Publisher	Comments
Air and Pizzicato-Staccato	Arthur Frackenpohl	Kendor	
Apollo Suite	Merle Isaac	Forest Etling	2–3
Axiom (Overture for Strings, Piano and Percussion)	Leland Forsblad	Hal Leonard	2–2½
Bach for Strings (Collection)	Irma Clark	G. Schirmer	2–3 (Also Ensemble)
Beautiful Music for Two Stringed Instruments (Collection)	Samuel Applebaum	Belwin-Mills	String Ensemble or duets
Bedfont Album, The ("Polychordia String Series")	Bach/James Brown	Galaxy	2–3
Beethoven Selections	Beethoven/J. Frederick Muller	Neil Kjos	2½–3 (Full also)
Brentwood Orchestra Folio (Collection)	Metcalfe	Pro Art	1–2
Calwood String Orchestra Folio (Collection)	Metcalfe	Pro Art	1–2
Canyon Sunset	John Caponegro	Kendor	
Caprice	Robert Frost	Southern	2½–3
Carpathian Strings	A. Cechvala	Wynn	2–3

Title	Composer/Arranger	Publisher	Comments
Cat and the Fiddle, The	Noah Klauss	Kendor	
Chamber Music for String Orchestra (Collection)	Samuel Applebaum	Belwin-Mills	
Children's Waltz, The	Phillip Klein	Kendor	
Chorale and March	Bach/Siennicki	Forest Etling	
Dance Suite for Strings	Maurice Whitney	Warner Bros.	
Danse Russe, No. 2	Russ Daly	Long Island	
Dorian Album for String Trio (Ensemble Collection)	Whistler-Hummel	Rubank	2–3
Double String Romp	Hastings	Alfred	
Dramatico (unison open strings)	Robert Hirsch	Tempo Publications	2–3 (Piano Solo)
Early Classics (Collection, String Ensemble)	C. Paul Herfurth		2–3
Edric Album, The (Polychordia String Series")	James Brown	Galaxy	2–3
Etudes and Ensembles (Collection)	J. Frederick Muller	Neil Kjos	2–3
Fiddling A-Round	John Caponegro	Kendor	2–2½
First Quartet Album (String Ensemble collection)	Whistler-Hummel	Rubank	2–3
First Trio Album (String Ensemble Collection)	Whistler-Hummel	Rubank	2–3
Five Carols for Christmas	Matteo Giammario	Musicians Publications	
Folk Fiddle (Collection)	Mel Bay	Mel Bay	2–3
Folk Song Set	Wesley Sontag	Galaxy	2½
Fumble Fingers	John Caponegro	Kendor	
Fun Way Strings (Collection)	Adamson-Young	Charles Hansen	
Gliding Swan, The	Mary Lou Farnsworth	Long Island	
Gavotte	Gossec	Carl Fischer	2–3
Gypsy Strings	Robert Martin-Emanuelina Pizzuto	Kendor	
Hornpipe	Robert Frost	Southern	2½–3
In Praise of Christmas	Edmund Siennicki	Forest Etling	2½–3
Largo	Alexander Von Kreisler	Southern	2–3
La Spagnola	Robert Brown	Pro Art	Also Full
Laurel Album, The ("Polychordia String Series")	James Brown	Galaxy	
Little Fugue	Edmund Siennicki	Forest Etling	
Matchmaker (from "Fiddler on the Roof")	Bock/Chase	Plymouth	2–2½
Minuet and Trio	Robert Frost	Kendor	2½–3
Mock Morris Dance	Wesley Sontag	G. Schirmer	
Musette and Minuet	Edmund Siennicki	Ludwig	2½–3
Ode to Joy	Beethoven/Giammario	Musicians Publications	
Orchestra Performance II (Collection)	J. Frederick Muller	Neil Kjos	2–3 (Full Orchestra also)
Petite Tango	C. B. Kriechbaum	Forest Etling	Piano not necessary

Title	Composer/Arranger	Publisher	Comments
Pizzicato Popcorn	Kingsley/Rizzo	Bourne	
Plink, Plank, Plunk	Leroy Anderson	Belwin-Mills	2–3
Procession	Alexander Von Kreisler	Southern	2–2½
Quinto-Quarto Suite	Merle Isaac	Forest Etling	2½–3
Rhumbolero	John Caponegro	Kendor	2½
Rhythms and Styles for String Orchestra (Collection)	Merle Isaac	Forest Etling	2–3
Sea Spray	George McKay	Elkan-Vogel	2–2½
Selections from "Fiddler on the Roof"	Bock/Baumel	Plymouth	
Set of Four, A	Wesley Sontag	Sam Fox	
Short Suite	Gerard Jaffe	Southern	2½–3
Sight Reader for Young Strings, Book II (Collection)	Norman Ward	Shawnee Press	
Slovakian Dances	Al Cechvala	Kendor	
String Colors (Oklahoma, Oh) (What a Beautiful Morning, etc.)	Bruce Chase	Chappell	2–3
String Music of Baroque Era (Collection)	Irma Clarke	Boston Music	2–3 (Also Ensemble)
Suite Christmas, A	Robert Ewing	Kendor	
Suite in C	Pleyel/Halen	Southern	2½–3
Tango Trocadero	Merle Isaac	Carl Fischer	2½
Thoughts of Spain	Samuel Quagenti	Long Island	
Two Excursions for Strings	Philip Gordon	Skidmore	
Walking Basses	Merle Isaac	Forest Etling	
Wreath of Carols, A	Ralph Matesky	Chappell	2–3

GRADE THREE

These materials could be used in the third and fourth year of playing or with an average junior high orchestra. Students need to have completed a Book Three method. Keys of G, D, C, F, B-flat and possibly E-flat will be used. There may be some simple shifting required. Piano is no longer required in most cases. Rhythms, bowings and time signatures are more difficult. An awareness of musical styles will be necessary.

Title	Composer/Arranger	Publisher	Comments
Air for Strings	Norman Dello Joio	Belwin-Mills	3–3½
Andante and Allegro	Mozart/Isaac	Forest Etling	
Boulderollicks	Jean Berger	European-American Forest Etling	3½
Brandenburg Concerto No. No. 3	Bach/Isaac	Forest Etling	
Chimes	Robert Frost	Kendor	
Colorado Suite	Francis Fees	Young World	
Concerto Grosso (Opus 11)	Sammartini/transcribed Paul Glass	Associated	3–4

Title	Composer/Arranger	Publisher	Comments
Concerto in E minor	Avison/transcribed Paul Glass	Associated	3½–4
Concerto in G minor	Scarlatti/transcribed Paul Glass	Associated	3½–4
Contra-Dance No. 1	Beethoven/J. Frederick Muller	Neil Kjos	3–4
Contradanse	Salierer/Fendler	Boosey Hawkes	
Dance Suite	Mozart/Thor Johnson	Neil Kjos	3–4
Danza	Vaclav Nelhybel	European-American	3–4
Divertimento for Strings	Alexander Von Kreisler	Southern	3–3½
Early American Suite	Traditional/Isaac	Forest Etling	3½–4
Elegy	Darrell Richardson	Kendor	
Entrancing Sound of Strings (Collection)	J. Frederick Muller	MCA	3–4
Fantasia for Orchestra	Tartini/Bauerschmidt	Lydian	3½
Festival at Newport	Francis Feese	Young World	
Fiddle Fable	J. Frederick Muller	Neil Kjos	
Finale from "Water Music"	Handel/Roy Douglas	Sam Fox	3–4
Gotham Collection of Classics (Collection)	Clifford Barnes	Jack Spratt	
Holiday Music for Strings	Robert Frost	Kendor	
Hungarian Dance No. 6	Brahms/Isaac	Forest Etling	
Hopak	Moussorgsky/Isaac	Forest Etling	
Intermediate Etudes and Ensembles (Collection)	J. Frederick Muller	Neil Kjos	
Introduction to String Quartets (Collection)	Irma Clark	Boston	String Ensemble
Introit for Strings	Persichetti	Elkan-Vogel	3–4
Larghetto	Karl Forssmark	Shawnee Press	
Man of La Mancha	Leigh/Applebaum	Belwin-Mills	
Marcello Suite	Marcello/Siennicki	Forest Etling	
Mazas, Opus 38, No. 2 (Famous Violin Duet)	arr. Carson Rothrock	Musicians Publication	
Menuetto from Brandenburg No. 1	Bach/Gordon	Warner Bros.	
Minuet and Rondo	Marpurg/Scarmolin	Ludwig	
Minuet, Aria and Minuet	Schubert/Johnson	Neil Kjos	
Mogul Set	H. Schramm	Boosey Hawkes	3–4
Odyssey in Strings, Volume I and II (Collections)	Ralph Matesky	Belwin-Mills	3–4
Olympiad	Paul Whear	Elkan-Vogel	
Pavan	Byrd/Collins	Sam Fox	3–4
Pavane	Ravel/Isaac	Carl Fischer	
Prelude and Courante	Eccles/Isaac	Forest Etling	
Prelude for Strings	A. Kreisler	Southern	3–3½
Preludio	Paul Whear	Ludwig	3½–4
Quartet in D	Hambourg	Balwin-Mills	String Quartet
Red Rocks Suite	Francis Feese	Young World	3½–4
Rodgers and Hammerstein String Colors	arr. Chase	Williamson	3–4
Rondeau and Chaconne	Purcell/Isaac	Forest Etling	

Title	Composer/Arranger	Publisher	Comments
Selections from Carnival	Merrill/Holesovsky	Robbins (Big Three)	3–3½
Serenade for String Orchestra	Norman Leyden	Plymouth	
Serenade for Strings	Robert Washburn	Oxford Univ.	3½
Shades of Blue	Carson Rothrock	Musicians Publications	
Shadow of Your Smile	Mandel/Holesovsky	Robbins (Big Three)	3–3½
Sinfonia in D	Stamitz/Elizabeth Green	Carl Fischer	3–4
Sleigh Ride	Anderson/Applebaum	Belwin-Mills	
Sonata de Chiesa (Opus 1, No. 2 in E minor)	Corelli/transcribed Paul Glass	Associated	3½
Sonata from "The Fairy Queen"	Purcell/transcribed Paul Glass	Associated	3½–4
Song of the Heather	Mendelssohn/Henderson	Kendor	
Suite for Strings	Vitali/Analee Bacon	San Fox	3½
Suite for Strings	Robert Washburn	Oxford Univ.	3½–4
Suite from "The Fairy Queen"	Purcell/transcribed Paul Glass	Associated	3½–4
Three Bagatelles	Daninov/Brian Phillips	Kendor	
Three Baroque Chorales	Phillip Gordon	Kendor	
Three Pieces for Strings	Noah Klauss	Tempo	

GRADE FOUR

These materials require that students know keys up to three flats and three sharps and have a knowledge of basic positions. This music can be played by an exceptional junior high group or an average high school orchestra.

Title	Composer/Arranger	Publisher	Comments
American Celebration (An Overture)	Bill Holcombe	Musicians Publications	2–4½ (Also full Orch.)
Arioso (from Kantate No. 156)	Bach/Tommy Fry	Carl Fischer	
Basic Scales and Two-Part Inventions (Collection)	J. Frederick Muller	Neil Kjos	
Bon Bons 'n Bossa	Francis Feese	Young World	Opt. winds
Brook Green Suite	Gustav Holst	G. Schirmer	
Canon for Strings	Pachelbel/Ades	Shawnee	
Christmas Pastorale	Corelli	Galaxy	4–5
Colloquy for Strings	Abbe Gesben	Warner Bros.	4–4½
Concerto, D minor	Vivaldi	Belwin-Mills	Violin Solo and Tutti
Concerto Grosso for String Orchestra	Vaughan-Williams	Oxford	4–5
Concerto in G Major	Scarlatti/Glass	Associated	
Concerto Ripieno (C Major)	Vivaldi	Belwin-Mills	3 Violins, continuo, vla. ad lib
Divertimento (C Major)	Mozart	Belwin-Mills	
Divertimento III	Leopold Mozart/Whear	Ludwig	

Title	Composer/Arranger	Publisher	Comments
Divertissement	Jean Berger	G. Schirmer	4–4½
Eight Pieces	Paul Hindemith	Belwin-Mills	4½–5
Eine Kleine Nachtmusik (Serenade in Four Movements)	Mozart	Fischer, Klamus or Peters	4–5
Fantasia on Greensleeves	Vaughan-Williams/ Ralph Greaves	Oxford Univ.	4–5 (obligatc flute, harp)
Flonzaley Favorite Encore Albums (four volumes)	Alfred Pochon	Carl Fischer	4–5
Four Pieces from "Musick's Handmaid"	Purcell/Hunt	Carl Fischer	
Fugue for Strings	Benjamin Husted	Elkan-Vogel	1964 NSOA winner
Gigue and Fugue	Bach/Woodhouse	Boosey Hawkes	
Mass in G, No. 2	Schubert/Martin	Associated or Kalmus	4–5 (Strings and Chorus)
Nocturne and Dance	T. Kenins	Boosey Hawkes	
Organ Concerto in A minor (Themes by Vivaldi)	Bach/Paul Glass	Associated	4–5
Partita for Strings	Biber/Robert Currier	Kendor	
Pastel Blue	Norman Symonds	E. C. Kerby	
Petite Suite	Jean Berger	European-American	4–5
Petite Suite for Strings	Paul Whear	Ludwig	
Prelude and Fugue No. 22	Bach/Noah Klauss	Tempo	
Saint Paul's Suite	Gustav Holst	G. Schirmer	
Short Overture for Strings	Jean Berger	G. Schirmer	
Simple Symphony	Benjamin Britten	Oxford Univ.	4–5
Sinfonie (F Major)	W. F. Bach	Belwin-Mills	4½–5
Sometimes I Feel Like a Motherless Child	Traditional/ Murtaugh	Kendor	4–4½ (Alto flute solo)
Sonata III	Marcello/Richard Fote	Kendor	Solo Trombone
Square Dance/Hayride	Jean Berger	European-American	
Three Pieces	M. Semerlin	Southern	4–5
Winter Soliloquy	Francis Feese	Young World	

GRADE FIVE

These materials are for an exceptional high school orchestra that is able to play most of the standard symphonic literature (unsimplified).

Title	Composer/Arranger	Publisher	Comments
Brandenburg Concerto No. No. 3 in G Major	Bach	Kalmus or Associated	
Canon	Pachelbel	Belwin-Mills	3 violins & Continuo
Canon and Fugue for Strings	Riegger	Shawnee Press	
Christmas Concerto, Op. 6, No. 8	Corelli	Kalmus	5–6

Title	Composer/Arranger	Publisher	Comments
Concerto, G Major	Telemann/Baerenreiter	Associated	
Five Pieces	Paul Hindemith	Belwin-Mills	
Last Spring, The	Grieg-Reibold	Sam Fox/ Kalmus	Also full orchestra
Serenade, Opus 48	Tschaikovsky	Kalmus, MCA, Peters	5–6
Serenade for Strings	P. Warlock	Oxford Univ.	
Thirty-Seven Famous Quartets (Collection)	Haydn	Kalmus	5–6
Variations on Themes by Frescobaldi	A. Tansman	Editions Max	

GRADE SIX

These materials are for an extremely advanced high school orchestra. Most are usually used for university or symphony level orchestras.

Title	Composer/Arranger	Publisher	Comments
Adagio for Strings	Samuel Barber	G. Schirmer	
Holberg Suite, Opus 40	Grieg	Peters or Kalmus	
Serenade, Opus 22, E Major	Dvorak	Peters or Kalmus	
Suite for String Orchestra	Corelli	Broude	

Part Three

Sustaining the Program

Selection and Care of Instruments 11

PURCHASING INSTRUMENTS

Quality of Instruments

When purchasing instruments for school, or recommending instruments for purchase by parents, it must be kept in mind that an instrument is and should be a long time investment. Even a student line instrument of satisfactory quality will last indefinitely if it is taken care of correctly. Therefore, it behooves the teacher to be sure that the instruments are of sufficient quality from the standpoint of durability, adjustment, and tone quality.

Beginner Instruments

In choosing instruments that are to be used by elementary and junior high students, the durability of the instruments needs to be considered even more than the sound of the instrument. This is true because frequently a good sounding, carved instrument will be made of thinner, more easily broken wood than the sturdier school-type instrument. Also, in the case of cellos and basses, the larger, carved instruments crack more easily than the smaller instruments due to changes of temperature and humidity as well as from being bumped or dropped. Therefore, it is recommended, especially for elementary and junior high school-owned cellos and basses, that plywood cellos and plywood or fiberglass basses be used. The sound of plywood instruments may not be as good as the carved instruments, but the savings in time needed for routine care and in down-time that the instrument can't be used because of repairs of cracks, chips, etc., will more than make up for the relatively small loss of quality of sound.

"Step-Up" Instruments

When purchasing instruments for the high school or recommending full-sized instruments for purchase by parents, the emphasis must change from durability to *quality of sound.* No orchestra, however well-trained, can ever get the full, mature sound that it should have if it is using student line instruments. Even the best quality student line instruments do not have the quantity or quality of sound in them to allow a good orchestra sound.

When a student is ready to buy a full-sized instrument or their second instrument (if they started on a full-sized instrument), it is important that they "step-up" to an instrument that has more and better sound. These "step-up" instruments will be "carved" (not plywood) and they will be made of better, more resonant wood. Because more time, care and "handfitting" are involved, they will cost a minimum of twice what a beginner, student-line instrument costs (when bought new).

If the high school is supplying cellos and string basses for the students to use at school, the cellos should be of the carved variety and the basses should have at least the top carved from a solid piece of spruce instead of being all laminated wood as at the junior high level.

Chrome-Steel Strings

Another thing that must be considered in a special way for beginners is the type of strings to be used. From the standpoint of both teaching efficiency and financial economy, *only steel strings* (chrome-wound steel) *should be used.* All instruments also should be equipped with four adjusters (except bass). Further, if the students are going to have the instruments long enough to learn to tune the instruments (the second year at the latest), the instruments need to be equipped with patented adjustable pegs. *Warning:* Young students cannot be taught to tune instruments with conventional ebony pegs in a class situation without taking so much time that nothing else gets done.

There are several important reasons why chrome-steel strings, rather than gut or gut-wound strings, must be used by young students in a class situation. Among them are:

(1) Plain gut strings are just not being used at all by professional orchestral players except for a few "old school" bassists here and there that are definitely out of the "mainstream" of present day trends.

(2) Steel strings will stay better in tune than gut or gut wound strings, because they are not as much affected by temperature and weather changes. Also, gut wound strings go "false" much more quickly than steel strings. Because of these things, the use of steel strings makes the tuning of beginning classes easier and faster.

(3) Steel strings, although costing more initially, are more economical in the long run, because they will last much longer before going "false."

(4) Gut-wound strings have a softer sound, and although a little more refined, when used on a student type instrument, they give so little sound that they discourage the students who cannot be heard when playing in an orchestra.

Gut-Wound Strings

Gut-wound strings, however, do have a place in a high school or advanced junior high program. When the students have "stepped-up" to better quality instruments, the improved tone quality and volume of sound should now make it reasonable and advantageous to put the softer, but better sounding gut-wound strings on the instrument.

A fine instrument will usually not sound its best with four steel strings. A student who has a better quality instrument and studies privately with a good teacher should consult with the local string repairman/string craftsman about the best stringing for the instrument.

If an expert is not available, a safe stringing for a violin is a steel E-string and gut-wound A, D, and G strings. For viola and cello the stringing should be, depending on the individual instrument, either a chrome-wound steel A string and gut-wound D, G, and C string or a chrome-wound steel A and D string and gut-wound G and C string. For a better bass, the chrome-wound woven steel string will give the most refined sound.

MENC Instrument Specifications

When purchasing stringed instruments, it is best to insist that all instruments be in compliance with the original Music Educators National Conference (MENC) Specification (see the end of this chapter for the contents of the original MENC Specification).

All of the specifications are important and can result in problems for a student if they are not adhered to. However, technological developments and changes of opinion have obsoleted several of the recommendations found in the MENC Specifications. They are:

(1) Under *Strings,* as has been stated previously, gut strings are just not in general use in the United States today. Therefore, for artistic, as well as the financial and practical reasons, it would be unwise to buy gut strings for any instrument.

(2) Under *Bow sticks,* aluminum is given as the second choice for bow stick material. It is doubtful that aluminum bows are even available anymore. Rather, the second choice today would be the fiberglass-bow.

(3) Under *adjustment* there is an omission – the peg holes should be placed so that when the strings are installed, no string touches one or more of the lower pegs.

(4) Also, under *adjustment,* the specifications state that chalk is a satisfactory lubricant for pegs. This is incorrect because chalk is an abrasive, and it has been found that it will cause undue wear on the peg box and should

not be used. A good substitute is *graphite.* The lead from a pencil is very effective in lubricating a peg, and in many cases, stopping peg *slippage* when used in large enough amounts.

Bows

It is strongly suggested that fiberglass bows be purchased for school use. The fiberglass bows are recommended because they play as well or better than the average beginning bow (Brazil wood) and are less expensive. Also, they are not subject to warping if the students should forget to loosen them at the end of their practice sessions.

Bow Hair

There is no doubt that horse hair is the best substance for hairing a bow from the standpoint of sound. However, if maintaining the bows is to be the responsibility of the school, then serious consideration should be given to the processed bow hair that is available today. The quality is surprisingly good, it is considerably less expensive, and it is longer lasting.

By the time the students play well enough to make the horse hair a real advantage to use, they (the students) should be furnishing their own bows and taking care of the maintenance. For school instruments, especially before the senior high level, it is recommended that processed hair be used.

Pegs

Although properly fitted ebony pegs work very well for adults and the more advanced students, they are not recommended for school-owned instruments, but rather, a patented adjustable peg (wood) should be used (see Chapter II in Part II – Strings and Pegs).

The patented adjustable type pegs are better for school instruments used for younger, less experienced players, because they are turnable by even very young players. Even well-fitted ebony pegs, on the other hand, are not. Also, for ebony pegs to remain free and smooth working, they must be re-fitted periodically and in the long run will not only be less satisfactory but more expensive.

Endpins

Cellos and basses need to have end-pins that are adjustable. Small students may need to put the endpin all the way in, in order to get the instrument into the proper playing position. For larger students, the endpin must be long enough to raise the cello and the bass to proper playing height. Cellos and basses with an immovable peg are not satisfactory and should not be purchased. Cellos should have an endpin at least eighteen inches in length to be acceptable for a full-sized instrument purchased by a school system.

Summation

It is recommended that when purchasing stringed instruments and equipping them for school use, a compromise between the most expensive equipment (generally the best sound but expensive and troublesome to maintain) and the very cheapest equipment (generally the worst sounding and possibly least expensive to maintain) must be made. Therefore, for a reasonably good sound, coupled with the least amount of upkeep possible, it is strongly recommended that well adjusted (see MENC Specifications at end of chapter) plywood cellos and plywood or fiberglass basses be used equipped with steel strings (chrome wound solid core). All instruments should be furnished with fiberglass bows that are haired with processed hair.

All instruments, except string bass, should also be equipped with four adjusters and patented adjustable pegs. If violins and violas are to be furnished (not recommended) then they should be of good, solid construction (carved) and adjusted exactly as outlined in the MENC Specifications as amended in the previous paragraphs.

Writing Bid Specifcations for String Instruments

When writing specifications for string instruments, it must first be decided exactly which brand(s) of instruments are of sufficient quality to satisfy the demands to be made upon them.

Second, the specification should include the brand name (or names if more than one brand is satisfactory) and the model number from the manufacturer. A complete description of the instrument, including type of pegs, trimmings (fingerboard, saddle, tailpiece, etc.), strings adjusters (if desired), bow (material and/or model number) and case should also be included. To do this properly, a current catalogue listing the instruments and accessories must be available to the person making out the bid specification.

The term "or equal" should never be used on a bid specification because the "or equal" will be decided by the bidder instead of the purchaser and there have been many instances of unsatisfactory instruments purchased because of these two words.

Which Instruments Should Be Purchased By The School?

All violins and violas should be the responsibility of the students to furnish for home and school use (see Chapter I, Part I for rationales).

It is the authors' conviction that only cellos and bass should be purchased by the school system for use by the students at school on the secondary level. All cello and bass players should also own their own instruments, but because of their relatively large size and fragility, it is felt that daily transportation of the instruments from home to school and back is really an unnecessary hardship both in terms of inconvenience to the students and risk to the instruments. Therefore, it is suggested that all students (except possibly bass players for reasons of finances) be required to have an instrument at home to practice and that the school furnish the instrument only for rehearsals at the school. Thus, neither the students' instruments nor the school-owned instruments are subjected to unreasonable risk of damage.

The care of instruments logically divides into two categories, emergency repairs that must be taken care of immediately and routine maintenance. Any problem in either category will probably result in either loss of sound (quantity and/or quality), or in making the instrument harder to play.

Emergency repairs must, of course, be taken care of immediately – cracks, loose fingerboards, collapsed sound-posts, open joints, broken parts, broken strings, defective screw adjustments on bows, etc. These cannot wait and must be taken care of whenever they happen. However, equally important to remember are routine maintenance items which should be checked and repaired, if possible, on a fixed schedule. A good book that can help a teacher to learn about simple repairs is *You Fix Them* published by Scherl and Roth Inc. of Cleveland, Ohio.

Strings

Strings should be changed on a regular schedule and not just when they break! For steel strings, the minimum schedule for changing is generally as follows: (1) Violin and viola about every six months; (2) Cello about once a year; and (3) Bass every two years.

Steel strings will stay in one piece longer than this, but for passable sound and intonation, they should be replaced at least as frequently as recommended above. Even on this schedule, many of the strings will be "false" by the time they are changed, causing intonation problems and bad tone.

Installation of Strings

For maximum wear and best sound, the strings must be properly installed. Steel strings must be used with adjusters (see Figure No. 1).

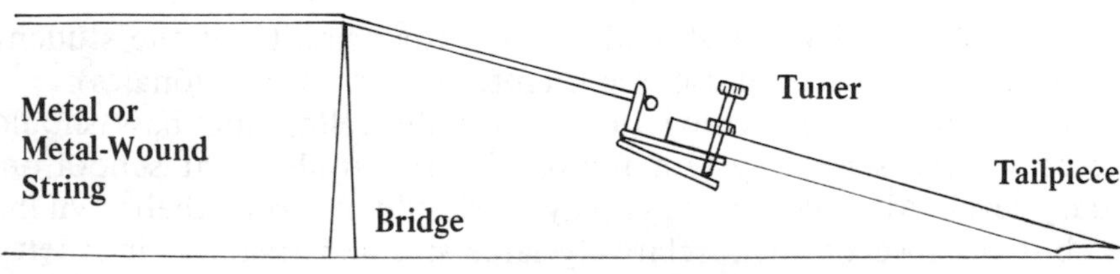

Proper Installation of Steel String On Adjuster
Figure No. 1

Gut-wound strings must not be used with adjusters. Note: The string is not to be pulled back through the loop on the end (see Figure No. 2).

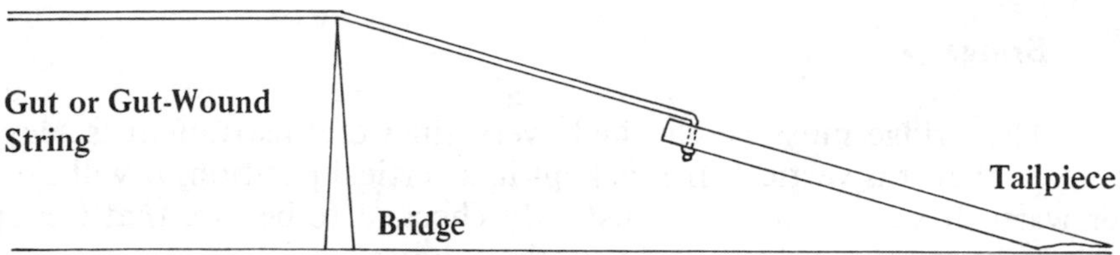

Proper Installation of Gut String (Without Adjuster)
Figure No. 2

For all of the instruments except the violin, the proper stringing is as shown in Figure No. 3. The reasons for this apparently "wrong" stringing order are as follows: The largest diameter string needs the least amount of bend possible, as the string goes over the nut. This allows the easiest movement of the string while turning and helps to avoid cracking of the winding thus making the string tune easier and last longer. Also, by attaching the string on the upper peg, the lowest string (which needs it the most), is given the most length to resonate.

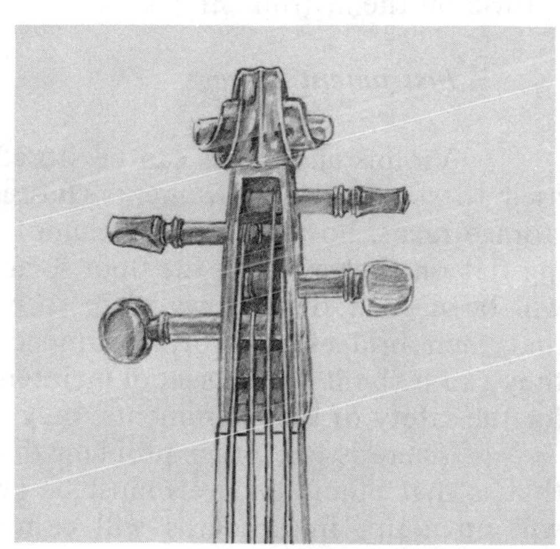

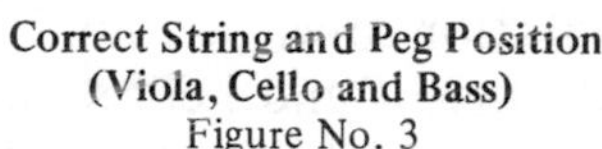
Correct String and Peg Position
(Viola, Cello and Bass)
Figure No. 3

Rehairing Bows

Every two years is probably the least often that bows can be scheduled for rehairing. They should not be used past the point that the hair does not extend completely across the ferrule and is at least a couple of hairs in thickness.

Bridge and Tailpiece Need Constant Checking

There are some things that need to be checked almost constantly. The students should be taught to be observant of these things. They are:

Bridge

The bridge must be checked every time the instrument is played to be certain that it is vertical. If it is kept in a vertical position, it will probably never warp. It should also be constantly checked to be sure that it is spaced exactly between the inside notches in the F-holes.

Tailpiece Adjustment

For the tailpiece adjustment to be correct it will need to be checked at least once a year. The tailgut must be drawn up short enough so that the end of the tailpiece is actually resting on the saddle. If it stretches, it should be shortened by tightening the brass nuts if there are any (Sacconi tailgut) or replacing it if there are none.

Keep Instrument Free of Rosin

The top of the instrument as well as the strings must be kept free of rosin, as a build-up of rosin deadens the tone and eventually will ruin the varnish on the instrument.

Instrument Storage

Violins and violas can be stored on the same type of shelves that are used to store band instruments. Basses and cellos will have to have special storage racks, however, as they cannot be stored safely and conveniently laying flat on shelves or on the floor so another solution must be found. A rack will be needed that allows them to be stored upright and held securely so that their bridges will not be bumped. These are available commercially or they can be built by the school maintenance department if desired. However, for the safety of the instruments, they are absolutely necessary.

There is one other problem that is peculiar to string instruments and that is that humidity levels must be kept within certain limits or the joints will open up, fingerboards will come loose, bass bars come unglued, the wood will crack, etc. This means that in a dry climate or in places that are heavily heated in the winter time, a humidifier will probably be necessary. In areas with high humidity, a de-humidifier will be necessary. In some places where there are large changes in humidity, it may be necessary to use both. This is true because excessive humidity causes the wood to swell and the glued parts to come undone. Too little humidity causes the wood to dry out and to shrink. Unfortunately, the various woods in stringed instruments do not expand and contract at the same rate. Any change in humidity causes stresses in the woods that can cause cracking if they are too severe. Therefore, keeping the humidity changes within a safe range can save many, many repair dollars and should be a consideration for the person responsible.

MINIMUM STANDARDS FOR STRING INSTRUMENTS USED IN SCHOOLS

THE STRING INSTRUCTION COMMITTEE of the Music Educators National Conference, in cooperation with committee representation from the Music Teachers National Association, believes that by encouraging the purchase of string instruments and accessories which meet the following standards, string instruction and school orchestra development can be materially advanced.

Because the playability of string instruments depends so much upon proper construction, correct adjustment and alignment, it is hoped that these "Minimum Standards for String Instruments in the Schools" will guide consumers and teachers in their selection of instruments regardless of their price bracket.

MEASUREMENTS AND TERMINOLOGY OF SIZES

Note: Measurements are given with a "plus or minus (+ or –) sign because instruments of different well-established makers (or even those of the same maker) will vary slightly. It is not the wish of the committee to rule out the many fine instruments that will vary somewhat from the accepted "standards."

A. INSTRUMENT MEASUREMENTS

	VIOLIN	
Standard (full)	(4/4) body length 14" (35.56 cm. + or –)	+ or –
Intermediate	(3/4) body length 13-1/4" (33.65 cm. + or –)	+ or –
Junior	(1/2) body length 12-7/16" (31.52 cm. + or –)	+ or –)
	VIOLA	
Standard	(4/4) (large) body length 16-1/2" and up (41.9 cm. and up)	
(full)	(4/4) body length 15-3/4" to 16-1/2" (40.9 cm. to 41.9)	
	(4/4) (small) body length 15" to 15-3/4" (38.1 cm. to 40.9)	
Intermediate	body length 14" (35.56 cm. + or –)	+ or –
Junior	body length 13-1/4" (33.65 cm. + or –)	+ or –)
	CELLO	
Standard (full)	(4/4) body length 29-5/8" (75.3 cm. + or –)	+ or –
Intermediate	(3/4) body length 27-5/16" (69.4 cm. + or –)	+ or –
Junior	(1/2) body length 25-1/2" (64.77 cm. + or –)	+ or –

BASS

Standard (3/4) body length 43-1/4" to 44-1/2" + or –
(109.85 cm. to 113 + or –)
String length from fingerboard nut to bridge
41-1/2" to 43-1/2" + or –
(105.4 cm. to 109.85 + or –)

Intermediate (1/2) body length 41-1/4" + or –
String length from fingerboard nut to bridge
38-1/4" + or –
(98.45 cm. + or –)

Junior (3/8) body length 36-5/8" + or –
(93 cm + or –)
String length from fingerboard nut to bridge
35" + or –
(88.9 cm. + or –)

B. BOW LENGTH (from tip end of screw button)

Note: Bows for use with a particular instrument should be the same proportionate size as the instrument, as follows:

Violin	(4/4)	29-1/4"	+ or –	(74.3 cm. + or –)
	(3/4)	27"	+ or –	(68.6 cm. + or –)
	(1/2)	24-9/16"	+ or –	(62.4 cm. + or –)
Viola	Standard	29-5/8"	+ or –	(75.2 cm. + or –)
	Intermediate	29-3/16"	+ or –	(74.1 cm. + or –)
	Junior	27-1/4"	+ or –	(69.2 cm. + or –)
Cello	Standard	28-1/8"	+ or –	(71.4 cm. + or –)
	Hair length	23-3/4"	+ or –	(60.3 cm. + or –)
	Intermediate	26-7/16"	+ or –	(67.1 cm. + or –)
	Hair length	22-1/6"	+ or –	(56.2 cm. + or –)
	Junior	24-1/2"	+ or –	(61.6 cm. + or –)
	Hair length	20-3/8"	+ or –	(51.8 cm. + or –)
Bass	French Model	28-1/16"	+ or –	(71.5 cm. + or –)
	Hair length	21-9/16"	+ or –	(57 cm. + or –)
	German (Butler) Model	30-3/8"	+ or –	(77.2 cm. + or –)
	Hair length	22-1/16"	+ or –	(56 cm. + or –)

MATERIALS AND CONSTRUCTION

A. INSTRUMENTS

1. Back, sides, scroll and top. Wood preferably seasoned seven years before use for instrument.
   a. Back sides and scroll – hard maple preferred. (carved).
   b. Top – spruce preferred (carved).
   c. Plywood approved for cellos and basses, thickness to be approved by committee.
2. Construction
   a. All joints glued tightly and reinforced with four full corner blocks and solid upper and lower blocks, fill lining inside of top and back. Inlaid purfling preferred.
   b. All edges glued securely.
   c. All cracks, if any, properly repaired (reinforced and glued).
   d. Inlaid purfling strongly preferred over painted purfling.
   e. Bass bar should be of harder spruce than wood used for top itself. Bass bar must be glued in and not carved out from top wood.

3. Trimmings
   a. Pegs – ebony, rosewood, boxwood or cocobola.
   b. Fingerboard:
      (1) First choice – ebony.
      (2) Second choice – rosewood treated to resist absorption (bass and cello only).
   c. Nut and saddle – ebony preferred.
   d. Tailpiece (copper wire loop accepted for elementary school instruments):
      (1) First choice – ebony.
      (2) Second choice – boxwood.
      (3) Third choice – rosewood (cello and bass only).
   e. Cello and Bass end pin:
      (1) Sturdy, metal adjustable, extra long.
      (2) Set screw, extra large "thumb – first finger" grip area.
4. Varnish
   a. Type: good quality of soft texture (oil type varnish preferred; thick, hard glossy finish discouraged).
   b. Neck should not be coated with any finish which prevents hand from sliding smoothly.

   Recommended process: Wood surfaced with 00 sandpaper and 00 steel wool. Wood wiped with water-moistened cloth to cause loose fibers to "burr," then again rubbed with 00 steel wool; surfaced again with 00 steel wool and, after a second application of linseed oil, polished with a chamois or wool cloth. (Other processes producing this result acceptable.)
5. Attachments
   a. Chinrest – ebony, boxwood or plastic, suitable size, without sharp edges. The Roth-Waller chinrest is most satisfactory for correct placement on the instrument and for maximum playing comfort.
   b. Strings – good quality fresh strings, properly matched.

   Note: The following are recommended for the majority of instruments in most school situations. Climatic conditions and differences in instruments may suggest some deviation.

      (1) Gauges for gut strings (medium):

* Violin	- E	steel, with adjuster. (See Item 4 "Tuners" below.)
		Single strand .010 (.25 mm.) aluminum wound on steel .011 (.27 mm.)
	A	.029 (.73 mm.) gut
	D	.034 (.85 mm.) aluminum on gut
	G	.032 (.80 mm.) silver on gut
* Viola	- A	.029 (.73 mm.) gut
	D	.035 (.85 mm.) gut or aluminum on gut
	G	.033 (.82 mm.) silver on gut
	C	.045 (.112 mm.) silver on gut
* Cello	- A	.044 (1.1 mm.) gut (metal smaller)
	D	.051 (1.126 mm.) gut (metal smaller)
		.056 (1.35 mm.) aluminum on gut
	G	.054 (1.36 mm.) silverplated wire on gut
		.053 (1.4 mm.) silver on gut
	C	.074 (1.75 mm.) silverplated wire on gut or silver on gut

*Obsolete – See P. 259.

* Bass - G .088 (2.20 mm.) gut
D .114 (2.85 mm.) gut
A .110 (2.75 mm.) copper or silver (or plated copper) on gut
E .138 (3.45 mm.) copper or silver (or plated copper) on gut

Note: Standardization of large gear box in bass is hoped for.

(2) Metal strings are supplied by manufacturer in balanced sets.

(3) For general school use, metal strings with tuners (see Item 4 "Tuners" below) approved as follows:

Violin - E single strand .010 (.25 mm.)
E aluminum wound on steel .011 (.27 mm.)
A steel core with chromium or aluminum winding over silk or plastic underlay .017 (.43 mm.)

Viola - A (same as Violin A) .017 (.43 mm.)
D (same as Violin A) .024 (.60 mm.)

Cello - A (same as Violin A) .025 (.625 mm.)
D (same as Violin A) .036 (.90 mm.)

(4) Tuners (adjusters):
Violin-Viola – type which will not tilt tailpiece or mar top of instrument.
Cello – extra sturdy.

B. BOWS

1. Bow stick.
   a. First choice: Pernambuco, seasoned at least 10 years.
   *b. Second choice: metal (aluminum).
   c. Third choice: brazilwood, seasoned at least 10 years.

2. Frogs and tip.
   a. Ebony frog preferred.
   b. Ivory tip preferred; plastic tip acceptable (metal tip acceptable on bass bows.)

   Note: Importers and dealers are urged to standardize eyelet threads on all bows.

3. Bow grip.
   Sterling silver wire with thumb leather at lower end and leather ring at upper end preferred. Leather at both ends securely glued or shellacked to stick, and wire held together by two runs of solder or other appropriate adhesive. In wrapped bow grips, the winding should not be loose. Thumb leather should be of proper length and thickness at upper end.

C. CASES

1. Type: shaped or oblong type. Hard shell plywood with Keratol, leather or other durable covering preferred. Cases must fit the instrument as well as being of proportionate body area. Special attention should be given to viola cases since there are varied sizes within the 4/4 or standard group.

2. Interior.
   a. Lining soft and attractive (plush material preferred).
   b. Bottom and sides well padded.

*Obsolete – See P. 259.

c. At least one accessory pocket and two bow holders.
d. Zipper instrument cover highly desirable.

3. Zipper cover for case desirable, especially in colder climate.
4. Cello and Bass bags – zipper openings preferred. (Cloth or leather between zipper and bouts.)

ADJUSTMENT

A. PEGS

1. Properly fitted for snug fit at both sides of peg box. The ends must not extend out beyond the peg holes.
2. Must be lubricated only with fresh yellow laundry soap, commercial peg soap, or ordinary chalk.

B. FINGERBOARD

1. Straight and proportioned correctly, but slightly concave with medium curvature.

C. NUT

1. Properly spaced and right height to allow small clearance below strings.
2. Over-all spacing of nut (full or standard size) center of string to string:

Violin	E to G 5/8"	(15.6 mm.)
Viola	A to C 11/16"	(16.9 mm.)
Cello	A to C 7/8"	(21.5 mm.)
Bass	G to E 1-3/16"	(29.6 mm.)

D. BRIDGE

1. Curvature.
   a. Same as the curvature of the fingerboard, but slightly higher on the G string side (E string side for bass).
   b. Material – hard maple
2. Grooves.
   a. Made just deep enough to hold the strings in place (only 1/3rd of string rests in notch, so 2/3rds of string is *above* bridge level).
   b. Bridge half round in shape and just large enough to accept the string which it is to accommodate.
   c. Ebony or equivalent inlay desirable under metal strings.
3. Height
   a. Should be high enough to give the following clearance between strings and end of fingerboard (standard or full-sized instruments; smaller instruments slightly less):

Violin	- E 1/8"	(3.12 mm.)
Violin	- G 3/16"	(4.6 mm.)
Viola	- A 3/16"	(4.6 mm.)
Viola	- C 4/16"	(6.25 mm.)
Cello	- A 1/4"	(6.25 mm.)
Cello	- C 5/16"	(6.80 mm.)
Bass	- G 7/16"	(10.9 mm.)
Bass	- E 11/16"	(17.17 mm.)

4. Feet must be shaped to fit instrument top, bridge tilted backward to form right angle between back side of bridge and top of instrument.

5. Unfitted bridge must be cut to medium thickness and tapered to top thickness as listed:
   Violin - 1/16" (1.55 mm.)
   Viola - 1/16" (1.55 mm.)
   Cello - 3/32" (2.32 mm.)
   Bass - 3/16" (4.67 mm.)
6. Proper string spacing at bridge (center of string to center of string), full size (smaller instruments slightly less):
   Violin - 7/16" (10.9 mm.)
   Viola - 1/2" (12.5 mm.)
   Cello - 5/8" (15.6 mm.)
7. Bridge should center on the inner F hole notches.

E. TAILPIECE

1. Should be just long enough so that end of tailpiece lines up with outside edge of saddle.
2. Saddle high enough so that tailpiece and ends of tailpiece loop are well in the clear over the top plate. Violin at least 1/16", proportionately more for other instruments.

F. SOUND POST

1. Location immediately behind the right foot (1st string side) of the bridge. Distance between back of bridge and front of sound post should be approximately one-half thickness of post (a little more for some instruments.)
2. Size:
   Violin - 1/4" (6.1 mm.) diameter
   Viola - 1/4" (6.1 mm.) diameter
   Cello - 7/16" (10.9 mm.) diameter
   Bass - 11/16" (17.1 mm.) diameter
3. Fitting – must fit snugly (but never glued), ends beveled to fit flush with top and back. (For best results, fitting should be done in the U.S.A.)

G. BOW

1. When the frog is in full forward position, the hair should be relaxed (not loose). The opposite test should also apply in tightening the bow screw.
2. Hair should be "sighted down" to make sure there are no cross hairs.
3. Stick (tightened 1-1/2 or 2 rounds for playing) should be "sighted down" to see that it is straight.
4. Frog should seat firmly on the bow, not rock from side to side.
5. Bow screw should work smoothly.
6. Bow grip should be properly attached. (See Item 3 under "Bow Materials").

Miscellaneous Considerations 12

INTRODUCTION

There are many areas that need to be considered, other than the actual teaching of the mechanics of playing, for an orchestra program to really be successful. Some of the more important areas that must be carefully thought out and then planned for include: how the staff will be utilized (teacher schedules, curriculum planning, and scheduling of activities), public relations and communication, fund-raising activities, and parents' organizations. The authors' views on these vitally important areas and their relationships to the size and quality of the orchestra program will be discussed in the paragraphs that follow.

UTILIZATION OF STAFF

Need For A Coordinator Or Supervisor

The authors feel that before a music department can be coordinated to work at utmost efficiency, a person must be designated to be in charge, and this person must have the responsibility and authority to make most of the decisions that affect the interaction of the department members' efforts. This is not to say that there cannot and should not be input from the members of the department, but when the decision is made, it should be made for the entire department. Obviously, all of this discussion applies only in school systems where there is more than one music faculty member.

One of the things that must be planned by the person in charge of the music department is the scheduling of music staff throughout the school system.

The administrator for the music department will be the person responsible for deciding who teaches what along with where and when. For the best qualitative utilization of the staff, and more success with the teaching in turn, the person in charge must look realistically and honestly at the personnel on hand before assigning positions. This probably should be done from time to time even after positions have been assigned – especially if problems arise.

The things that the music administrator must consider before assigning a faculty member his schedule are the person's experience, personality, and strengths and weaknesses in his teaching at various levels. For instance, assuming that all staff members are competent, it would not be the best scheduling for all concerned to place a first year teacher with an advanced secondary-level full orchestra, especially if a more experienced person is available. Also, some people might work better with junior high students – others may work better with either senior high or elementary students. A wise administrator will take these considerations into account when assigning teachers. However, it should be realized that if a teacher can only teach successfully at only one level, it probably would be better to replace him. Because the authors feel so strongly that the advantages of vertical scheduling enable a program to achieve better quality, it is felt that a person that can only teach on one level would be a detriment to a really fine program.

All teachers should be scheduled with an eye to their being able to grow and develop to their full potential. This means putting teachers into situations it is felt they are ready to handle and moving them gradually into positions requiring more experience and responsibility. So that every teacher can develop educationally and musically to his fullest potential, it is highly desirable to schedule each one with a secondary level performing group that would be capable of playing advanced music. This is important in fostering the feeling in each teacher that he has a stake in the results as young students progress into orchestras (or bands) that are mainly performance oriented organizations. *All* need to experience the "fun" of working with a large, more advanced group and seeing it progress from fall to spring into a mature, musical organization. Also, psychologically, it is good for every person to get some *public* recognition for the work he is doing.

Another way that strengths of the teachers can be utilized more fully is through team-teaching situations, either formally or informally. For instance, when assigning teachers to schools, if possible, a wind and a string major might both be scheduled to work with a performance orchestra.

STAFF PLANNING

Faculty Meetings

Having faculty meetings of all orchestra personnel and/or instrumental music staff several times during the year is very beneficial to the organization of the department so that the curriculum and activities of the music department can be planned and coordinated. It is also important that all faculty members share the same basic philosophy of teaching instrumental music so that the department doesn't go in separate directions towards different goals. The philosophy, as well as the curriculum or course of study used to accomplish the philosophy, should be worked out at these meetings and put into writing so as to be available to the school administration as well as any new music personnel who join the group. A coordinated curriculum is necessary for the development of highly competent groups. Without it, students will have no common backgrounds of abilities when they reach the secondary level.

A curriculum or course of study cannot be planned without deciding what method of technique books will be used at each grade level (order and choice of materials). This will need to be re-evaluated every year or so by the group and then a decision made by the music administrator. All teachers in the system should use the same basic books for technique building so that there will be coordination from school to school at the same grade level.

The music staff, along with the music administrator, should decide on a unified system of grading, try-outs, and policies pertaining to the groups giving concerts and going to contests. They should all also agree to similar regulations about students' obligations to participate in concerts so that parents will not be able to complain that teachers are not consistent.

Scheduling of Activities

It is very important that the music staff plan concert and other activity dates together and well in advance in order to avoid conflicts. If this is not done, a parent with children in two or more schools might have a problem getting to all of his childrens' concerts.

After dates are decided upon for recruiting, concerts, contests, festivals, etc., they should be placed on the music department calendar as well as the All-School calendar and the respective school calendars.

Multi-Level, All-City, or All-Area Coordinated Activities

Many school systems find it valuable to plan some type of activity where students from several schools can play together in large groups. This type of mass event can be set up in various ways – one grade level from a whole system playing together – several grade levels playing together or all grade levels playing together. It is probably best, however, to not have the entire concert consist of all of the students playing together at the same time. The spread of abilities over two or three grade levels is too great to allow optimum benefits for all if all of the music is played together by all of the students. No matter what type of mass events are used in a school system, it has been the authors' experience that they serve some very important purposes. First, students love to play in large groups with students of the same age from other schools, because it gives them a chance to make new friends who also participate in orchestra. Secondly, they really like the "feel" and the sound of playing in a large group. From this experience, they see how important it is that they learn to count correctly, follow the conductor, etc.

Another important aspect of this type of activity is that it gives the students and parents a chance to see what is ahead for the young player while the older students and parents can see how much progress they have made from when they started. This, of course, would only be true if several grade levels are featured on the same program. In this situation, it is best if each grade level plays several selections alone so that the parents can hear the differences in first year, second year and third year students. However, it has been found to be very exciting for both the parents and students involved if one or two numbers are done by two or more groups together. Both the sound and sight of a large, massed group playing well together can do much to inspire students, teachers and parents to go away from the concert convinced that this is an experience well worth all the time and effort.

Massed concerts are great morale builders for both the students and parents. They build much enthusiasm and help combat possible drop-outs that sometimes occur well into the year, because the students are beginning to tire of the sameness of the regular class routine. Working toward an activity where they get to leave school to go and rehearse with other students and/or a guest conductor is something they really look forward to. Events like this also serve as a good recruiting tool, because the students that are not involved in the string festival are aware of it from hearing about it from the students who are in it.

Having a massed festival does make necessary much coordination and planning between the staff to insure that the students are all prepared in the same way throughout the system and that a myriad of details are planned to provide the proper physical set-up. Some of the things that must be planned include: How many grades should be included? Should there be a guest conductor(s) or not? Where should the event be held?, etc. The authors suggest that events like this are most needed for the beginning year (fifth grade) through the third year (seventh grade). After this, the students should be scheduled in full orchestras that will have a busy performing schedule so they will regularly have the experience of playing in a large group.

One other advantage that should be mentioned about a festival of this type is that combining groups of students from various schools gives all teachers involved an opportunity to evaluate their work and see how it compares to other teachers' work. This type of event also gives them a chance to evaluate as a group the areas that are weak throughout the system and figure out what steps should be taken in another year to correct or avoid these problems.

IMPORTANCE OF EFFECTIVE COMMUNICATION

Introduction

No matter how strong a music department is in teaching and accomplishing goals musically with the students, it cannot exist very well and very long *without* effective communication in all areas. The entire music faculty, the school administration, the classroom teachers, the parents, and the community all must be aware of what the purposes and activities of the program are and feel as if they are a part of them. If this kind of situation does *not* exist, eventually some decisions involving the music department will need to be made, and someone involved may not understand what is going on, and as a result, hinder the music program rather than help it.

Types of Communication Needed

Music Faculty

The most important communication of all is between the music administrator and the various members of the music faculty. It must appear to all outsiders that the group is working together for the same goals and purposes with the music students. It is very important that all faculty members know what other music faculty members are doing. The responsibility for keeping the others informed is an equal responsibility of the music administration and the music faculty. If the teachers expect the music administrator to stand behind them and back them up when problems arise, they must keep him informed of what is happening and be asked for advice when there are problems. Likewise, the music administrator must communicate openly and often with his staff, both individually and as a group, to make sure all understand and carry out the policies established for the department.

The School Administration

When there are decisions to be made involving city-wide musical activities or policies, it will be the music administration's responsibility to inform and/or work out the necessary details with the appropriate members of the school administration. Once the decision is made, the music administration should then inform the music faculty of the decision. The music faculty in turn have a responsibility to discuss and keep the individual principals informed ahead of time about activities that may involve a change in the regularly-scheduled classes so that they can readjust the schedule (if possible) and/or inform the appropriate classroom teachers.

Classroom Teachers

If instrumental music faculty will take the time to build a good relationship with the classroom teachers, it can be very beneficial to the instrumental music program. Especially at the elementary level, it pays great dividends for music faculty members to get acquainted with the teachers that have the instrumental music students in their rooms and make them feel that they are important to the music program. It is also wise to be interested in the school and its activities. Introducing the principal and the classroom teachers from whose rooms the instrumental music students come from at the P.T.A. meeting when the students perform is a very good way to let everyone know that their cooperation and support for the instrumental music program is appreciated. *Remember:* The principal and the classroom teachers have much influence on both the students and their parents. It is wise to develop good relationships with them.

Students

ELEMENTARY LEVEL

At the elementary level, one of the most important communications involves making sure that the other students in the building are aware of what the instrumental music students are doing so that the other students will want to join the orchestra program. The director must try to create the feeling among the students that the instrumental music program is a large, active, fun program and that anyone not involved in it is really missing something. If this feeling can be accomplished, then much of the next year's recruiting will automatically be taken care of.

Students playing in the instrumental music classes should be encouraged to help advertise the program to friends, neighbors, relatives, small brothers and sisters, scouts, church, sports groups, etc. If they are enthusiastic in talking about it, other students will want to join. Students sell students!

SECONDARY LEVEL

At the secondary level, communication will mostly involve the director and officers of the music group making sure that written material and photos about the various activities are passed on to the school and local newspapers and the yearbook. Often, posters will need to be printed or made by the students to put up in the halls, stores in the community, etc., to advertise concert activities.

Community

Communication with the community is also very important if the music program is to have the status it deserves in the area. It is, of course, very important that the community know of the music program's purpose and activities so that it will support it by attending concerts, helping with any fund-raising that may be necessary, and in general, feel that the school orchestra is an important cultural asset to the community. It should be realized that when people hear a lot about something, they assume it is important, but if they don't hear much about it, they will assume that it must *not* be important.

NEWSPAPERS, RADIO AND TELEVISION MEDIA

Other than the enthusiasm of students in the orchestra, the best way to advertise music department purposes and activities is through newspaper, radio, and television publicity. The teacher should realize, however, that the news media are really looking for news releases that have a different newsworthy slant to them. Perhaps an article about what students like about being in an orchestra, what it feels like to play music, how individuals in the group prepare, etc., would be of more interest to a community audience than just a report of the upcoming event (try centering on something interesting like the purpose of the event). Articles about school activities should be taken to the *school editors* of the various media.

FUND-RAISING ACTIVITIES

Introduction

With today's constant crunch on the money allocated to the schools from local taxes, most instrumental music departments are finding it more and more necessary to have fund-raising activities to support some of the activities that are necessary to keep the students in the program (trips to music educators conventions, exchange concerts, going to festivals, clinics, contests, etc.). Events like this are necessary both musically and socially for fine secondary level groups, yet are costly and most school systems cannot subsidize them. In most school systems, the majority of the fund-raising activities are handled by the music students with the music director's assistance. Sometimes, if there is a strong parents organization, parents also do some fund-raising.

Types

There are numerous kinds of projects that have been proven successful for raising money. Some of the more popular ideas used in today's schools for fund-raising include:

(1) admission fee for concerts
(2) selling magazines
(3) selling calendars
(4) selling candles
(5) selling fruitcakes
(6) tag days
(7) marathon concerts
(8) car washes
(9) rummage sale, garage sale, or flea market
(10) slave auction of music students (hourly labor)
(11) spaghetti dinner
(12) pancake breakfast
(13) bake sales
(14) mile of penneys
(15) program advertising
(16) patron contributions listed on programs), etc.

While fund-raising activities are hard work on everyone's part, they can contribute positively in ways other than financing. First, the group interaction between the students working on these projects provides a social outlet as well as helping to develop a real sense of pride in belonging to the organization. Second, the community really becomes aware of the group and its activities when the students are out in the community working on these fund-raising activities. All in all, they are an activity that every teacher dreads, but he realizes that the benefits are far greater than the time taken to do them.

IMPORTANCE OF PARENT ORGANIZATIONS

Introduction

Parents' organizations can be a very valuable asset to a music department if handled correctly. However, it is imperative that from the very outset, the members understand they are there only to assist the music directors and their groups in any way that they can. It should be written into their constitution that they have no function in the administration of the musical groups. If a parent's group tries to make decisions about the running of the music department or policy, it is the authors' recommendations that it be disbanded immediately. However, any music department that doesn't have a parent organization is depriving itself of valuable help. Unless the school system is a huge city system, it has been found that it is best for there to be only one instrumental music parents' organization that all parents of these students belong to. Most of the projects can then be larger all-school projects with common goals.

Types of Activities

Successful parents' organizations usually sponsor various types of fund-raising and service activities to support the instrumental music department. Some possible service activities include:

(1) Purchase of uniforms needed for secondary level groups

(2) Scholarships to summer music camps for outstanding instrumental students

(3) Calling committees to assist the director in notifying parents of events, problems, etc.

(4) Banquets or picnics at end of year for high school music students

(5) Gifts for graduating instrumental music students

(6) Awards for outstanding music students

(7) Selling advertising for concert programs

(8) Helping with publicity for departmental activities

(9) Chaperoning for trips

(10) Serve refreshments after concerts, at parents' meetings, etc.

In conclusion, the right kind of parents group is an asset beyond comparison. Not only are they helpful in the areas mentioned above but also as a ready-made public relations group for the music department. The authors feel that they can be quite effective in selling the instrumental music program to both the school administration and the community.

Conclusion: Thoughts for the Future 13

WHERE WE HAVE COME FROM

Summary of School Orchestra Movement in the United States

The development of the high school orchestra has followed a long and erratic course. Orchestras were apparently the first type of instrumental music group to be connected with the public schools in the United States. As early as 1878 there were orchestras found in the high schools.[1] By the 1890's and very early 1900's, there is record of numerous orchestras in the high schools and even some in the elementary schools.[2] These early orchestras bore little resemblance to our present day orchestras as they were very small (10-18 students), the instrumentation was determined strictly by chance (whatever was available), and the players were all students who studied privately and already knew how to play. The rehearsals were very informally organized – they were not during school and sometimes were not even at the school. The directors were frequently not even trained musicians, but rather students or teachers of other subjects. Sometimes even the principal was known to direct the orchestra.[3]

By the time of World War I, there were school systems in several parts of the country who were making class instrumental lessons available to their students to insure a balanced instrumentation and steady supply of students to play in their school bands and orchestras. Orchestras continued to grow in number and quality until the early thirties when the band movement, fueled by the popularity of military bands during World War I, the uniforms for the young men, use of the bands at football games, and the national band contests that were first sponsored and then vigorously supported by the band instrument manufacturers gradually eclipsed interest in the orchestras. One can only speculate upon why this happened. One of the important reasons seems to be that because stringed instruments were, and still are, almost all imported from Europe, there was no organization of manufacturers in the United States to promote orchestras in the way the band instrument manufacturers promoted the bands during that era.

[1] *History of Public School Music In The United States* by Edward Bailey Birge. Music Educators National Conference, 1966, p. 166.

[2] *Ibid.*

[3] *Ibid.*

Another reason, though more difficult to substantiate, seems probable. That is that string and orchestra teachers were for many years much slower than the band teachers in adopting large group class teaching techniques. Because of this reluctance on the part of many string teachers to recruit large numbers of students and to teach them in large classes, the string programs suffered in two ways. First, it was found that young students liked to be in larger classes, and therefore they chose band instruments. Second, many administrators felt that string programs were too expensive for their budgets.

For a period of about twenty-five years (1935-1960), the orchestra movement seemed to be dying, and appeared about to become a thing of the past in many parts of the United States. Then, about 1960, a change for the better was signaled – stringed instrument sales began to increase noticeably! Orchestras and string programs around the country were established or, in some cases, re-established. Again, one can only speculate as to why this happened. There were undoubtedly many reasons for this resurgence of interest in strings and orchestra programs, but some things were happening about this time which probably had a bearing on this development.

Even though very fine string method books had been written for heterogeneous string-class teaching as early as 1923 (*Universal Teacher for Orchestra and Band* by T. P. Giddings and J. A. Maddy, *A Tune A Day,* C. P. Herfurth, 1927, and the *Merle Isaac String Class Method,* 1938), it was not until the early 1950's that anyone actively promoted the concept of heterogeneous string-class teaching to any extent beyond their own local communities. Starting in those years, men like Gilbert Waller of the University of Illinois and J. Frederick Müller, later to become Educational Director for the Scherl and Roth Company, were writing articles and doing clinic demonstrations advocating heterogeneous string-class teaching. About this same time, Heinrich Roth, President of the Scherl and Roth, Inc., saw that if the orchestra movement was to ever gain its rightful place in music education, it was going to need to be actively promoted and financially supported just as the band movement had been some twenty-five years earlier. At first Heinrich Roth sponsored Gilbert Waller, author of the *Waller String-Class Method* and professor of music at the University of Illinois, in clinics to demonstrate his heterogeneous class-teaching procedures. About the same time, Joseph Bornoff (author of Bornoff's *Finger Patterns)* was also active in the Eastern United States with clinics promoting heterogeneous string-class teaching.

Observing the successes of these and other clinics, Scherl and Roth, Inc., then a very small stringed instrument company in Cleveland, Ohio under the guidance of Heinrich Roth, created an Educational Division to promote strings and orchestras on a national level. J. Frederick Müller was engaged to be its first Director. Müller very actively promoted orchestras and heterogeneous string-class teaching through clinics, workshops, articles, guest conducting and consulting work with school administrations throughout the United States.

During the 1950's, with the exception of J. Frederick Müller, there was not much activity of the national level in promoting string instruments and orchestras. The 1960's, however, blossomed into a period of great activity with many advocates of orchestras and heterogeneous string-class teaching.

The 1960's saw the publication of the *Müller-Rusch String Method* (J. Frederick Müller and Harold W. Rusch), *The String-Builder Series* (Samuel Applebaum), *Playing and Teaching of Stringed Instruments* (Ralph Matesky and Ralph Rush), and Elizabeth Green's many books on string teaching and orchestral techniques (*Orchestral Bowing, Teaching Stringed Instruments in Classes,* etc.), among others. During this decade, these authors of methods and textbooks, among others were also very active in promoting strings and orchestras through articles, clinics, and workshops.

Another movement, while not a heterogeneous class approach, nor even primarily orchestra-oriented, was also beginning its rise to prominence in the U. S. during the 1960's. Shinicki Suzuki at this time received worldwide acclaim and recognition for the outstanding work he was doing with his Talent Education Program with very young violinists in Japan. The interest in his violin teaching methods, and the results he achieved, led to the founding of the American Suzuki Association, and most certainly improved the American public's concept of string playing even though his basic intent was not to develop or encourage the growth of school orchestras.[4]

In retrospect, the orchestra movement apparently slowed down and fell behind the band movement for two main reasons: One, there was no comparable financial support from business firms selling stringed instruments (due in part to the fact that there were no large firms in the field, only small dealers); and two, the decision (albeit a tacet one), to stress the older "conservatory" approach (one to one) in the teaching of strings instead of the large group string class methods developed and used to such great advantage by the teachers of band instruments. When these two problems were corrected by Scherl and Roth, Inc. lending financial support and teaching help to the string movement through its Educational Division and the advocacy of heterogeneous large group instruction by many respected authorities, the string and orchestra movement began to move toward achieving its deserved place in the total music education program.

During the 1970's, the upsurge of interest and participation in string and orchestra programs has continued at an even more rapid pace. The interest in class-teaching continues unabated, and at least four new series of method books are on the American market for perusal of the string educators of today: *Learning to Play* by Ralph Matesky, the *Etling String-Class Method* by Forest R. Etling, the *Learning Unlimited String Program* by Thomas Wisniewski and John Higgins, and *The Conceptual Method* by Samuel Applebaum.

WHERE WE ARE TODAY

More Orchestra Programs

Today the pendulum is swinging back towards the establishment of many new orchestra programs. According to music industry statistics, for the past several years, the sales of stringed instruments has increased while the sales of band instruments have leveled off or even declined slightly.[5]

[4]Waltraud Suzuki, "Methods and Misconceptions," *American Suzuki Journal,* Vol. 5, No. 3, September 1977, p. 1.

[5]*The Instrumentalist,* December 1976, p. 98.

Many Are New

Many school systems with strong, established band programs are realizing that their music programs are not complete and are adding strings to their programs. The incompleteness is felt, because without an orchestra, there is a vast quantity of some of the finest music written that cannot be experienced by the music students. Also, there are students whose personality make-up is such that they will not become involved in the instrumental program if they *have* to play in a band. For these two reasons, as well as others, more and more school music programs are adding string classes and orchestras to their music programs at an ever increasing rate.

Many Band Directors Entering the Field

Because of the increase in interest in strings and orchestras and the relatively small number of string music education majors graduating from the university music schools, there are not enough string majors available to do all of the string and orchestra teaching required in the United States. So, many band-trained people, seeing this need as an opportunity, are going into the orchestra field first and then later (after a clinic or two to re-train) get into the actual teaching of string techniques.

Other band teachers are getting into the orchestra-string field because their administrations have notified them that either they must teach strings and/or orchestras or they will be replaced by someone who can. This happens more often than one would suspect because of dropping enrollment in the band program and/or dropping school enrollment in general. With the smaller enrollments of the late 70's, the administrators have the choice of letting the music teachers go or finding additional courses for them to teach. Because of the up-surge of strings mentioned earlier, when the administrator needs someone to start a string program, it must be taught by one of the present band teachers or he will have to be replaced by someone that is willing and able to teach both winds and strings. The third important reason that band directors are being asked to take over strings is that in many instances the present string person has let the program dwindle to the point that the administration feels it cannot justify a full-time salary for a string specialist. At this time, there are many band and former band people involved in orchestra and string teaching, and many of them are doing an outstanding job.

Why Is Quality High?

Class Teaching Expertise Developed

The orchestra programs of today, even though they are often times relatively new, are of surprisingly high quality because of the instrumental class teaching expertise that has been developed over the past thirty years. This expertise, which was developed primarily by the teachers of wind instruments, has been put to good use by band leaders teaching strings and by some of the more progressive string specialists. This accounts for the fact that, although orchestra programs on their "second time around" are relatively new, the quality is very close to many of the older established band programs in many places and even ahead of them in others.

Other Reasons

Another reason for the apparent sudden growth in quality of string programs is that, contrary to common belief, strings have been found to be as easy, if not easier, to teach than winds (not necessarily to play) if they are both taught by equally enthusiastic and competent teachers.

There are several other reasons why the quality and number of fine teachers in the string teaching field is steadily growing:

(1) The colleges are doing an ever improving job of teaching prospective music teachers about strings and orchestras.

(2) There are many string clinicians striving to disseminate information to aid orchestra directors to do a better job.

(3) Professional associations of music educators in the string and orchestra field, such as the National School Orchestra Association (NSOA) and the American String Teachers Association (ASTA), and State Music Associations sponsor many workshops every year.

(4) Educational Divisions of instrument manufacturers and music publishers sponsor many diverse programs to promote string teaching and teaching methods and orchestras.

(5) Music conventions at the national, state and local level are scheduling string and orchestra teaching sessions with increasing frequency.

(6) As a result of the interest and enthusiasm of teachers for attending clinics and workshops and the many clinics available to choose from, there is a growing spirit of optimism in regard to the future of string and orchestra teaching.

FUTURE OF SCHOOL ORCHESTRAS

Looks Very Positive

The future of school orchestras has never been as bright as it is today. Because of the large number of potential students, the improved teaching methods, and the disenchantment by a large part of the student population with the regimentation of bands, the potential for many large and excellent orchestra programs is greater than it has ever been in the past.

It is the feeling of the authors that the orchestra movement is now in the same position that the band movement was back in the 1930's right before it literally exploded from relatively few schools with bands to a situation where a school without a band was a rarity.

The road to professional recognition is wide open in the orchestra field, because the means to success are readily available and there are relatively few teachers at this time in the string and orchestra field. Now is the time for teachers, string majors and/or non-string majors, to get in on the "ground floor", because the competition will never be less than it is today. Now is the time for a new teacher to establish a reputation in a relatively wide-open field.

The trend is now toward all instrumental music education students at the university learning *more* about strings. The competition *is* going to increase in the orchestra field, because more and more of the teacher-training institutions are encouraging all music students to learn to teach strings. This is because there exists a shortage of positions for people who are limited to teaching only winds and percussion. The idea that only string majors can teach strings and/or orchestras is being challenged more and more, because non-string majors in the string and orchestra field are proving that it can be done; and further, competition for jobs is causing increasing numbers of non-string majors to favorably consider this area of instrumental music teaching as a very realistic and satisfying alternative to not teaching instrumental music at all.

GAINING, MAINTAINING, AND IMPROVING ORCHESTRA TEACHING SKILLS

As most students today cannot be depended on to take private lessons, the teacher must be prepared to teach all of the students through a rather advanced level of achievement. It is, of course, much easier for a music student to prepare for a career in string and orchestra teaching while at the university.

Play In An Orchestra

The first step in preparation for teaching is for the music student to go to a school with a good orchestra and an excellent orchestra director-teacher. Then play in the orchestra. During rehearsals, string majors should observe carefully how the wind and percussion instruments work, ask questions of the wind and percussion players, and listen and observe what the director says and does to achieve various results. Wind majors should observe the string players carefully to crystalize a picture in their mind of what the basic positions of the various string instruments are and how the bow looks when being drawn properly. The right and left-hand positions must be imprinted on their minds because, when teaching strings, the teacher (string or wind major) must know how the string player must look and then make them look that way. In string teaching, everything is out in the open for all to observe, therefore, if the teacher knows what to look for, he can easily supervise and improve the progress of his students.

Study the Stringed Instruments

University students should also take class and private lessons on the various instruments that are not in their major field.

Attend Clinics and Workshops – Get on Mailing Lists

University students, and teachers in the field alike, need to constantly evaluate, up-date, acquire, or reject new concepts and methodology in the teaching of strings and orchestra. Music for strings and orchestra should be reviewed by attendance at clinics and workshop seminars that are held by music dealers, universities, and conventions such as the Midwest National Band and Orchestra Clinic, Music Educators National Conference and its various affiliated state organizations, NSOA and ASTA. Teachers should ask publisher and manufacturer representatives to put their names on string and orchestra promotion mailing lists. Write directly to those not contacted at conventions. Subscribe to professional publications like the *Instrumentalist, School Musician* and *Music Journal.*

Attend Concerts and Rehearsals

A great deal can also be learned by attendance at high school, college and professional symphony concerts and rehearsals. It is always possible to learn from any rehearsal or concert whether good or bad, but it is always possible to learn more from a good one. Therefore, the serious student and teacher out in the field needs to find out where the best work in the area's schools is taking place and attend concerts and rehearsals there if the directors will allow it.

DIRECTING SCHOOL ORCHESTRAS DIFFERS FROM COLLEGE OR PROFESSIONAL ORCHESTRAS

Directing a school orchestra successfully is a completely different task than directing a university or professional orchestra. Therefore, to learn this skill, observation of a fine high school director will usually be much more helpful for learning to work with high school students than watching the finest professional or university director. Although the university or professional conductor must know what he wants and be able to explain it, he can usually depend on the orchestra members to be able to give him what he wants. The fine high school director, however, must know, not only what he wants and how to explain it to the students, but he must also be able to teach them how to do what must be done to get the effects desired. Phrasing, dynamics, rhythmic nuances, intonation, style and many other things that a professional conductor takes for granted can and must be objectively taught by the high school director.

Associate with Other Directors and "Experts" in the Field

At conventions and clinics, much can be learned outside as well as inside the actual clinic and/or demonstration sessions. Many times, very usable and practical information about teaching and maintaining a program can be learned by talking to successful directors and visiting clinicians in an informal conversation over dinner, coffee or drinks, because the situation is informal rather than formal. Above all, the teacher must get out of his classroom regularly and find out about what is being done by other people who are emerging with new ideas or who are in the forefront of the orchestra movement! The teacher should be aggressive and seek out other teachers – ask questions, observe rehearsals, invite others to work with his own group. Ask them to watch and critique his own rehearsals as well. One should not feel that this is an admission of any incompetence, because all artists and teachers have learned much from others in this way throughout history.

PERSONAL REWARDS OF SCHOOL ORCHESTRA TEACHING

For the teacher who wants to learn, improve, and aggressively pursue the goals mentioned in this book, the authors feel that directing an orchestra and/or teaching strings at any level is a task that is challenging and rewarding enough to keep a person completely engrossed for a long and exciting career. This is true not only because of the nature of the work, but because the school orchestra movement in the schools today is on the threshold of its greatest growth and potential. The opportunities are unlimited for the person who is willing to continue to grow professionally, and give unstintingly of his time and effort.

It is also the feeling of the authors that the *possibilities for outstanding orchestra programs are unlimited* for the teacher who can work positively at seeking solutions and then implementing them rather than complaining about the problem(s). The possibilities for professional and personal success and fulfillment as an orchestra director never have been greater, and are better than any other field of music education because of the lack of sufficient numbers of qualified string teachers. It is the authors' sincerest wish that this book will help make the accomplishment of the highest goals in the school orchestra field possible to its readers, and that they too will find the fulfillment that the authors have received during a lifetime of working with youthful musicians in the orchestra program.

General Index

Kjos West/Neil A. Kjos, Jr., Publishers
4382 Jutland Drive
San Diego, California
1978